Creating
White Australia

Edited by Jane Carey
and Claire McLisky

SYDNEY UNIVERSITY PRESS

Published 2009 by Sydney University Press
SYDNEY UNIVERSITY PRESS
Fisher Library, University of Sydney
www.sup.usyd.edu.au

Reproduction and communication for other purposes

National Library of Australia Cataloguing-in-Publication entry

Title: Creating white Australia / edited by Jane Carey and Claire
                McLisky.
ISBN: 9781920899424 (pbk.)
Subjects: White Australia policy.
                Racism--Australia.
                Australia--Emigration and immigration--History.
                Australia--Race relations--History.
Other Authors/Contributors:
                Carey, Jane, 1972-
                McLisky, Claire.
Dewey Number: 305.80094

Cover design by Evan Shapiro, University Publishing Service, The University of Sydney

Contents

Contributors..v

Introduction
Creating White Australia: new perspectives on race, whiteness
and history..ix
Jane Carey & Claire McLisky

**Part 1: Global framings: Australian whiteness
in an international context**..1

1   White, British, and European: historicising identity
    in settler societies 3
    Ann Curthoys
2   Reworking the tailings: new gold histories and the cultural
    landscape 25
    Benjamin Mountford & Keir Reeves
3   Trans/national history and disciplinary amnesia: historicising
    White Australia at two *fins de siècles*.........................44
    Leigh Boucher

**Part 2: Whiteness on Indigenous missions
and reserves** 65

4   Colouring (in) virtue? Evangelicalism, work and whiteness on
    Maloga Mission 67
    Claire McLisky
5   'A most lowering thing for a lady': aspiring to respectable
    whiteness on Ramahyuck Mission, 1885–1900.................85
    Joanna Cruickshank

6   Calculating colour: whiteness, anthropological research
     and the Cummeragunja Aboriginal Reserve,
     May and June 1938 103
     Fiona Davis

Part 3: Writing and performing race: creation and disavowal 121

7   Theatre or corroboree, what's in a name? Framing Indigenous
     Australian 19th-century commercial performance
     practices 123
     Maryrose Casey

8   The Wild White Man: 'an event under description' 140
     Maggie Scott

9   Perpetuating White Australia: Aboriginal self-representation,
     white editing and preferred stereotypes 156
     Jennifer Jones

Part 4: Gender and whiteness 173

10   A word of evidence: shared tales about infanticide and
     others-not-us in colonial Victoria 175
     Marguerita Stephens

11   White anxieties and the articulation of race: the women's
     movement and the making of White Australia,
     1910s–1930s 195
     Jane Carey

12   Whiteness, maternal feminism and the working mother,
     1900–1960 214
     Shurlee Swain, Patricia Grimshaw & Ellen Warne

Contributors

Leigh Boucher is a lecturer in the Department of Modern History, Politics and International Relations at Macquarie University, Sydney. He is the co-editor (with Katherine Ellinghaus and Jane Carey) of *Re-orienting whiteness* (Palgrave, 2009) and is currently researching the relationship between historical writing, settler colonialism and political rights in the 19th-century British world.

Jane Carey holds a Monash Fellowship at Monash University where her current research explores the politics of population in British settler colonies. She is the co-editor (with Katherine Ellinghaus and Leigh Boucher) of *Re-orienting whiteness* (Palgrave, 2009) and has published articles in *Gender and History* and the *Women's History Review*.

Maryrose Casey lectures in theatre and performance studies at Monash University. Her research focuses on the practice and cross-cultural reception of theatre by Indigenous Australian practitioners. Her publications include the multi-award winning *Creating frames: contemporary Indigenous theatre* (UQP 2004) and with Aileen Moreton-Robinson and Fiona Nicoll, *Transnational whiteness matters* (Rowman & Littlefield, 2008).

Joanna Cruickshank is a lecturer in history at Deakin University. She has published on 18th- and 19th-century religious history in Britain and Australia. Forthcoming publications include an article on the friendships of British Methodist women in the *Journal of Eighteenth-Century Studies*, a co-authored chapter (with Patricia Grimshaw) on Moravian missionaries in far north Queensland and a book on the 18th-century hymn writer Charles Wesley, to be published by Scarecrow Press in late 2009.

Ann Curthoys is ARC Professorial Fellow at the University of Sydney. Her most recent book is Ann Curthoys, Ann Genovese and Alexander Reilly, *Rights and redemption: history, law, and Indigenous people* (UNSW Press, 2008). For something completely different, see Ann Curthoys and Ann McGrath, *How to write history that people want to read* (UNSW Press, 2009).

Fiona Davis is a postgraduate student in the School of Historical Studies at the University of Melbourne. Her PhD thesis topic is 'Black, white and shades of grey: the story of cultural exchange on Cummeragunja, 1900–1950'.

Patricia Grimshaw is a Professorial Fellow in the School of Historical Studies at the University of Melbourne, where for several decades she taught Australian and American history and contributed to the Gender Studies Program. She has written extensively on women's history, and engaged with the history of settler colonialism and whiteness studies. With Shurlee Swain and Ellen Warne, she is currently completing a book, 'Balancing acts: working mothers in twentieth-century Australia'.

Jennifer Jones holds an ARC Post Doctoral Fellowship at the Australian Centre, School of Historical Studies at the University of Melbourne. Her project examines rural women's cross-racial collaboration in the Country Women's Association of NSW during the assimilation era. Jennifer's first book, *Black writers and white editors: episodes of collaboration and compromise in Australian publishing history*, was published by Australian Scholarly Publishing in 2009.

Claire McLisky is a white Australian woman descended from colonial-era Scottish and English settlers. She grew up on Bundjalung land in northern New South Wales. In early 2009 Claire was awarded her PhD in Australian history, from the University of Melbourne, with a thesis exploring faith, power and subjectivity in the lives of Protestant missionaries Daniel and Janet Matthews. She has recently set off for two years travelling, living, and working overseas.

Benjamin Mountford is a Rae and Edith Bennett Travelling Scholar, reading for a DPhil in Imperial History at Exeter College, Oxford. His doctoral research examines the importance of 19th-century perceptions of China in shaping an Anglo-Australian understanding of the British Empire.

Keir Reeves is a Monash Research Fellow co-housed in the Tourism Research Unit and the National Centre for Australian Studies at Monash University. Keir is the exhibition reviews editor for *History Australia*, and an editorial board member of *Sporting Traditions*, and the Heritage Council of Victoria. He is a contributing co-editor of *Places of pain and shame: dealing with difficult heritage* (Routledge, 2009) and *Deeper leads: new approaches in Victorian goldfields history* (Ballarat Heritage Services, 2007).

During her studies at the University of Melbourne, Maggie Scott was inspired by lecturers such as Tracey Banivanua-Mar and Jane Carey to pursue research into historical and contemporary Indigenous resistance to colonialism, critical race theory and alternative narratives of history. In 2008 Maggie completed a thesis encompassing some of these interests in the story of William Buckley. She currently tutors 'Writing Angles' and 'Popular Culture and the Moving Image' at RMIT and is adapting her thesis into a screenplay.

Shurlee Swain is a professor at Australian Catholic University and a Senior Fellow in the School of Historical Studies at the University of Melbourne. She has written extensively on the history of women, children and welfare, and is currently completing a book with Patricia Grimshaw and Ellen Warne, 'Balancing acts: working mothers in twentieth-century Australia'.

Marguerita Stephens was a working gardener before returning to study history at the University of Melbourne. Her PhD on race relations in colonial Victoria, with a close focus on the Coranderrk Aboriginal Station, was awarded the Dennis-Wettenhall Prize for Research in Australian History, 2004. She holds a Research Fellowship in the School of Historical Studies, University of Melbourne and is a participant in the Manuscript Sponsorship Program at the University's Writing Centre for Scholars and Academics.

Ellen Warne is a lecturer in history at Australian Catholic University where she teaches in a range of Australian and international history units. She has written on Christian women's use of maternal activism to achieve political aims in 19th- and early 20th-century Australia, and is currently completing a book with Shurlee Swain and Patricia Grimshaw, 'Balancing acts: working mothers in twentieth-century Australia'.

Introduction

Creating White Australia: new perspectives on race, whiteness and history

Jane Carey, Monash University
Claire McLisky, University of Melbourne and University of Copenhagen

As the promulgation of the White Australia Policy in 1901 would seemingly demonstrate, 'whiteness' was crucial to the constitution of the new Australian nation. And yet historians have paid remarkably little attention to this in their studies of Australia's past. 'Whiteness', as a concept, has only recently been recognised as a significant part of the story of Australian nationalism. In seeking to understand the operations of 'race', historians have primarily looked towards Indigenous peoples and other 'non-white' groups. *Creating White Australia* takes a fresh approach to the questions of Australian national formation and the crucial role of race in Australian history. Including contributions from some of the leading scholars in Australian history as well as the work of emerging historians, it argues that 'whiteness' has been central to the racial regimes which have so profoundly shaped the development of the Australian nation.

This collection is the first to draw together an array of studies dealing with the question of whiteness in Australian history as their central theme. It demonstrates that Australia's racial past can only be understood by recognising whiteness too as 'race'.

By revealing what 'white' meant in a particular place and time, each of these chapters contributes to the elucidation of how race and whiteness have, in effect, 'created' the historical, geographical and imagined entity known as Australia. They show the multiple, and often contradictory, ways in which whiteness was understood, manifested, and seen, and, sometimes, how it failed to be seen. The new understandings they offer have considerable significance for how we approach the question of race in Australian history, as well as its more recent operations. Many chapters explore the colonial origins of whiteness, and its growing dominance, which culminated in the adoption of the White Australia Policy as the foundation of the new Australian nation. Others pursue the continuing evolution and impact of whiteness into the 20th century, from the heyday of White Australia through to more recent times, revealing the enduring nature of these racial structures. From the relationship between white identities and British identities and the destructive impact of colonisation in the Australian colonies, to the broader dynamics which shaped race relations in settler colonies, to the 'half-caste' menace and policies of biological absorption, to Indigenous resistance to the impositions of whiteness and racial classifications, to white interpretations of Aboriginal cultural practices, to the 'hidden' histories of the Chinese on the goldfields. From studies of the ambivalent figure of William Buckley (the escaped convict who lived with the Wathurung people for 30 years), to the recurrent stories of Aboriginal infanticide, to the eugenic obsession with creating an ideal white race in the early 20th century, to the appropriation of Aboriginal women's life stories by white writers in the 1970s. These chapters pursue the study of whiteness into previously uncharted territory—particularly into missionary contexts, and in terms of the relationship between women, gender and whiteness.

But the purpose of this book is certainly not to reposition white people at the centre of historical narratives. The devastating impact of whiteness on those deemed 'not-white' is at the heart of this book. The studies presented here show how whiteness was given meaning only in relation to 'other' races, and the attributes of power and privilege it accrued had severe implications for these groups. They thus provide important new insights into the experiences particularly of Indigenous Australians, but also other 'non-white' groups such as the Chinese.

This work, of course, has not emerged in a vacuum. It has its roots in the spate of foundational works of whiteness studies which appeared in the United States in the early 1990s. David Roediger's 1991 publication, *The wages of whiteness*, was quickly followed by what would become equally influential works by Toni Morrison, bell hooks, Ruth Frankenberg and Cheryl Harris.[1] As Eric Arnesen has noted, since this time, 'Few branches of the humanities and social sciences have escaped the increasing gravitational pull of "whiteness studies".[2] Where previously 'race' had been seen only to refer to 'others', this scholarship established whiteness too as racial category, and one that was in urgent need of interrogation. As Richard Dyer has put it, 'As long as race is something only applied to non-white peoples ... [white people] function as a human norm. Other people are raced, we are just people.'[3] Aileen Moreton-Robinson, Australia's leading scholar in this field, has similarly observed: 'As long as whiteness remains invisible in analyses "race" is the prison reserved for the "Other".[4] In other words, race has primarily been viewed as a problem only for 'non-white' people. Thus Ruth Frankenberg argued that to 'speak of whiteness is ... to assign *everyone* a place in the relations of racism' since it is 'more difficult for white people to say

---

[1] David Roediger, *The wages of whiteness: race and the making of the American working class* (London/New York: Verso, 1991); bell hooks, 'Representations of whiteness in the literary imagination', in *Black looks: race and representation* (Boston: South End Press, 1992); Toni Morrison, *Playing in the dark: whiteness and the literary imagination* (New York: Vintage, 1992); Cheryl I. Harris, 'Whiteness as property', *Harvard Law Review* 106.8 (June 1993): 1707–91; Ruth Frankenberg, *White women, race matters: the social construction of whiteness* (Minneapolis: University of Minnesota Press, 1993).

[2] Eric Arnesen, 'Whiteness and the historian's imagination', *International Labor and Working-Class History* (Fall 2001), 2. Homi Bhabha similarly remarked upon the 'blizzard of "whiteness studies"': Homi K. Bhabha, 'The white stuff', *Artforum* 36 (1998): 24.

[3] Richard Dyer, *White* (New York: Routledge, 1997), 1.

[4] Aileen Moreton-Robinson, *Talkin' up to the white woman: Aboriginal women and feminism* (Brisbane: University of Queensland Press, 2000), xix.

"Whiteness has nothing to do with me—I'm not white" than to say "Racism has nothing to do with me—I'm not a racist".[5] These insights have important ramifications for the study of Australian history, which the essays in this volume pursue in diverse ways. In doing so, they offer significant new perspectives.

Most studies of whiteness are based in present-day America. While this work has revealed the hegemonic and structural, but often invisible or disavowed, power of contemporary whiteness, the obviously important facts both of its historical formations and its manifestations in diverse locations across the globe have tended to be overlooked. While much American scholarship remains determinedly insular, some work from outside, and to a lesser extent from within, the United States, has pushed whiteness studies in important new directions.[6] As Aileen Moreton-Robinson, Maryrose Casey and Fiona Nicoll have argued, 'whiteness is a transnational process of racialization, which exceeds containment within fixed boundaries of identity and nation'.[7] It cannot then be understood only through narrowly American-centred analyses. And there is indeed a significant and growing body of scholarship on contemporary Australian formulations of whiteness, which this collection clearly builds on. Largely due to the influence of Aileen Moreton-Robinson, Australian scholars have produced the largest body of contemporary whiteness scholarship outside of the United States.[8] The key difference of this Australian work,

---

[5] Frankenberg, 6.

[6] See for example Alfred Lopez, ed., *Postcolonial whiteness: a critical reader on race and empire* (Albany: State University of New York Press, 2005), which analyses constructions of whiteness in the postcolonial world (where postcolonial is used in its temporal sense); Sara Ahmed, 'A phenomenology of whiteness', *Feminist Studies* 8.2 (2007): 149–68; Lynette Russell and Margery Fee, '"Whiteness" and "Aboriginality" in Canada and Australia: Conversations and Identities', *Feminist Theory* 8.2 (2007): 187–208.

[7] Aileen Moreton-Robinson, Maryrose Casey and Fiona Nicoll, 'Introduction: virtue and transnational whiteness', in *Transnational whiteness matters*, eds. Aileen Moreton-Robinson, Maryrose Casey and Fiona Nicoll (Lanham: Lexington Books, 2008), x.

[8] See for example *The Australian Critical Race and Whiteness Studies Association Journal*, 2005; Susanne Schech and Ben Wadham, eds. *Placing race and localising whiteness*,

as Moreton-Robinson notes, is its focus on the colonial context and Indigenous dispossession. '[T]he problem with American literature', she observes, 'is that it tends to locate race and whiteness with the development of slavery and immigration rather than the dispossession of Native Americans and colonization ... there is a refusal within the American work to acknowledge America as a former colony of Britain'.[9]

Despite its obvious implications for history, and more particularly the history of European colonialism, whiteness studies have remained overwhelmingly concentrated on contemporary contexts.[10] As Leigh Boucher, Jane Carey and Katherine Ellinghaus have argued, while recently the terms 'white' and 'whiteness' have been widely adopted by historians, 'the specificities of how, historically, white identity was formed and shaped are only starting to be examined'. There is still a clear need for whiteness to be more robustly historicised.[11] Most of the small corpus of historical

---

(Adelaide: Flinders University, 2004); and other works cited in this introduction. The implications of this Australian scholarship, however, have yet to be addressed within American whiteness studies, most of which remains determinedly insular. For further discussion on this see Jane Carey, Leigh Boucher and Katherine Ellinghaus, 'Historicising whiteness: towards a new research agenda', in *Historicising whiteness: transnational perspectives on the construction of an identity*, eds. Leigh Boucher, Jane Carey and Katherine Ellinghaus, (Melbourne: RMIT Publishing, 2007), vi–xxiii; Jane Carey, Leigh Boucher and Katherine Ellinghaus, 'Re-orienting whiteness: a new agenda for the field', in *Re-orienting whiteness: transnational perspectives on the history of an identity*, eds. Leigh Boucher, Jane Carey and Katherine Ellinghaus (New York: Palgrave, 2008), and Peter Kolchin, 'Whiteness studies: the new history of race in America', *Journal of American History* 89.1 (2002): 154–73. For a key example of the failure to take account of Australian scholarship see Steve Garner, *Whiteness: an introduction* (London: Routledge, 2007).

[9] Aileen Moreton-Robinson, 'Preface', in *Whitening race: essays in social and cultural criticism*, ed. Aileen Moreton-Robinson (Canberra: Aboriginal Studies Press, 2004), viii. On this issue see also Radhika Mohanram, *Imperial white: race, diaspora and the British empire* (Minneapolis: University of Minnesota Press, 2007), especially xvi–xxi.

[10] This is clearly evident in Garner.

[11] Carey, Boucher and Ellinghaus, 'Historicising whiteness', vii. For examples of the ways whiteness has begun to feature in historical scholarship see: Catherine Hall, *Civilising subjects: metropole and colony in the English imagination 1830–1867* (Cambridge: Polity, 2002); Philippa Levine, ed., *Gender and empire: the Oxford history of the British empire*, 6 (Oxford: Oxford

treatments of whiteness is also based in the United States, but some work has begun to pursue its formations in other locales.[12] Again, it is Australian scholarship which stands out here. Foremost among this work is Warwick Anderson's 2002 book *The cultivation of whiteness*, which, focusing on the early 20th century, examined 'medical and scientific visions of what it meant to be white in Australia during a period in which the colonial settler society came to refashion itself as a nation'. These visions, he argued 'helped to set the nation's racial agenda'.[13] Angela Woollacott's previous work on Australian women's journeys to London in the early 1900s also contained some significant discussions of colonial whiteness, and how this travelled across national borders.[14] The significant transnational dimensions of whiteness have also been the subject of Marilyn Lake and Henry Reynolds' important recent work, *Drawing the global colour line* (2008). While drawing on Australia as a key case study, this work approaches the appearance of whiteness in the early 20th century as 'a mode of subjective identification that crossed national

---

University Press, 2004); Ann Laura Stoler, ed., *Haunted by empire: geographies of intimacy in North American history* (Durham, NC: Duke University Press, 2006).

[12] For American historical works see for example: David Roediger, *Wages of whiteness*, and *Working toward whiteness: how America's immigrants became white* (New York: Basic Books, 2005); Noel Ignatiev, *How the Irish became white* (New York: Routledge, 1995); Karen Brodkin, *How Jews became white folks and what that says about race in America* (New Brunswick: Rutgers University Press, 1998); Matthew Frye Jacobson, *Whiteness of a different color: European immigrants and the alchemy of race* (Cambridge, Mass.: Harvard University Press, 1998); Matt Wray, *Not quite white: white trash and the boundaries of whiteness* (Durham/London: Duke University Press, 2006). For work on other contexts see for example Alistair Bonnett, *White identities: historical and international perspectives* (Harlow/New York: Prentice Hall, 2000).

[13] Warwick Anderson, *The cultivation of whiteness: science, health and racial destiny in Australia* (Melbourne: Melbourne University Press, 2002), 1.

[14] Angela Woollacott, '"All this is empire I told myself": Australian women's voyages "home" and the articulation of colonial whiteness', *American Historical Review*, 102.4 (1997): 1003–29. See also her *To try her fortune in London: Australian women, colonialism, and modernity* (New York: Oxford University Press, 2001).

borders and shaped global politics.[15] Its more specific focus is on the emergence of what came to be termed 'white men's countries'—the United States, Australia, Canada, New Zealand and South Africa (all former British settler colonies)—through tracing the ways that politicians and intellectuals constructed this racial/territorial concept. Transnational historical perspectives were also the focus of a collection of essays published in 2007, *Historicising whiteness: transnational perspectives on the emergence of an identity*. This collection encompassed new perspectives on the science and politics of whiteness, but also tracked its impact into numerous other spheres. In many ways this present volume builds directly on this collection, not least because it contained a large number of specifically Australian studies.

While acknowledging the importance of the transnational, other work has emphasised the significance of the colonial encounter in the historical trajectories of whiteness.[16] As Carey, Boucher, and Ellinghaus have argued, 'the construction of whiteness and the phenomena of European colonialism are fundamentally interconnected, and … whiteness studies must be "Re-Oriented" to take this into account'. They highlight how 'whiteness was differently constituted under colonial regimes' and how settler colonies in particular—including the United States—were:

> critical sites for the historical emergence of whiteness and its later trajectories. It was these colonies that had the greatest impact on Indigenous peoples, and where racial beliefs about the capacities and entitlements of white settlers were so crucial to validating the scale of this

---

[15] Marilyn Lake and Henry Reynolds, *Drawing the global colour line: white men's countries and the question of racial equality* (Carlton: Melbourne University Publishing, 2008), 2. See also Marilyn Lake, 'White man's country: the trans-national history of a national project', *Australian Historical Studies* 34.122 (2003): 346–63.

[16] This was in fact the focus of many of the essays in Boucher, Carey, and Ellinghaus, *Historicising whiteness*. Ann Stoler explored some of these interconnections in *Race and the education of desire: Foucault's* History of sexuality *and the colonial order of things* (Durham, NC: Duke University Press, 1995), 46–7, 99–100, 149–64, 177–83.

violent expropriation ... It took considerable discursive and legislative work to inscribe settler colonies as 'white spaces'. And strident assertions of whiteness were a significant component of settler colonies' transition into autonomous nation-states.[17]

By contrast, this collection seeks to return to the significance of the nation, which in the Australian case necessarily encompasses the colonial. It is based on the recognition that, as the advent of 'White Australia' demonstrates, although new understandings of whiteness were transnationally generated, they were most frequently deployed within nationalist terms.[18] Moreover, particular national and local contexts had a significant impact on specific local formations of whiteness, and there could be substantial differences between these. There is, then, a need for more detailed national studies. This collection stands out as one of the very few broad historical examinations of how whiteness has operated outside of the United States. Warwick Anderson's book remains the only historical monograph on Australian formulations of whiteness. The Australian case, we suggest, has much to offer to wider understandings of the changing historical constructions of whiteness. Indeed, with its settler colonial origins, and national foundations firmly based in the White Australia policy, it may well prove exemplary.

Creating White Australia substantially expands on the existing body of historical work on whiteness in Australia by exploring the multiple and often divergent tropes of whiteness in circulation throughout the 19th and 20th centuries. The chapters analyse sources created by a diversity of historical actors, in a range of settings and genres, and across disparate chronologies: from Christian missions to mid-19th-century goldfields;

---

[17] Carey, Boucher and Ellinghaus, *Re-orienting whiteness*, 1, 10.

[18] For further discussion of this point see Carey, Boucher and Ellinghaus, *Re-orienting whiteness*. See also Lake and Reynolds, 4. On the wider implications of the transnational turn in historical scholarship, see Leigh Boucher in this collection, and on the need for the nation still to be addressed see Antoinette Burton, 'On the inadequacy and the indispensability of the nation', in *After the imperial turn: thinking with and through the nation*, ed. Antoinette Burton (Durham, NC: Duke University Press, 2003), 1–23.

colonial cities to pre-colonial camps and settlements; legal institutions to women's groups and anthropological societies. The studies are linked both by their theoretical sophistication and their strong historical and geographical groundings. The volume is enriched by the wealth of exciting new approaches and methodologies, with contributions informed by disciplines as diverse as performance studies, archaeology, creative writing, women's studies, and postcolonial theory. Its chapters venture into fields which remain under-explored in whiteness studies—particularly in terms of the intersection between whiteness and colonialism, but also, for example, in relation to women and gender. The question of whiteness in missionary history, which several of the chapters address, has only recently begun to be explored. The chapters range from broad studies tracking the emergence of 'whiteness' as a racial designation to micro-histories which examine the pervasive reach of 'race' into everyday activities and intimate personal interactions. These novel approaches allow us to see the history of whiteness in Australia through many lenses, and in many voices, from the early 19th century—when it was relatively uncommon for Britons to speak or write of themselves as 'white'—through to the nation's fascination with the idea of its own whiteness at the turn of the 20th century, and well beyond.

The continent's shift from a set of disparately linked colonies to a federated nation state was a crucial moment in the construction of Australian whiteness. But how was whiteness defined in the years prior to federation, and how did understandings of whiteness change during the early and middle decades of the 20th century? As Ann Curthoys points out in her chapter, there is a need to tease out the competing and overlapping nature of identities such as white, British, European, and Australian, and the relationship between colonial/national, imperial and racial identifications. Elsewhere, noting the 'lack of specificity about the racial status of the coloniser population' in mid-19th-century Victoria (who were 'termed "Anglo-Saxon," "English," "British," "colonist" or, very, very rarely, "white"'), Leigh Boucher has urged the need to pay closer attention to specific 'grammars' of racial difference: 'precisely because designations of whiteness ... emerge at particular times, this demands a more robust historicisation of what populations we are referring to when we deploy this category in our analysis'.[19] Nevertheless, it was the White Australia Policy which was promulgated in 1901, indicating the degree of significance which adhered to this identification by the early 20th century. Both the race and the perceived 'white'-ness of non-Indigenous Australians were invoked as identities from the very beginning of European settlement of the continent. These ideas were used, sometimes explicitly, and sometimes implicitly, as the basis for claims to power, land and influence, but they also impacted on the social, cultural and geographical landscape in a variety of ways. It is these important issues which this collection addresses.

The opening section of the collection situates the understanding of Australian whiteness within its broader context, both in terms of the transnational and the competing, coexisting modes of identification. Thus, Ann Curthoys unpacks the terms 'white', 'British', 'European' and 'Western' and places them in both their Antipodean and global contexts. She points particularly to the importance of seeing Australian colonialism as a global 'British' phenomenon, positioning Australian history in conversation with the colonisation of Canada, New Zealand, and the Cape Colony, and identifying a paradoxical sense of 'British entitlement' which informed colonial claims for self-government, and the assumption of governance over Indigenous peoples. In the next chapter, Benjamin Mountford and Keir Reeves approach the global contextualisation of Australian whiteness from a different perspective. Exploring the mid-19th-century central Victorian cultural landscape through the life of one Chinese emigrant and goldseeker, Lee Fook Shing, they open a window into how race, ethnicity and whiteness were (and continue to be)

---

[19] Leigh Boucher, 'Whiteness, geopolitical reconfiguration and the settler empire in nineteenth century Victorian politics', in Boucher, Carey and Ellinghaus, *Re-orienting whiteness*.

spatially inscribed in the settler-colonial context. Their analysis, as well as making an important intervention into the field of Chinese-Australian history, demonstrates what a focus on diasporic, or transnational, histories can add to our understanding of the development of whiteness in Australia. While the advantages of both Curthoys', and Mountford and Reeves', global approaches to Australian history are undeniable, a broader question about the utility of a 'national' (or, for that matter, a 'transnational') history of whiteness remains. The final chapter in this section, by Leigh Boucher, takes as its subject this problem of how to historicise White Australia when both national and transnational historiographical approaches leave much to be desired. Through an investigation of trends in history-writing at the ends of the 19th and 20th centuries, Boucher demonstrates the long history of transnational histories, in the process countering recent invocations of the transnational as a radical new approach and as a panacea for the limitations of nationally bounded historical writing. Ultimately, Boucher argues, the central 'problem' of history-writing is not in fact the nation state, but the universalising claims of liberalism which refuse to be contained within national boundaries.

The second section considers the place of whiteness on Indigenous missions and reserves in Australia during the 19th and early 20th centuries, exploring how racialised ideas about labour, gender, respectability and science could both entrench and unsettle the privileges of whiteness. In such institutions, whiteness was understood by missionaries and reserve managers as embodying a whole range of 'virtuous' qualities, including productivity, civility, piety and rationality. Yet, as these chapters also show, whiteness in these contexts was a particularly fragile construct, due both to the universalism of Christian doctrine and the marginalised position which white workers on Indigenous reserves and missions occupied in settler-colonial society. This latter theme is explored in Claire McLisky's chapter, which analyses the relationship between work and whiteness on Maloga Mission in colonial New South Wales between 1874 and 1888. Building on the work of Australian labour historians, her chapter explores how racialised constructions of Aboriginal labour affected the politics of work and productivity in the late-19th-century settler-colonial mission field. The next chapter, by Joanna Cruickshank, investigates the intersections between gender and whiteness on Ramahyuck Mission in Victoria between 1885 and 1900. With a focus on Ellie Hagenauer, daughter of Moravian missionaries Louise and Friedrich Hagenauer, Cruickshank explores the dilemmas which missionaries faced when the physical and emotional proximity of mission life conflicted with the racial distance required by respectable whiteness. The section's final chapter, by Fiona Davis, interrogates the trip of two well-known anthropologists, Joseph Birdsell and Norman Tindale, to the Cummeragunja Aboriginal Reserve in May and June 1938. Drawing on original oral history testimony gathered by the author, this chapter explores what Davis calls the 'the unspoken, unarticulated power of whiteness' which, although always present, came to the fore with special clarity during their visit.

The chapters in the next section consider how whiteness has been understood, embodied, and challenged by both Indigenous and non-Indigenous writers and performers since the 19th century, and, indeed, how whiteness affects the creative process itself. Firstly, Maggie Scott explores colonial reactions to the story of the 'wild white man', William Buckley, showing the ways in which 19th-century historians and commentators' framing of Buckley's story were deeply imbued with ideas about race and whiteness. Representations of Buckley, she concludes, 'lent authority to the labelling, categorisation, and naming of Indigenous peoples and culture', and 'illustrate the depths of colonial anxieties and desires which were projected onto the Indigenous Other'. In the following chapter, on cross-racial collaboration, Jennifer Jones explores how the white 'privilege' of editorship—a privilege which is in her case study inflected also by gender—can obscure the richness, nuance and (to a white audience) inexplicable difference of Aboriginal oral testimony. The textual suppression of Indigenous perspectives, she suggests, demonstrates how white collaborators continued, in many cases, to prioritise the needs of White Australia throughout the 20th century and beyond. The final chapter in this section, by Maryrose Casey, takes this exploration of white privilege in the literary and performative fields one step further. Drawing upon extensive 19th-century primary descriptions of Aboriginal performances, Casey shows how the meta-structures of nomenclature, and even genre, can limit our potential for understanding the multiple meanings of past and present Aboriginal cultural practices. Using European terms to describe these practices, she argues, 'would, in effect, make these performances part of a norm that privileges European practice as originary'; as such, we need a new vocabulary to describe Aboriginal performance practices.

The final section investigates the relationship between gender and whiteness in the Australian context. Marguerita Stephens' chapter focuses on gender and violence in the construction of Australian colonial whiteness by examining the contested question of Aboriginal infanticide. Charting the persistence of the idea of Aboriginal infanticide from the late 18th century onwards, Stephens shows how 'what was, in all likelihood, an exceptional and incidental practice amongst Aboriginal people ... was raised up by the interaction of European and Aboriginal fears of the other into a morally and racially defining trope that marked whole communities as "infanticidal", and as people whose common rights could be morally suspended'. Despite the far-reaching consequences of this trope for all Aboriginal Australians, it was the figure of the 'depraved' and 'dysfunctional' Aboriginal mother who was at its centre, and who bore the brunt of settler society's twin attempts to erase and to 'rehabilitate' Aboriginality through its policies of segregation and, later, forced assimilation. The regulation of motherhood to achieve 'utopian' racial and social ends was not, of course, limited to Aboriginal mothers, as Jane Carey's chapter on how ideas about race and whiteness were mobilised by the early-20th-century Australian women's movement explores. The movement's concern with racial fitness did not apply only to racial 'others', but was also firmly embedded in ideas about health and whiteness. Long thought of as the realm of women, maternal health was an area in which women activists could claim a certain degree of expertise, and therefore exercise power. Carey places theses racial anxieties in contrast to the movement's relatively limited discussions of the contemporary 'Aboriginal problem'. This theme is continued in the final chapter, which deals with whiteness and maternal feminism between 1900 and 1960. Here, Shurlee Swain, Patricia Grimshaw and Ellen Warne observe how the campaigns of the women's movement during this period were 'grounded in a mostly disguised racial discourse'. In a climate of fear about the continuing vigour of the white race, they argue, mothers came to be valued for their whiteness, a state of affairs which in turn allowed women's rights campaigners to argue for reforms such as the child endowment payment. Thus, 'Feminists who sustained a watching brief on women's labour issues could exclude quite unthinkingly Indigenous women and migrant women of colour from their conceptual frame'.

The charge that whiteness studies problematically returns the focus of historical scholarship back to its traditional subjects is a potent one. As Daniel Wickberg has noted, 'Just when [historians] thought they had moved whites out of the centre of history, here they are, back in a new and different form ... Why, of all people, one hears whispered in the hallways, do white people now need a history when it has been their history all along?'[20] Critical studies of whiteness can only be warranted if the oppression it creates remains clearly and explicitly at the centre of the endeavour. Thus, it is the effects of white power and privilege on those who lost—and still lose—the most from its operations that are the focus of the studies presented here. Rather than approaching race as a burden

---

[20] Daniel Wickberg, 'Heterosexual white male: some recent inversions in American cultural history', *Journal of American History* 92.1 (2006): 137–38.

reserved for and experienced only by 'others', they reposition whiteness as the source of this 'problem'. They demonstrate that, throughout the 19th and 20th centuries and continuing into the 21st, many white people in Australia have been, and continue to be, able to create and maintain for themselves positions of power through racialised constructions of rationality, civility, knowledge, authority, sex, labour and violence. These observations are particularly poignant given the demonstrated effects they continue to have on the way Australians—white and non-white, Indigenous and non-Indigenous—see themselves and their 'others'. As the recent Apology to the Stolen Generations, the Northern Territory Intervention, and continuing controversies over asylum seekers reveal, the issues addressed here have enormous contemporary resonance. Indeed, few issues are more contentious than race relations in present-day Australia. The 'History Wars' dramatically highlighted the ongoing struggles white Australians experience in confronting and comprehending the colonial past, and how the 'problems' of 'race' are usually attached only to 'non-white' people. By presenting a substantial new understanding of the racial, transnational, and gendered frames animating the settler-colonial project in Australia, the new perspective offered by this collection will help to overcome these impasses. Yet, perhaps more importantly, the collection demonstrates beyond a doubt that whiteness was never, and indeed is not, a stable or monolithic concept. By exploring the many faces of whiteness—acknowledged and unacknowledged, hidden and exposed—we are better able to confront its power.

Part 1

Global framings: Australian whiteness in an international context

1

White, British, and European: historicising identity in settler societies

Ann Curthoys, University of Sydney

This chapter explores three key terms—white, British, and European—in order to ponder their connections and disconnections. My title pays homage to Catherine Hall, noted scholar of the 'new imperial history' especially in her path-breaking book, *Civilizing subjects*. The title echoes that of her earlier book, *White, male, and middle class*, which explored through a series of essays the connections between racial identity, gender identity and the operations of class. I want to explore these too. In addition, I want to tease out the connections and dissonances historically between white, British, and European identities, and the relationship of all three to the destructive impact of settlement in Britain's settler colonies. I want to investigate further the relationship between racial identity and colonising practice. Considering these questions means thinking about the ways in which the distinct fields of whiteness studies, the 'new' imperial history, and European political theory currently relate to one another, and the possibilities for further dialogue between them in the future.

White

First, of course, the term 'white', and the profound and enduring phenomenological and existential social condition that goes with it—whiteness. Many people have pointed to the origins of the field in American labour history, as historians like David Roediger reprised a brilliant idea of W.E.B. du Bois, the idea of the wages of whiteness. Du

Bois and Roediger pointed to the benefits for working class white people of being white, a psychological reassurance that helps compensate for the oppression and/or exploitation that goes with being waged workers. It was their sense of superiority, of having particular rights and entitlements, which led white workers to refuse to make common cause with black ones, and so weakened working class solidarity and bargaining power as a whole. At least, that is the general argument. Subsequently many scholars followed suit by examining groups that, for socio-political reasons, were seen to be on the margins of whiteness, which sought and eventually gained acceptance as white—Irish, Italians, and Jews, among others.[1]

In fact, my own introduction to whiteness studies was a little different. I was influenced by Ruth Frankenberg's wonderful book, *White women, race matters*, which appeared in 1993. I think for many of us, our introduction to whiteness studies came through our feminist scholarship, our attempts to think through the importance of race in dividing women. An American sociologist, Frankenberg interviewed a range of white American women about the continuing importance of race in American society. She found these white women had a wide variety of ways of conceptualising racial difference; together these ways of thinking constituted a contemporary spectrum of whiteness self-identity. Some of these ways of thinking were relatively new; others had a long history, having once been dominant and now surviving as a minority view. We should therefore understand whiteness, as an identity and a mode of

---

[1] David Roediger, *The wages of whiteness* (London, New York: Verso, 1991); Karen Brodkin, *How Jews became white folks and what that says about race in America* (New Brunswick, NJ: Rutgers University Press, 1998); Noel Ignatiev, *How the Irish became white* (New York: Routledge, 1996); Stefano Luconi, *From Paesani to white ethnics: the Italian experience in Philadelphia* (Albany: State University of New York Press, 2001); Jennifer Guglielmo & Salvatore Salerno, eds., *Are Italians white?: how race is made in America* (New York: Routledge, 2003); Matthew Frye Jacobson, *Whiteness of a different color: European immigrants and the alchemy of race* (Cambridge: Harvard University Press, 1998).

thinking about racial difference, as a palimpsest. Whiteness is composed of layer upon layer of thinking through, with, or about white privilege.

The other important point Frankenberg made was that white people often did not think of themselves as white, or see their whiteness as an important part of their identity or their social position. Where non-white people are constantly categorised in terms of their skin colour, white people see themselves simply as people, as an unmarked category against whom everyone else must identify themselves. As she put it, '"whiteness" refers to a set of cultural practices that are usually unmarked and unnamed'.[2] This lack of marking was also a sign of lack of recognition of privilege, of a taking-for-granted of privileges that others might have to fight hard for, or perhaps never be able to achieve. As cultural theorist Richard Dyer put it in the same argument in 1997, 'other people are raced, we are just people'.[3] This point struck home to many, and there has been considerable scholarship exploring the idea of a white assumption of privilege, and the lack of understanding by white people of how race silently and pervasively operates as a form of power, status, and inequality.

Since then, the field has developed internationally, and moved beyond its initial focus on the United States. There have been two main arguments. The first is that we need to understand whiteness not only in relation to black and immigrant workers, but also in relation to Indigenous peoples, that is to say, in relation to the processes of colonisation and its aftermath. As such the *history* of whiteness needs to be specified, from the time of earliest contact between Indigenous peoples and European explorers and settlers, through to periods of frontier conflict and violence, and on through the history of segregation, incarceration, assimilation, and into our time with its notions of Indigenous self-determination. The second argument is that far from

---

[2] Ruth Frankenberg, *White women, race matters: the social construction of whiteness* (London: Routledge, 1993), 1.

[3] Richard Dyer, *White* (London: Routledge, 1997), 1.

being unmarked and invisible, whiteness in settler societies has been explicitly named and highly visible, as evident in the White Australia Policy and its counterparts in Canada, New Zealand, and the United States, and especially in South Africa with its policy of apartheid. From the late 19th century to the middle of the 20th, whiteness became something to be proud of, protected, and asserted, from official discourse to popular culture.

Only with the end of the Second World War did whiteness begin to fade into the invisibility Frankenberg originally wrote about, if it did at all. In place of the aggressive attachment to whiteness characterising the period from the 1880s to the 1940s, the postwar period ushered in a new era of opposition to racial discrimination, as indicated in the United Nations Universal Declaration of Human Rights, adopted on 10 December 1948. Ruth Frankenberg, in a later essay, 'The mirage of an unmarked whiteness', critiqued her own earlier work. Whiteness she now saw as invisible to some white people some of the time, perhaps, but not to others and not most of the time.[4] The task of whiteness studies has been to demonstrate the continuing power of whiteness in a world in which it is not *supposed* to matter at all.

A new history of whiteness

The appearance in 2008 of Marilyn Lake and Henry Reynolds' book, *Drawing the global colour line*, has significantly augmented the history of whiteness as a form of identification and privilege. The book traces how, in what the authors call 'white men's countries'—that is, the United States, Canada, Australia, New Zealand, and South Africa, and their colonial forerunners—the world's multiplicity of peoples, nations, and religions came from the late 19th century to be understood through a binary distinction between white and non-white. The book argues that the

---

[4] Ruth Frankenberg, 'The mirage of an unmarked whiteness', in *The making and unmaking of whiteness*, eds. Birgit Brander Rasmussen et al. (Durham: Duke University Press, 2001), 73.

increased attachment to whiteness as a form of identification and power had serious practical consequences, including racially-based immigration restriction policies and other forms of racial discrimination. These racially constructed regimes ended, at least in theory, in the decades after the Second World War, with South Africa holding out the longest until the end of the apartheid regime in 1994. Whiteness, then, has a broad transnational history, and this is its story.

Lake and Reynolds also examine some alternative traditions and forms of racial identification, including an older British imperial tradition that valued British subjecthood across racial lines. The book traces the developing code of international law and ideas about racial equality, and its challenge to whiteness as a form of power and privilege. Political activists and thinkers, frequently of African and Asian origin—people like Lowe Kong Meng, W.E.B. du Bois, and Gandhi—opposed the claims of white people to dominate and control, and sought various forms of freedom and independence for themselves. In their campaigns for an end to racial discrimination in the immigration policies of these 'white men's countries', China and Japan looked to international law and emphasised ideas of freedom of movement.[5]

In developing their analysis, the authors consider debates within each of these countries and the ways they looked to each other for example, inspiration and ideas. The idea of a literacy test as a means of excluding non-white people from entering a country, or enjoying voting or other rights, circulates from the American South to Natal to Australia with remarkable rapidity. In this period the nation became the site of exclusion (and some of these nations, such as Australia and South Africa, were formed in the period of study) but each nation shared similar aims and technologies for protecting white privilege. One of the key insights of the book, shared with some other historians of race in settler societies, is that

---

[5] Marilyn Lake and Henry Reynolds, *Drawing the global colour line: white men's countries and the question of racial equality* (Carlton: Melbourne University Press, 2008), 26.

a certain kind of egalitarianism and racism go together. While conservatives with a hierarchical view of society can envisage very well a lower social position for non-white people to occupy, especially as labourers, plantation workers, and so on, those who sought an egalitarian and democratic society envisaged no position for non-white people at all. As a result, liberals, radicals, and democrats insisted that democracy requires social homogeneity, so that all can participate. In their view, this meant it was necessary to exclude those thought unable to enter the society on equal terms. Both forms of thinking—the hierarchical and the egalitarian—rested in these white men's countries on notions of racial hierarchy, but only one, the democratic, became rigidly exclusionary. As the authors of this book say, 'white men's countries rested on the premise that multiracial democracy was an impossibility'.[6]

Australian racial exclusionism was taken up by German political theorist, Carl Schmitt, in the preface to the second (1926) edition of his book, *The crisis of parliamentary democracy*. Schmitt argued that democracy is inherently exclusionary in some way, and should not be confused with liberalism, which he saw as inclusive. In this context, he wrote:

> Every actual democracy rests on the principle that not only are equals equal but unequals will not be treated equally. Democracy requires, therefore, first homogeneity and second—if the need arises—elimination or eradication of heterogeneity.[7]

Australia, Schmitt thought, was an excellent illustration of this general principle. He noted that it used its immigration laws to exclude potential immigrants who are not the 'right type of settler'. And he drew on Myra Willard's classic book, *A history of the White Australia Policy*, which

---

[6] Ibid., 6.

[7] Carl Schmitt, 'Preface to the second edition (1926): on the contradiction between parliamentarianism and democracy', in Carl Schmitt, *The crisis of parliamentary democracy* (Cambridge: The MIT Press, 1985), 9.

defended the policy as it narrated its history, and which had appeared just three years earlier. He quotes from Willard in an endnote:

National self-preservation is the object of the policy. Australians feared that non-European immigration … might radically alter, perhaps destroy, the British character of the community. They knew that racial unity, though not necessarily racial homogeneity, was essential for national unity, for the national life. The union of a people depends on common loyalty to common ideals … to preserve the unity of their national life, a people can admit emigrants from alien races only if within a reasonable time they show a willingness and a capacity to amalgamate ideally as well as racially with them … [Australians] believed that at present non-Europeans of the labouring classes have neither this willingness nor this capacity.[8]

This quote from Willard draws our attention not only to the racial basis of immigration exclusion, but also to something else, something that is a key point in this essay. Notice the easy slide from the terms 'non-European' to 'British' to 'alien races' to 'Australians'. In 1923, when Willard was writing, the identity 'white' was jostling with many competitors. Indeed, it had always done so. In the mid-19th-century Australian colonies, for example, as both Leigh Boucher and Penelope Edmonds have indicated, the identities 'white', 'British', 'Anglo-Saxon', and 'European' were all significant and used interchangeably.[9] This observation neatly leads me to my next major term, 'British'.

---

[8] Schmitt, 90.26. Thank you to John Docker for drawing this discussion to my attention. See John Docker, 'Dissident voices on the history of Israel/Palestine: Martin Buber and the bi-national idea, Walid Khalidi's Indigenous perspective'; and Alexander Reilly, 'The inherent limits of the Australian Government Apology to the Stolen Generation', both in *New worlds, new sovereignties: frontier of possibility in the emerging global order*, eds. Julie Evans, Ann Genovese, and Alexander Reilly, forthcoming.

[9] Leigh Boucher, '"Whiteness" before "White Australia"?'; and Penelope Edmonds, 'White spaces? Racialised geographies, Anglo-Saxon exceptionalism and the location of empire in Britain's nineteenth-century Pacific rim colonies', both in *Historicising whiteness: transnational perspectives on the construction of an identity*, eds. Leigh Boucher, Jane Carey, and Katherine Ellinghaus (Melbourne: RMIT Publishing, 2007).

British

In the Australian context, as in similar societies with large populations of British descent, Britishness is both salient and elusive. For over a century but especially since the Second World War, a sense of Britishness has often been suppressed in favour of the identity 'Australian'. That is, a new inclusive Australian identity is held to supersede the sense of Britishness felt by those of British descent. In the particular kind of egalitarianism of mid-20th-century Australian society that existed when I was growing up, there was little interest in or indeed knowledge of one's British descent. While we could speak of class differences and conflicts, we did not speak of ethnicity, in my world at least, and our particular British origins were lost in the mists of time. The Cold War, for all its bitter divisiveness, did not seem to suggest strong ethnic identifications. Many of us did not even know if our ancestry was English, Scottish, Welsh, Irish, or other European, much less where our ancestors had come from in narrower regional terms or when they arrived. There was, in retrospect, a certain kind of Australian nationalism that insisted on being Australian and *not* British. It was this kind of nationalism that chafed at the continuing Britishness of many public institutions, such as the playing of the British national anthem in cinemas, and made it such a daring thing to keep sitting down as the anthem played. It had academic consequences as well. When New Zealand-born political theorist J.G.A. Pocock called in 1974 for a new British history, which saw the Dominions as an integral part of British history, he met only a limited response. The British were not interested in us and we in the former Dominions—the Australians, Canadians, New Zealanders, and so on—were more interested in distinguishing ourselves from them. More national histories and identities were the order of the day.

By the 1970s, and even more so by the 1980s, this denial of Britishness had created a problem for Australians confronted with the history of the devastating consequences for Indigenous people of colonisation. Being 'Australian' rather than 'British' provided an alibi, an ability to say, 'We were not there'. After all, it was not *Australians* (who did not yet exist as such), but mainly *Britons* who seized the country and then sought to displace and replace the Indigenous population with wave after wave of migration. When acknowledgement of a destructive colonial history came into public consciousness, especially around the time of the bicentennial in 1988, insistence on being Australian and not British increasingly looked like an evasion, a failure to acknowledge the history of colonisation that brought so many of us here. In some versions, an assertion of Australian nationality became a statement of belonging in Australia and nowhere else, of feeling indigenous to the country.

At times, Indigenous commentators were clearer than we were that we came from elsewhere, pointing out that our ancestors had come from Britain, not so very long ago; for them our forefathers and mothers were emissaries from another country who had seized the land and displaced its Indigenous inhabitants. We can see this awareness in Hobbles Daniyarri's account, given to anthropologist Deborah Bird Rose in the early 1980s, of colonisation from 'Big England'. As Daniyarri succinctly explained: 'Lotta man in Big England, and they start there looking for 'nother land'. They were colonisers who came and stayed without permission: 'He should have come up and: "hello", you know, "hello"'. The white man should have sought permission to stay, and if he did not gain it, gone away.[10] We can see the same awareness of British colonisation in Burnam Burnam's claiming of England for Aboriginal people by standing on the beach at Dover and raising the Aboriginal flag on Australia Day, 26 January 1988, an event widely covered in both the British and Australian media. In the face of stories and statements like these, we can no longer avoid the British nature of the invasion. Thinking about

---

[10] Deborah Bird Rose, *Hidden histories: black stories from Victoria River Downs, Humbert River and Wave Hill Stations* (Canberra: Aboriginal Studies Press, 1991), 15, 17. See also Maria Nugent, *Captain Cook was here* (Melbourne: Cambridge University Press, 2009), 120–27.

Britishness becomes part of the process of acknowledging and understanding colonisation.

So I have been thinking about Britishness, both personally and academically. Personally, it's meant getting into family genealogy, and tracing the English convicts, one a Yorkshire weaver convicted of treason for rioting and sentenced to transportation for life, and another convicted of theft, both arriving at Van Diemen's land in the early 1820s; then finding the Cornish tin miners who came to the gold rushes in the 1850s; the mechanics from the west of Scotland who set up a coach-building business in Mittagong in the 1860s; and the middle-class educated immigrants from Bristol and Staffordshire and Wales in the 1870s and 1880s. This meant recognising both the regional mixture that migration brings about, blurring distinctions between English, Scottish, and Welsh and thus reinforcing the identity 'British', yet also noticing the tendency of these mainly west country immigrants to find each other and stick together, at least for a generation or two. It meant also a deeper understanding of the history of migration.

Academically, in the 1990s, the study of diasporic Britishness that Pocock had advocated in the 1970s finally came onto the historical agenda. In Britain and the US, this was influenced by the work of historians like Linda Colley, who explored the complex nature of Britishness around the world. A focus on Britishness has also been important in the international shift in British imperial historiography that has been going on now for 15 years or more. This new imperial history has been strongly influenced by feminist scholarship, just as whiteness studies has been. It is marked by an interest in gender in colonial situations, recognition of the two-way interaction and influences between periphery and centre, a tracing of transnational networks and circulation of ideas, people, and goods, and its emphasis on race, specifically on whiteness and its construction. A key figure here is Catherine Hall, whose book *Civilizing subjects* demonstrates the creation of consciousness of both Britishness and whiteness in the context of colonialism in Jamaica.

Also important for understanding settler identities and the circulation of ideas around the British Empire is the work of Tony Ballantyne. Those who study intellectual history, he argues and demonstrates, should not continue to focus their analyses on the imperial centre, but should rather ground their study, at least in part, in the ideas and life in the colonies. 'We must', he writes, 'be especially vigilant to strike a balance within the historiography of Britain and its empire so that we do not privilege metropolitan perspectives and thus, even inadvertently, marginalize the brute realities of colonial power and cultural change in the periphery'.[11] As he puts it, we need to study horizontal (colony-to-colony) as well as vertical (Britain to colony and back to Britain) connections, and much of his own work traces these horizontal connections in detail. Ideas about Britishness are thus produced not only in Britain and by British settlers themselves, but also in other parts of the empire, notably in India, and by Indigenous peoples in the British settler colonies.

Britishness has also come under scrutiny from 'four nations' historiography, which refuses to equate Englishness and Britishness, as has so often been done, and productively investigates the mutual interactions of Scots, Irish, Welsh and English histories in British society and the British imperial project since the 16th century. There is now a considerable body of scholarship in Scotland considering just why Scots were such willing foot soldiers of the British empire, as administrators, soldiers, medical men, and educators and in many other ways; in Ireland, scholars are considering the ways in which the Irish were both victims and beneficiaries of British imperial adventures. Suffering the effects of colonial occupation themselves, many Irish migrated to the settler

---

[11] Tony Ballantyne, 'Religion, difference, and the limits of British imperial history', *Victorian Studies* 47.3 (Spring 2005): 447.

colonies and, after initial difficulty, did rather well in the process.[12] It is a challenge for historians, now, to meld 'four nations' and the new imperial history to come to a nuanced understanding of Britishness both at home and abroad.

Historians in both Australia and New Zealand have in recent times emphasised the scale and impact of these waves of British migration to the settler colonies, and later the independent nations that arose from them. New Zealand historian James Belich's study of British settlement in North America and Australasia emphasised the explosive population growth resulting from British expansion and migration in the late 19th century and early 20th century, and its huge impact on the world economy and social, political, and natural environments. He noticed also the strengthening rather than the weakening of the relationship between Britain and the rest of the Anglophone world via trade and culture in the early 20th century.[13] Eric Richards has charted the history of British migration to Australia in considerable depth, and emphasised the longevity and ubiquity of British emigration generally.[14]

Britishness in the Australian colonies

Britishness was not only a foundational aspect of settler identity in the mid-19th-century Australian colonies, but also a means of claiming political rights. In his study of the movement for responsible government in New South Wales, *Colonial ambition*, Peter Cochrane points out that British entitlement was a vital aspect of the demand for self-government and democracy: 'entitlement was an insistence on inclusion, not

---

[12] T.M. Devine, *Scotland's Empire 1600 to 1815* (London: Penguin, 2003); Kevin Kenny, ed., *Ireland and the British Empire* (Oxford: Oxford University Press, 2004).

[13] See James Belich, 'The rise of the Angloworld: settlement in Australasia and North America 1784–1918', in *Rediscovering the British world*, eds. P. Buckner and D. Francis (Calgary: Calgary University Press, 2005), and also his book, *Replenishing the earth: the settler revolution and the rise of the Angloworld* (Oxford: Oxford University Press, 2009).

[14] See Eric Richards, *Britannia's children: emigration from England, Scotland, Wales and Ireland since 1600* (London: Hambledon, 2004).

rebellion; an expression of loyalism rather than republicanism'.[15] Recent research work by Jessie Mitchell and me on the relationship between Indigenous-settler history and the coming of self-government to the Australian colonies in the 1850s supports this view. During the 1840s and 50s, we find again and again that when colonists claimed their rights to local, representative, and eventually responsible government, they did so on grounds of equal British subjecthood.[16] At a banquet held in Sydney in 1856 to mark the beginning of responsible government, for example, Richard Thompson's account of the evening reminded readers that many Australian colonists were 'the equals in education, and general intellectual habits, of those who ordinarily find their way into the British House of Commons'.[17]

Feelings were similar in the other colonies. In Tasmania, influential writer John West, after acknowledging that the colony's convict beginnings had prevented representative government at first, went on to point out that colonists' British character and heritage prevented the government from sliding into disgraceful European-style tyranny. 'The genius of British freedom', West writes, 'has ever overshadowed the British colony, and awed the despotic ruler, while it has encouraged and sheltered the feeblest colonist'.[18] In South Australia, the *South Australian*

---

[15] Peter Cochrane, *Colonial ambition: foundations of Australian democracy* (Carlton: Melbourne University Press, 2006), 8.

[16] The research reported in this section was undertaken by Jessie Mitchell, and parts of it are reported in three articles: '"The Gomorrah of the Southern seas": population, separation and race in early colonial Queensland", *History Australia*, 6.2 (2009).; '"The galling yoke of slavery": race and separation in colonial Port Phillip', *Journal of Australian Studies*, 33.2 (June 2009), 125–37; and '"Are we in danger of a hostile visit from the Aborigines?" Dispossession and the rise of self-government in New South Wales', *Australian Historical Studies*, 40.3 (2009), 294–307.

[17] Richard Thompson, ed., *Report of the proceedings at the National Banquet, held at the Prince of Wales Theatre, Sydney, on the 17th of July, 1856, to celebrate the establishment and inauguration of responsible government in the colony of New South Wales* (Sydney: Thomas Daniel, 1856), 4.

[18] John West, *The history of Tasmania*, 2 (Launceston: Henry Dowling, 1852), 339–40.

Register in 1843 described representative government as 'a right to which every Briton has an indefensible and an indisputable claim'.[19] One landowner, speaking at a public meeting in 1849 about the proposed new constitution, objected to the prospect of an unrepresentative legislature: 'They were Britons; and they felt the spirit of Britons as much in South Australia as they had done when they were in Old England itself'.[20]

In Port Phillip (Victoria) and Moreton Bay (Queensland), those campaigning for separation from New South Wales strongly expressed similar ideas. In Moreton Bay, the *Courier* rallied its readers in 1853 against the threat of NSW retaining portions of the northern districts, declaring that this must 'meet with that resistance which any man of British spirit aught to oppose to those who seek his enslavement'.[21] Without local government, the paper stated, colonists were left in an 'un-English political condition'; 'What we want is no more than the birthright of every Englishman—a voice in the making of our own laws, and a power to dispose of the public revenues to which we contribute'.[22] In Port Phillip, an 1844 petition to the House of Commons requested separation on grounds of 'the spirit which should pervade every people who have inherited the feelings of which the British Constitution is the parent and guardian'.[23]

When Victoria's independence was finally declared in November 1850, the celebrations combined passionate regional and imperial loyalty with a nascent hint of federation, as well as an interestingly gendered tone. This was apparent in the public celebrations in Melbourne, which

---

[19] *South Australian Register*, 21 September 1839, 4; 21 December 1839, 5; 26 August 1843, 2; 20 August 1851, 2.

[20] W. Snell Chauncy, *A guide to South Australia* (London: E. Rich, 1849), x; *South Australian*, 25 December 1849, 3.

[21] *Moreton Bay Courier*, 13 August 1853, 2.

[22] *Moreton Bay Courier*, 15 September 1855, 2; 27 October 1855, 2.

[23] Committee of the Separation Society, *The petitions of the District of Port Phillip (Australia Felix) for separation from the territory of New South Wales* (Melbourne: W. Clarke, 1844), 20.

promoted the message that British loyalty could best be enjoyed and expressed through colonial self-determination. The Mechanics' Hall featured a picture of the Queen with the words 'Loyal, Separate, and Free'. The Bush Inn displayed a transparency of Britannia separating two quarrelling children (NSW and Port Phillip) and saying 'Phillip, my boy, go, and be sure you behave like a man'.[24] Victorian anthems written for the occasion by colonial political commentator Nathaniel Kentish implied similar messages. One of his works, *Commemoration national anthem* ('respectfully inscribed to the Ladies of Victoria'), featured repeated phrases like 'Rule AUSTRALIA, VICTORIA rule the waves—For BRITAIN'S SONS shall ne'er be Slaves!' and 'Rule BRITANNIA— AUSTRALIA rule the waves,—VICTORIA'S Sons shall ne'er be slaves!' The song also implied that Britain's best traditions could be enjoyed and strengthened in the colonies—'All Nature's seeds from BRITAIN cold, in this mild climate but improve'—and implied a certain reinvigoration of gender in this pioneer setting.[25]

All this assertion of Britishness did not mean colonials were uncritical of Britain itself. Some colonial commentators complained that while they were loyal Britons, they were unimpressed by the treatment they received from the Home government. When the Australasian League protested against the continuance of transportation, they threatened that colonists, possessing a natural superiority inherited from Britain, were losing their patriotic attachment to the home country 'which has hitherto been their pride and boast'.[26] They and others saw

---

[24] *Argus*, 14 November 1850, 2.

[25] Nathaniel Kentish, *Commemoration national anthem. Victorian-Australian 'Rule Britannia', composed in celebration of the glorious separation, respectfully inscribed to the Ladies of Victoria* (Melbourne: S. Goode, 1850).

[26] Australasian League, *Sessional papers, etc etc, of the Australasian League Conference held in Hobart Town and Launceston, Van Diemen's Land, in the month of April and May 1852* (Launceston: 1852), 16.

colonisation itself as developing qualities of initiative and determination, perhaps making the British colonist a superior form of Briton.

Britishness arises with a special urgency in the context of Indigenous Australian history. As Angela Woollacott has pointed out, the return to imperial perspectives in Australian history joined up with more inward-looking studies of the history of Indigenous-colonial relations, leading to comparative and transcolonial approaches.[27] The study Jessie Mitchell and I are undertaking into the relationship between Indigenous-settler relations and the granting of self-government to the Australian colonies necessarily connects imperial policy, settler identity, and Indigenous dispossession. With independent government for the colonies seen as depending on their quintessential Britishness, Aboriginal people were by definition seen as outside the polity, beyond the scope of those seeking self-government. Colonists acknowledged Indigenous people as British subjects, but only in a technical sense. In the many debates over separation and self-government, speakers scarcely ever addressed the possibility of their inclusion in the political process.[28]

Woollacott has focused on the nature of masculinity in the British colonial situation. She questions 'the legend that self-government in the Australian colonies was won by a progressive reform movement that operated in a purely political realm divorced from the messy realities of the frontier.'[29] Leading advocates of self-government for the white colonies, such as Henry Chapman in New Zealand, Van Diemen's Land, and Victoria and Thomas Murray-Prior in Queensland were, she demonstrates, either involved in or approving and aware of frontier violence themselves. Her research, and ours, into the connections

---

[27] Angela Woollacott, 'Whiteness and "the imperial turn"', in *Historicising whiteness: transnational perspectives on the construction of an identity*, eds. Leigh Boucher, Jane Carey and Katherine Ellinghaus (Melbourne: RMIT Publishing, 2007), 10.

[28] *South Australian Colonist* 1.3, 24 March 1840, 41; *South Australian Register*, 2 July 1851, 2.

[29] Angela Woollacott, 'Frontier violence and settler manhood', *History Australia*, 6.1 (2009), 11.4.

between the demand for and granting of self-government on the one hand, and Indigenous-settler relations on the other, promises a reworking of the history of Australian democracy which has the potential to place racial identities and relationships in the centre of the story.

European

British settlers and colonists were not only, in their own eyes, white and British; they were also European. Their Europeanness meant they shared with other Europeans—French, German, Italians, and others—a history of thinking about the non-European. 'European' in this context meant not only people who had arrived in the colonies directly from Europe, but also Americans of European, including British, descent. What mattered was not where people now lived but rather their descent and their political and cultural heritage.

In recent years, political theorists have been probing the history of European thought since the 18th century, investigating the changes in thinking about human difference and its implications for political freedom and autonomy. Generally, they have traced the nature and timing of the shift in European thought from some kind of universalist appreciation of human difference and variation towards racialised understandings. Influential here have been two books, one by Sankar Muthu, entitled *Enlightenment against Empire* (2003) and the other by his wife, Jennifer Pitts, *A turn to Empire* (2005). Where Muthu traces the anti-colonial, anti-imperialist and anti-racist strands in Enlightenment thought, Pitts investigates how these largely gave way to a full embrace within European thought of colonialism, imperialism, and racism by the mid-19th century.

Muthu explores in depth just what Enlightenment intellectuals in the later 18th century thought about colonisation and the differences between peoples. One of his interesting arguments is that while we find strands of anti-imperial thought in a wide variety of thinkers, it is only in continental European thought, in people like Diderot, Kant and Herder, that we see thoroughgoing forms of critique of colonisation. British critics nearly always focused on the particular forms of colonisation here or there, as with Edmund Burke on India, but they rarely if ever mounted the wholesale attacks that some continental thinkers did. We are reminded what anti-imperial and anti-colonial thought actually looks like when we read Diderot. Diderot wrote sections of the *History of the two Indies*, which came out in several editions, the most important in 1780. The book was extremely popular, in French and in English, until the 1820s, when it sank into oblivion, rediscovered only in the late 20th century. The 'two Indies' in the title are the East Indies (meaning India and East Asia), and the West Indies (meaning North and South America).

Writing in the 1770s, Diderot ridicules the absurdity of the New World conquests in which Europeans claim lands to be their rightful property not because they are uninhabited but because they are unoccupied by anyone from the Old World. The creed of the coloniser, he says, is as follows:

> Let all perish, my own country and the country where I rule, the citizen and the foreigner, even my associate, provided that I grow rich on his remains. All places in the universe are as one to me. When I have laid waste, sucked dry and exhausted one region, there will always be another to which I can take my gold and where I can enjoy it in peace.

He sees the effects of this European expansion as everywhere catastrophic: 'ruins have been heaped on ruins; countries that were well-peopled have become deserted'. Europeans, says Diderot, typically use corrupted principles of international law and fantastical half-baked theories to justify mass injustice, such as expropriating American Indian land. He is especially devastating on the role of the British in India, and makes the point that even countries that are not despotic at home will act despotically abroad.

To the colonised peoples, he says, beware. Beasts, he says, 'are less fearsome than these colonisers ... The tiger may tear you apart, but it will take from you only your life. These creatures will steal your innocence and your liberty'. You are too trusting 'and you do not know them'. The answer is to confront the Europeans with brute force. 'Do not waste your time with protests about justice to which they will pay no heed; it is with your arrows that you must speak to them'. Of the settlers, he says, 'Living in lands to which they have come in order to grow rich, they easily forget to be just'. They enter into a 'spirit of depredation' manifested in horrible violence. The only solution is to decolonise and give up imperial holdings, and to refuse to colonise any further.

Diderot was writing in France in the 1770s, living under an autocratic regime. His antipathy to his own society is thoroughgoing, and lays the basis for his opposition to imperialism. In Britain, as indicated earlier, there was no real equivalent; the tendency was not so much to criticise imperial and colonial projects *per se* as to urge they be carried out with humanity and justice. We can think here of Andrew Fitzmaurice's book, *Humanism and America*, which explores English ideas of colonisation in early modern England. Since early modern times, the English have wished to see themselves as kindly, caring, and honourable colonisers.[30] Jennifer Pitts in her *A turn to Empire* considers British thinkers such as Adam Smith, Edmund Burke, Bentham, James and J.S. Mill, alongside the French theorists de Tocqueville and Condorcet. Her narrative is one of increasing attachment for both British and French to racial paradigms. Europe's progressive civilisation, these thinkers argued, gave Europeans the authority to suspend their usual moral and political standards when dealing with non-European societies.

In the Australian colonies, non-British Europeans were included within colonial public life. British colonists generally welcomed non-British Europeans as valued colonists and settlers with shared values and customs. As Jessie Mitchell has noted, the *Argus'* coverage of the celebrations to mark Port Phillip's separation in 1850 emphasised the joyous coming together of all ages and classes of colonial society. She

---

[30] See John Docker, *The origins of violence* (London: Pluto, 2008), passim.

notes local authorities permitted and even encouraged a certain multicultural inclusion; in the grand parade held in Melbourne to mark the opening of Prince's Bridge across the Yarra, the German Union carried German and British flags together and the St Patrick's Society displayed Irish and British symbols.[31] A few years later, during the gold rushes, British, Germans, Italians, French and other European goldseekers intermingled freely.

The sense of European brotherhood was especially clear in the hostility European goldseekers expressed towards the Chinese. The Lambing Flat riots of 1861, where European goldseekers drove Chinese goldseekers away from the Lambing Flat goldfield, involved a German band, and the joint action of British and other European goldseekers. As one of the goldminers involved in anti-Chinese agitation on the goldfields in New South Wales so eloquently put it, they welcomed 'men of all nations except Chinamen'. By 'all nations', they meant 'all European nations'; Europe was in this assured view the site of civilisation, as in the idea of European civilisation that superseded all previous cultures and civilisations.[32] The anti-Chinese movement prompted some puzzled debate at times over how to distinguish who was acceptable and who was not. After the Lambing Flat riots, for example, a Bill was presented to parliament aiming to restrict the immigration of Chinese into New South Wales. The original Bill provided for the exclusion of 'aliens', that is, it distinguished on the basis of nationality rather than race. Yet the colonists did not want to exclude immigrants from Europe and the US and there was a lively discussion in the Assembly over the virtues of aliens such as Germans and Americans; as one member of parliament put

---

[31] *Argus*, 13, 14 and 19 November 1850, cited in Mitchell, 'The galling yoke of slavery'.

[32] See Ann Curthoys, 'Men of all nations, except Chinamen: Chinese on the New South Wales goldfields', in *Gold: forgotten histories and lost objects of Australia*, eds. Iain McCalman, Alexander Cook and Andrew Reeves (Melbourne: Cambridge University Press, 2001), 103–24.

it, 'although aliens in country [they] were not so in blood and civilisation'. After further discussion, the Bill was amended to exclude only Chinese.[33]

It is important to remember, though, that despite this sense of European brotherhood, Britishness (and British subjecthood) was to remain primary. While European civilisation was important, the colonies would not become 'European' in the sense of a fusion of all European nationalities into a new 'European' colonial society. They were to remain undeniably British in character and allegiance, and adaptation could only be one way. Ultimately, it was the colonial expansionist mission of Britain, rather than that of Europe, which was to be consolidated and vindicated.

Conclusion

A focus on British imperial and colonising history helps strengthen the insight that whiteness has always to be understood relationally, and in process. The appeal to whiteness does not necessarily displace other identifications, such as British and European and Western, though it certainly can and does change the ways in which they were deployed in given circumstances. Whiteness faces competition not only from alternative forms of identification such as European and British, but also from long-standing ideals of equality and mutual respect. While there is a long history of racism dominating the relations between white settlers and various others, there is also a significant history of resistance, opposition, and critique. White settler societies generally have liberal and humanitarian traditions and sets of institutions that at times come into direct conflict with racial thinking, action and policy.

It is important to keep connecting the study of the past and the present. Just as Ruth Frankenberg found layer upon layer of historical race thinking in contemporary white American thinking about race, so we find similar layers in Australian consciousness of race and colonialism. No racial idea remains dominant forever, and no racial idea

---

[33] *Sydney Morning Herald*, 2 May 1861.

ever quite goes away. The shock that many in Australia felt in response to Pauline Hanson in the late 1990s and Keith Windschuttle in the early 2000s is one of realisation that there is no secure progressivist narrative for race relations in Australia. Ideas that had been thought long defunct, such as the denial of rights relating to prior occupation, or belief in the noble coloniser who was too civilised and Christian to destroy the foundations of life of Aboriginal people or to attack Aboriginal people themselves, continue to have purchase. Whiteness as an assumption of destiny, nevertheless, is especially under pressure in the new millennium. In world terms, with the presence of a black President of the United States and the rise of China and India as world economies and powers, it will be interesting to observe just what happens in future to white people's so-far-resilient fantasies of being the bearers of history.

2

Reworking the tailings: new gold histories and the cultural landscape[1]

Benjamin Mountford, University of Oxford
Keir Reeves, Monash University

For a number of years now, cultural historians have looked to the experiences of Chinese migrant communities to interrogate established narratives of national cultural development. In recent years, Chinese diaspora studies has consolidated its position as a vital stream in a broader shift away from historical frameworks centred on the nation state and towards considerations of the transnational. In Australia, this realignment is challenging a number of long-accepted interpretations of whiteness and otherness, as emerging scholarship produces more nuanced and sophisticated readings of our colonial past. For historians considering the Australian goldfields, the emergence of a strong Chinese focus in readings of colonial history has cast new light on the cultural complexity of the era.

With this context in mind, this chapter touches upon a larger research framework and a methodological approach that we have been

[1] The authors would like to thank Antoinette Dillon; the Registry of Births, Deaths and Marriages, Victoria; Heritage Victoria; Valerie Lovejoy and Kirsty Marshall for permission to use images; and Exeter College, University of Oxford. Keir Reeves would like to acknowledge the students who took his 2007 'Heritage Workshop: Chinese in Australia' fourth-year honours seminar at the University of Melbourne; much of the fieldwork and ideas for this chapter were formulated as part of this unit. This chapter is an outcome of an ARC Linkage Project (LP0667552) entitled 'Layers of meaning: historical studies in central Victoria's regional heritage 1834–1950' and fieldwork was made possible by a University of Melbourne Faculty of Arts seeding grant.

exploring and refining, in consultation with a number of colleagues, over the last few years. It focuses on the advantages of using a range of historical methods to explore the Chinese experience on the Australian goldfields, and in doing so raises a number of broader questions on the merits of competing approaches. It argues that historians, and other cultural practitioners, can look to a number of different sources in order to interpret and reinterpret colonial history. This approach is particularly valid when seeking out a more sophisticated understanding of the goldfields Chinese and when evaluating notions of cultural hegemony and long-standing European interpretations of the Victorian goldseeking experience.

As Ann Curthoys reminds us in her work on New South Wales, the experiences of the thousands of Chinese goldseekers who arrived in the 19th century continue to cast a long and often dark shadow over Australian colonial history.[2] There are a number of important stories that remain to be told. This chapter explores an evolving approach to rediscovering some of these hidden histories and navigates some of the challenges that have emerged (or may emerge) from a rapidly growing historiography.

The remaking of Chinese-Australian history

For much of the 20th century, Australian historians paid relatively little attention to the thousands of Chinese goldseekers who came to this country in the 19th century and to the broader patterns of cultural transmission of which they were a part. Obscured in both celebratory and radical nationalist readings of our colonial past, the extent and significance of the Chinese experience in Australia was generally underrated.

---

[2] Ann Curthoys, '"Men of all nations, except Chinamen": Europeans and Chinese on the goldfields of New South Wales', in *Gold: forgotten histories and lost objects of Australia*, eds. Andrew Reeves, Iain McCalman and Alexander Cook (New York: Cambridge University Press, 2001), 103.

The recent upsurge in interest in Chinese-Australian history has provided an opportunity to link local research with parallel work being carried out overseas. Studies of Chinese migration networks, political and native-place organisations, financial interests, and other patterns of social and cultural transmission across the globe have added new dimensions to our understanding of the overseas Chinese and their role (as both sojourners and settlers) in shaping the character of Australian society.[3] In considering future directions and implications of cultural research in this country, ethno-histories, and in particular diasporic studies, provide an opportunity to locate Australian history in a global context. As such, historians of the Chinese in Australia have considerable scope to contribute to a more worldly Australian history and move away from some of the insular preoccupations of the past.[4]

Without downplaying the significance of recent advances, it remains vital that historians seeking new histories of the Chinese in colonial Australia continually refine their research methodologies. This process involves balancing insights gained from emerging studies and the continuous release of new source material (as archives move to accommodate shifts in community and academic interest) with a consideration of alternative viewpoints and approaches. Engaged in 'a new and proliferating subject' we must resist a tendency to skew our work toward established traditions and audiences.[5] In their recent study *The*

---

[3] John Fitzgerald's *Big white lie* considers a number of these themes and seeks to relate the Chinese-Australian case to contemporaneous overseas developments. John Fitzgerald, *Big white lie* (Sydney: UNSW Press, 2008).

[4] Adam McKeown, 'Introduction: the continuing reformulation of Chinese Australians', in *After the rush: regulation, participation, and Chinese communities in Australia: 1860–1940. Otherland Literary Journal* 9, eds. Sophie Couchman, John Fitzgerald and Paul Macgregor (Kingsbury: Otherland, 2004), 1. Here McKeown echoes Ann Curthoys' call for historians to consider 'global and transnational' dimensions in their approaches to Australian history. Ann Curthoys, 'Does Australian history have a future?', *Australian Historical Studies Special Issue: Challenging histories: reflections on Australian history* 33.118 (2002): 147.

[5] John Darwin, *The end of the British Empire: the historical debate* (Oxford: Basil Blackwell, 1991), preface.

Chinese in Britain, for instance, Benton and Gomez provide a timely reminder of the risks of overstating the transnational aspects of overseas Chinese experience.[6] As Australian historians seek to liberate Chinese goldseekers from traditional depictions as faceless troupes of labourers or the passive victims of racial chauvinism, we must be wary of establishing equally crude transnational stereotypes, where individuals and considerations of identity-formation become lost in grand narratives of migration and cultural internationalism.

Personal history and cultural landscape

With these challenges in mind, this chapter considers two areas of Chinese-Australian history that the authors feel require further investigation. The first relates to the need to seek out personal perspectives and biographical histories of goldfields Chinese. Despite recent advances, Chinese-Australian studies have had limited success in seeking out individuals and their stories, particularly in the colonial era.[7] To some extent this omission is unavoidable. Despite the significant number of Chinese immigrants to Victoria in the 19th century, no central body of archival documents from the community survives. This limitation makes writing a conventional history of the colonial Chinese difficult, irrespective of its desirability. This challenge is particularly pronounced when it comes to seeking out personal histories. Viewed though the fragments of evidence in which colonial society documented their existence, Chinese miners have often been portrayed collectively as

---

[6] Gregor Benton and Edmund Terence Gomez, *The Chinese in Britain, 1800–present: economy, transnationalism, identity* (Basingstoke: Palgrave Macmillan, 2008), 1–20.

[7] Some exceptions here include Robert Travers, *Australian Mandarin: the life and times of Quong Tart* (Kenthurst: Rosenberg, 1981); Keir Reeves, 'Goldfields settler or frontier rogue? The trial of James Acoy and the Chinese on the Mount Alexander diggings', *Provenance: Journal of the Public Records Office of Victoria* 5 (2006); Yuanfang Shen, *Dragon seed in the Antipodes: Chinese-Australian autobiographies* (Melbourne: Melbourne University Press, 2001).

isolated and passive participants in goldfields communities.[8] Unchallenged by rich, personal stories, an enduring characterisation of the faceless, shabby alluvial digger, eking out a living at the fringes of society, dominates both sympathetic and hostile readings of period.

The second research pathway, one that we contend has been under-utilised, relates to the interpretation of relic mining landscapes of the central Victorian Goldfields (see figure 1). Often confusing and contradictory, shaped by varied combinations of human impact and revegetation, these multifaceted spaces present a challenge to historians and heritage professionals alike. Despite a recent acceleration in attempts to provide themed interpretation on the goldfields (including the provision of audio-visual material at Castlemaine and Bendigo) there remains a need for continuing critical analysis and refinement.

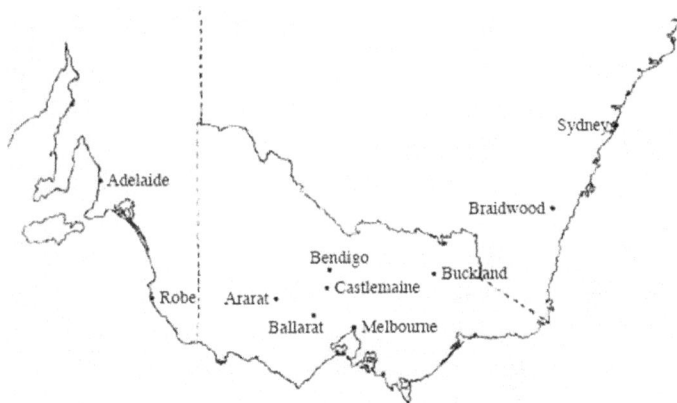

Figure 1: Map of South Eastern Australia Showing Key Goldmining Sites. Courtesy of Antoinette Dillon.

---

[8] For a discussion of the problems with sources see Kathryn Cronin, 'Chinese in colonial Victoria: the early contact years' (PhD thesis, Monash University, 1977), v; Kathryn Cronin, *Colonial casualties: Chinese in early Victoria* (Melbourne: Melbourne University Press, 1982), 6.

This task presents a number of obvious challenges. Moving from subtle bushland ruins to iconic regional centres such as Bendigo and Ballarat, interpreting the goldfields as they appear today requires a fluid and pragmatic investigative model. One flaw of heritage studies to date has been the lack of serious theoretical precepts for analysing the past in the present day. Unlike history, there is no established canon from which to draw historiographical insight or critique. Our response is to take landscape as an evidentiary medium; one that enables the practitioner to put history back into place. One important aspect here is the development of a framework for better understanding landscapes by inscribing them with human narratives. Through this process historical landscapes, such as the Chinese precinct of the goldfields city of Bendigo, can be better interpreted. Complex (and sometimes contradictory) understandings of Chinese-European relations also start to emerge. These relations highlight an ambiguous cultural encounter and can provide the historian with a glimpse of Chinese subaltern perspectives.

In responding to the often distorted nature of source material relating to the colonial Chinese and to the complexity of reading remnant colonial landscapes, we have attempted to devise a tandem approach, with personal insights and landscape analysis supporting one another. This strategy follows Keith Jenkins' assertion that historical writing can draw on a range of complementary methodologies.[9] To date, the most effective proponents of this style of approach in Chinese-Australian studies have been Jane Lydon, Grace Karskens and Alan Mayne.[10] By creating a new cultural history framework for the central Victorian

---

[9] Keith Jenkins, *On What is history? From Carr and Elton to Rorty and White* (London: Routledge, 1995), 178.

[10] Jane Lydon, *Many inventions: the Chinese in the Rocks, Sydney, 1890–1930* (Melbourne: Monash Publications in History, 1999); Grace Karskens, *Inside the Rocks: the archaeology of a neighbourhood* (Sydney: Hale & Iremonger, 1999); Alan Mayne, *Hill End: an Australian goldfields landscape* (Melbourne: Melbourne University Press, 2003).

Goldfields, one that encompasses both people and place, we can begin to unpack a regional historical narrative.

This process rests on an understanding of the concept of the 'cultural landscape'. When using the term cultural landscapes we refer to the remnants of the built environments created as a consequence of gold discoveries together with the collateral visual, oral and documentary material that assists in the interpretation of these environments. This concept is especially useful for an analysis of diverse heritage sites across the central Victorian diggings and is particularly appealing for Chinese-focused studies because of the relatively scarce nature of archival sources. Cultural landscapes provide an important conceptual tool for investigating how human activity has shaped the built environment and how, in turn, the natural environment has impacted on human activity.[11] This approach to interpretation is also of relevance to a broad audience as it provides a methodology for a range of cultural practitioners (including curators, heritage consultants, and site managers) to identify and interpret successive layers of heritage. In Australian history, these layers of past may include the Indigenous presence, convict settlement, pastoralism, or the impact of the agricultural, maritime, military or timber industries.

For the historian seeking new insights to the experience of the Chinese on the Australian goldfields, the value of landscape analysis is enriched when it is combined with personal or biographical studies. This relationship is mutually supportive, as a research framework incorporating a reading of a subject's surroundings can open new avenues of investigation for the biographer exploring personal impressions of the colonial Chinese. In both scenarios, by linking a reading of remnant goldfields landscapes to a consideration of day-to-day life, we can begin to investigate subtle interactions between people and

---

[11] This approach was first outlined in Keir Reeves, 'A hidden history: the Chinese on the Mount Alexander diggings, Central Victoria, 1851–1901' (PhD thesis, University of Melbourne, 2005), 26.

place. This complementary approach allows the historian to bring together a range of disparate sources and may in time help repopulate ambiguous historical spaces (and surviving visual records) with vibrant individual narratives. By seeking an understanding of cultural landscapes, and setting them as a cultural and spatial context to individual narratives, historians of the goldfields Chinese can supplement documentary records and relocate the individual into the *mise en scène*.

Fook Shing and the Bendigo diggings

To demonstrate this process, the authors are currently engaged in a research project that centres on the story of Fook Shing, a prominent goldfields personality, who settled in Victoria and served as a police detective in the years after the rush. By taking a complementary approach and synthesising a range of historical sources, we are attempting to unearth some of the complex patterns of social interaction that characterised Fook Shing's life on the Bendigo diggings in the 1850s. The aim of this approach is to seek out a more detailed understanding of one Chinese-Australian's goldfields experience and to draw on that individual narrative to uncover new insights into the hidden history of the region.

For the historian seeking a personal window to the Chinese in colonial Victoria, Fook Shing (sometimes Bay Fok Sing, Fok Sing, Fook Ching, Fook Sing, Fook Shing and finally Henry Fook Shing) has left behind a wealth of material.[12] Though a more detailed examination of Fook Shing's personal narrative forms the basis of our broader study, a brief survey of his involvement in the Bendigo community during the 1850s provides an indication of the sophistication of Fook Shing's goldfields experience. From a methodological perspective, Fook Shing's personal story also offers a number of insights into how a biographical history might complement a reading of Bendigo's cultural landscape.

---

[12] For a more detailed account of Fook Shing's life on the goldfields and a complete catalogue of associated references see Benjamin Mountford, 'In search of Fook Shing: detective stories from colonial Victoria' (Honours thesis, University of Melbourne, 2007).

Fook Shing was a ubiquitous figure across the colony of Victoria throughout much of his professional life. A native of Guangzhou, he arrived in Victoria via Adelaide in January 1854, making his way quickly to the goldfields at Bendigo.[13] Like so many of the Chinese gold diggers who arrived in Victoria in the 1850s, his family farmed the land in troubled Guangdong province. As rapid population growth and political instability shook the region, Fook Shing joined the mass of his countrymen seeking new opportunities abroad.[14] He took work as a ship's steward and a serving boy at Singapore, reaching Victoria as his countrymen began to arrive *en masse*.[15]

At Bendigo, Fook Shing took an active role in the rapidly expanding local community. As both a formative leader of the Bendigo Sheathed Sword society, a triad organisation representing his Sze Yup countrymen, and a headman in the Victorian government's Chinese Protectorate system, he established significant local authority. He took an active role in cultural and political life, attacking Christian missionaries and their efforts to convert Chinese diggers, campaigning against the Victorian government's efforts to restrict Chinese immigration, and playing a prominent role in the erection of a Chinese temple.[16] Fook Shing was also

[13] According to his certificate of naturalisation, Fook Shing arrived in Adelaide via Singapore aboard the Swan and then travelled to Melbourne aboard a ship 'the name of which ... [he] could not remember'. 'Naturalisation Papers: Fook Shing', Series A 712/1, Item 1859/L10690, National Archives of Australia (NAA), Canberra.

[14] Geoffrey Serle, *The golden age: a history of the colony of Victoria, 1851–1861* (Melbourne: Melbourne University Press, 1963), 320; Jean Gittins, *The diggers from China: the story of Chinese on the goldfields* (Melbourne: Quartet, 1981), 8.

[15] *The Courier of the Mines*, 4 September 1857. The Chinese population of Victoria (approximate) increased dramatically from 2373 in 1854 to 25,424 in 1857 and was estimated at 42,000 in 1859. G.A. Oddie, 'The Chinese in Victoria 1870–1890' (Master's thesis, University of Melbourne, 1959), 184.

[16] In addition to serving as places of worship, Chinese temples were social spaces and meeting points for local communities. Jutta Niemeier, 'The changing role of the See Yup Temple in Melbourne, 1866–1993', in *Histories of the Chinese in Australasia and the South Pacific: proceedings of an International Public Conference held at the Museum of Chinese Australian history, Melbourne, 8–10 October 1993*, ed. Paul Macgregor (Melbourne: The

involved in a range of business ventures on the goldfields. As Protectorate employment declined in the later 1850s, he began touring a successful Chinese theatre company across central Victoria and opened a store at Ballarat. Ongoing research shows he may also have been the 'Fok Sing' involved in the construction of a large brick kiln uncovered at Bendigo's PepperGreen Farm (see below). By the end of the 1850s, Fook Shing had become a naturalised Briton, and had purchased a house and land package across from the government reserve in Bendigo.

For a snapshot of the complexity of Fook Shing's goldfields narrative, we turn our attention to an episode that took place in 1856. On 3 November of that year, at Castlemaine's Primitive Methodist Chapel, the Reverend William Young delivered a report on the local Chinese mission.[17] Frustrated by what he perceived to be a prevalence of idolatry in the goldfields camps, Young castigated the Chinese for their lukewarm response to Christian teaching, expressing great disappointment that 'the seeds of divine truth … [had made] no deep religious impression'.[18] Elaborating on the failure, he recalled a recent visit to the Clinkers Hill Chinese camp, where he had been ridiculed by two headmen.[19] Most vocal was a leader from Bendigo:

> When he was told there was but one God, he replied—Englishmen may worship one God, we Chinese worship hundreds of gods. When I offered

Museum of Chinese Australian History, 1995), 328. For an overview of Fook Shing's goldfields activities see Mountford, 9–29.

[17] Reverend William Young was a church missionary of Scottish and Malaysian decent. See Keith Cole, *The Anglican mission to the Chinese in Bendigo and Central Victoria 1854–1918* (Bendigo: Keith Cole Publications, 1994), 11–12; William Young, 'Report on the condition of the Chinese population in Victoria', in *The Chinese in Victoria: official reports and documents*, ed. Ian McLaren (Ascot Vale: Red Rooster Press, 1985).

[18] Cronin, *Colonial casualties*, 108.

[19] According to the *Mount Alexander Mail* concerns were mounting about growing idolatry among the Chinese toward the end of 1856. On average 612 Chinese had been attending the mission Sunday services. The Chinese chapel on Clinkers Hill had been successfully renovated to improve conditions in summer and completely at the expense of the local Chinese community. *Mount Alexander Mail*, 10 November 1856.

him a copy of the bible he rejected it with disdain, and said he could not read or understand that book, and that he liked Chinese books better.[20]

As Young left the camp in defeat, the headman called out to him:

You sir, go about teaching the Chinese with a view of making them Christians. I can tell you a very easy method by which you can do that; just promise to give each man £3 a-week, and, I will pledge myself to bring you fifty Chinese Christians.[21]

Though the Bendigo headman is not named, Young's detractor was almost certainly Fook Shing, who made similar anti-Christian affirmations elsewhere.[22] His identity is affirmed by a number of factors, such as Young's assertion that the headman he encountered at Clinkers Hill had 'taken a prominent part in the erection of the Joss house at Long Gully ... Bendigo and was champion of idolatry there.'[23]

This vibrant episode is one of many from Fook Shing's personal story that provide the historian with a vignette of day-to-day life in the Chinese camps. As well as raising a number of questions about the influence of missionary activity and Christian teaching on the Victorian Chinese communities, Fook Shing's treatment of Young prompts considerations of broader patterns of cultural transmission and community identification. By taking his personal perspective as our focal point, we are able to approach these complex questions at the micro-level, taking into account

---

[20] Ibid.

[21] Ibid. For an account of the work of missionary societies amongst the colonial Chinese see Cronin, Colonial casualties, 107–23.

[22] Mountford, 20–3.

[23] Mount Alexander Mail, 10 November 1856. Fook Shing is recorded as having acted as headman at 'Long Gully' and 'Golden Gully', two of the largest Chinese camps at Bendigo. Cronin, 'Chinese in colonial Victoria', 37–9; David Horsfall, March to big gold mountain (Ascot Vale: Red Rooster Press, 1985), 52; Yolande Collins, 'Chinese communal arrangements in Bendigo and health officer surveillance, 1870s–1905', in Histories of the Chinese in Australasia and the South Pacific: proceedings of an International Public Conference held at the Museum of Chinese Australian History, Melbourne, 8–10 October 1993, ed. Paul Macgregor (Melbourne: The Museum, 1995), 394–408.

relationships between the individual and the collective. Fook Shing's actions at the Clinkers Hill Camp can thus be read as an expression of Chinese community resistance to missionary endeavour but also understood as a concerted effort by a government employee to emphasise his Chinese cultural affiliations and to downplay his role as a colonial agent. By setting himself in opposition to those Asian-Australians (like Young) actively promoting Western values, he fortified his own position amongst the parochial diggings Chinese.[24] The suggestion that Fook Shing's anti-Christian stance rested on political (rather than spiritual) foundations is supported by his readiness to marry spinster Ellen Mary Fling in a Christian ceremony, held at Melbourne's Congregational and Independent Church in July 1857 (see figure 2 below).[25]

Though only touched upon here, Fook Shing's story demonstrates the capacity of personal ethno-history to substantially enrich our understanding of colonial society. In contrast with the enduring image of the faceless, downtrodden Chinese digger (or the usual counterpoint, the flamboyant, urban Chinese entrepreneur) which dominates Australian history, his goldfields narrative provides a framework for interrogating a number of long-standing perceptions of the Chinese in 19th-century Australia. Neither simply 'collaborator' nor pro-Chinese 'chief', he offers a more complex, pragmatic image of the Chinese on the diggings. His readiness to adapt to Australian society and commitment to carving out a place in his adopted home provides a personal dimension to ongoing arguments over the sojourning mentality of Chinese goldseekers.[26]

---

[24] Cronin, *Colonial casualties*, 119.

[25] 'Marriage Certificate of Fook Shing and Ellen Mary Fling', 6 July 1857, no. 3225, Victorian Registry of Births, Deaths and Marriages.

[26] This commitment remained strong for the rest of his life. After the collapse of the Chinese Protectorate system in 1859, Fook Shing went on to serve as government interpreter and eventually became Victoria's longest-serving Chinese detective. In the large number of personal and professional records so far uncovered, Fook Shing gives no indication of any intention to return to China.

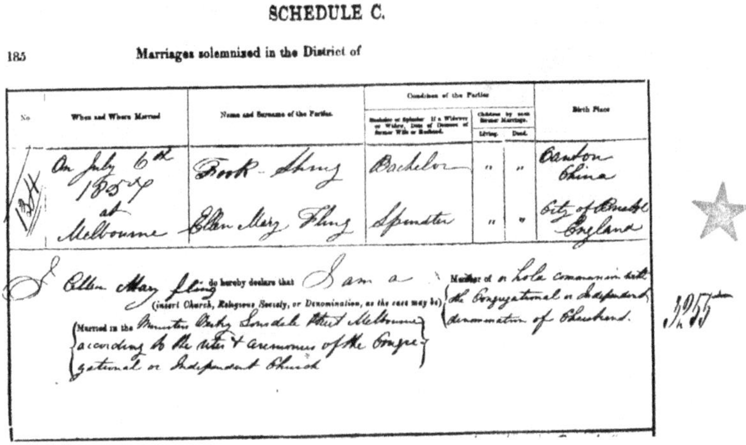
SCHEDULE C.

185 Marriages solemnized in the District of

No	When and Where Married	Name and Surname of the Parties	Condition of the Parties: Bachelor or Spinster. If a Widower or Widow, Date of Decease of former Wife or Husband	Children by each former Marriage: Living	Dead	Birth Place
	On July 6th 1857 at Melbourne	Fook Shing	Bachelor	"	"	Canton China
		Ellen Mary Fling	Spinster	"	"	City of Bristol England

I Ellen Mary Fling do hereby declare that I am a Member of no sole communion but the Congregational or Independent denomination of Churches. (insert Church, Religious Society, or Denomination, as the case may be)

Married in the Minister's Vestry Lonsdale Street Melbourne according to the rites & ceremonies of the Congregational or Independent Church

Figure 2: Marriage Certificate of Fook Shing and Ellen Fling, 1857. Courtesy of Registry of Births, Deaths and Marriages, Victoria.

Reading the historical layers of White Hills, Bendigo

In moving from personal history to a discussion of landscape we suggest that by considering people and place together, a more sophisticated analysis of heritage sites can be realised. The need for greater heritage interpretation has only recently been acknowledged by cultural heritage practitioners in general and Australian historians in particular.[27] Accordingly, we contend that Fook Shing's historical experience cannot be fully understood independently of the cultural landscape of White Hills, Bendigo (see figure 3), where he spent much of his time on the goldfields. Equally, it is only by anchoring the biographical details of his life to defined places that a deeper understanding of colonial Bendigo can be achieved.

[27] Tom Griffiths, *Forests of ash: an environmental history* (Melbourne, Cambridge: Cambridge University Press, 2001), 15.

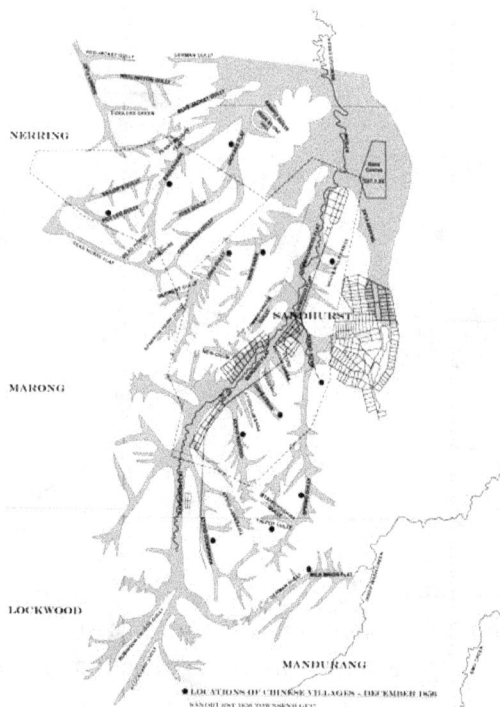

Figure 3: Map of Gullies at Bendigo Showing Chinese Villages in December 1856. Courtesy of Valerie Lovejoy. Adapted by Jacqueline Lovejoy from 'Sandhurst in 1856' by Townsend. GF 37, Department of Primary Industries, Victoria.[28]

White Hills, Bendigo, Fook Shing's former stamping ground, offers an excellent case for reading a cultural landscape. It should be noted that heritage professionals are mainly in agreement about the existence of cultural landscapes and their significance, yet the defining characteristics of such landscapes are not so easily identified. The Ironbark Camp, now

---

[28] This image appears in Valerie Lovejoy's doctoral thesis, Valerie Lovejoy, 'The fortune seekers of Dai Gum San: first generation Chinese on the Bendigo Goldfield, 1854–1882' (PhD thesis, La Trobe University, 2009).

known as the Chinese Camp, is the key Chinese heritage site in White Hills. The Ironbark Camp, also known in colonial administrative circles as the Chinese Protectorate, was the largest and most enduring camp in Bendigo. Situated at the northern terminus of the Bendigo tram, Ironbark Camp and its surrounding precinct comprise the key 19th-century Chinese heritage sites of the city. The Chinese temple, which is still known locally by the derogatory term Joss House, was where Chinese goldseekers practised their religious custom and engaged in many social activities. Today it stands as a remarkable relic of the goldrush era and as a reminder of the enduring Chinese presence throughout the region.

Figure 4: Excavation of Chinese Kiln and Market Garden, PepperGreen Farm. Courtesy of Heritage Victoria.

Until recently the Chinese temple comprised a single element of Chinese culture in an otherwise European streetscape. However, in 2005 a community access program undertook a fencing project at PepperGreen Farm, situated some 200 metres from the Chinese temple (see figure 4). During the project participants uncovered a large brick-kiln. Originally constructed by A'Fok, Fok Sing and Co in 1859, a subsequent excavation by Heritage Victoria revealed a large conical structure, much of which remained buried underground. This startling find represented one of the largest archaeological discoveries of Chinese activity outside of China and highlighted the extent of the Chinese role on the Bendigo diggings during the rushes.

It transpires that PepperGreen Farm was also previously a Chinese market garden. It is probable that the Chinese who operated the kiln concentrated their work on the market following the kiln's closure during the 1880s. Archaeological excavation carried out in 2006 revealed a range of smaller artefacts that indicated the kiln was part of a significant commercial concern whose products were for both Chinese and European clientele. Market gardening on the site continued well into the 20th century. The scale of the market gardens and the varieties of fruit and vegetables produced indicate the Chinese community's role in providing nutritious food to a notoriously dry region of Victoria.[29]

Perhaps the most enduring, and well-known, continuous physical presence of the Chinese community in Bendigo is manifested at the White Hills cemetery. While most of the Chinese goldseekers returned to China, a significant minority were not sojourners and instead remained in regional Victorian goldfields centres such as Bendigo, Castlemaine and Ballarat. A major replacement of headstones and the preservation of the burning tower make it a key Chinese burial ground in the southwest Pacific (see figure 5). The scale of the headstones in the Chinese burial

---

[29] Warwick Frost, et al., 'Interpreting the Chinese precinct', in *Deeper leads: new approaches to Victorian goldfields history*, eds. Keir Reeves and David Nichols (Ballarat: Ballarat Heritage Services, 2007), 203–23. See also Warwick Frost, 'Migrants and technological transfer: Chinese farming in Australia, 1850–1920', *Australian Economic History Review* 42.2 (2002): 113–31; Keir Reeves, 'Historical neglect of an enduring Chinese community', *Traffic* 3 (2003): 53–78.

ground section challenge the sojourning stereotype of the typical Chinese goldseeker. As Warwick Frost has pointed out:

> the very physicality of the cemetery, both its presence and its size, makes apparent tensions within the Chinese goldfields narrative … [and] suggests another story of Chinese life on the Victorian goldfields in which the Chinese became settler Australians.[30]

Figure 5: A Chinese headstone, White Hills cemetery. Courtesy of Kirsty Marshall.

Bendigo's historically layered landscape highlights the broader cultural themes of goldseeking and migration that are central to understanding

---

[30] Frost et al., 'Interpreting the Chinese precinct', 205–6.

the region. While White Hills can be read as a vernacular landscape (as Jackson has done in America) it is one that is also intricately linked with underlying historical forces of global capital and colonial settlement.[31] If we consider the temple, the kiln, the White Hills cemetery, and the market gardens as an assembly of Chinese heritage sites, then the claim of national and international significance is a tenable assertion. These heritage locations are, however, in many respects subtle parts of the cultural landscape and require human narratives in order to bring a greater depth of meaning and historical context. Without historical interpretation they stand as peripatetic elements in a little-known cultural landscape.

Though we seek to foreground the individual narrative in this interpretation, it is important to avoid setting Fook Shing and his contemporaries as stylised Chinese-antipodean caricatures or, conversely, to elevate them uncritically as universalising cultural metonyms. It is necessary, rather, to interpret personal histories as part of a broader global movement of people and transmission of ideas that underpinned the 19th-century gold discoveries. As such, Fook Shing can be equally understood as a Protectorate headman in the employ of the Victorian colonial authorities; a nefarious Chinese community leader; a businessman with a stated interest in the White Hills brickworks; and a pioneer with a vested interest in the development of Bendigo and, in turn, the machinations of the British Empire. These traits should not be treated as mutually exclusive.

Conclusion

In this chapter we have argued that it is necessary to consider people and place together in order to historically analyse the Chinese experience in the predominantly British colonial setting of goldrush-era Bendigo. Here

---

[31] An excellent example is J.B. Jackson, 'The abstract world of the hot-rodder', in *Landscape in sight: looking at America*, eds. J.B. Jackson and H.L. Horowitz (New Haven, Connecticut: Yale University Press, 1997).

we have been particularly concerned with exploring a methodology that we hope will inspire new considerations of Chinese perspectives within colonial history. By linking people and place (individuals and historical landscapes) we have an opportunity to uncover another layer of history on the diggings and to reinterpret the physical legacy of this history in the present day. Recognising the complexity of cultural identification on the goldfields, particularly across boundaries of race and ethnicity, promises new insights into 19th-century Australian society and our understanding of the importance of 'whiteness'.

3

Trans/national history and disciplinary amnesia: historicising White Australia at two *fins de siècles*

Leigh Boucher, Macquarie University

> What should ... form the field of history? ... States and politics will be the chief part of its subject, because the acts of nations and of the individuals who have played a great part in the[ir] affairs have usually been more important.
>
> Besides the thirty-five millions of the United Kingdom, there is in America and the British colonies and dependencies an English-speaking population of nearly seventy millions, who form ... virtually one people with the inhabitants of the old country [and history should] appeal to an audience of the whole race. [1]

(White) Australia has a problem with its past. As the venom in the recent 'history wars' suggests, these problems aren't produced by a straightforward tussle over historical truth; these cultural battles were energised by contestations over the meaning of that past in and for the present.[2] Indeed, current questions about identity, belonging and territorial entitlement inevitably underpin our historical engagements. In concrete ways, the historical stories we tell bind present-day communities together, police their boundaries of inclusion and exclusion, and legitimate their territorial claims. Moreover, there is little question that,

---

[1] 'Prefatory note', *English Historical Review* 1.1 (1886): 3–4.
[2] On the contours of the 'history wars' see Stuart Macintyre and Anna Clark, *The history wars* (Carlton: Melbourne University Press, 2004).

culturally speaking, the nation functioned as the dominant category of 20th-century historical consciousness in the Anglophone world; these battles were thus inevitably shaped by the culturally-naturalised ideologies of nationalism.[3]

As Benedict Anderson reminds us, however, nation-states rely on the collective imagination of communities; by implication, historians should be wary of the ways in which our disciplinary practice neatly discerns the origins of these contemporaneous communities in the past.[4] Regardless of our claims to empirical voracity, professional historical practice is, at the very least, epistemologically implicated in the framing of these political dynamics. Academic historians have been similarly bound by a 'narrative contract' with the nation-state for much of the discipline's history. Thus in a moment of disciplinary 'birth' in 1886, the *English Historical Review* directed the nascent profession to discern the acts of nations as its fundamental project.[5]

Furthermore, in settler-colonial states like (white) Australia, historians might do well to rethink the nation-making imperatives of our territorially-bounded writings because the territorially-possessive logic of settler (national) identity seems incompatible with an acknowledgment

---

[3] I don't want to enter the muddy debate about the 'character' and 'origins' of nationalism as an ideological formation. However, importantly, most theorists and historians of nationalism suggest that a crucial character of nationalism is a claim on territorial possession and legitimate sovereignty by a 'people'. Most importantly, these 'people' (and their correlative territorial claims) are buttressed by historical narratives. As Eric Hobsbawm writes, 'my profession, which has always been mixed up in politics, becomes an essential component of nationalism ... because nations without [history] are a contradiction in terms'. Eric J. Hobsbawm, 'Ethnicity and nationalism in Europe today', *Anthropology Today* 8.1 (1992): 3–8.

[4] Benedict R. Anderson, *Imagined communities: reflections on the origin and spread of nationalism* (Cambridge: Cambridge University Press, 1991), 6.

[5] The phrase 'narrative contract' is taken from Antoinette Burton, 'Thinking beyond the boundaries: empire, feminism and the domains of history', *Social History* 26.1 (2001).

of continuing (Ab)original sovereignty.[6] If the (white) Australian nation and its imagined community are necessarily given foundation by the mythic legitimacy of settler territorial expropriation, does writing national histories in the present inevitably uphold these (il)legitimacies? Indeed, in many ways Indigenous histories represent an historiographic paradox; the category of (Ab)original Australians functions as a constant reminder of the wholesale theft that underpins the Australian nation-state.[7] It's no coincidence that the doomed race theory was at its height around the time of federation. It safely (dis)placed (Ab)original Australians in the pre-historical past; the remaining Indigenous population became a temporal 'remnant' with no place in the historicised national present and future.[8] Whilst the inclusion of (Ab)original voices into Australian history from the 1970s addressed the great (white) Australian silence, the ensuing 'history wars' suggest that this incorporation opened a serious epistemological rift.[9] In these contexts, wars about 'our' national history, then, are less than surprising. If historical writing answers past and present questions about who belongs where, Australian History—the story of European conquest and national emergence—is always going to struggle to escape the expropriating dynamics of settler colonialism.

Thinking transnationally about the past, then, offers a tempting solution to these problems because it seems to reframe the boundaries of

---

[6] See, Patrick Wolfe, 'Nation and miscegenation: discursive continuity in the post-Mabo era', *Social Analysis* 36 (1994), 111; Aileen Moreton-Robinson, 'Terra Nullius and the possessive logic of patriarchal whiteness', in *Changing law: rights, regulation and recognition*, eds. Rosemary Hunter and Mary Keyes (Aldershot: Ashgate, 2005), 123–33.

[7] Drawn from Bain Attwood, *Telling the truth about Aboriginal history* (Crow's Nest: Allen & Unwin, 2005), 11–35.

[8] On the 'doomed race' theory in Australia, see Russell McGregor, *Imagined destinies: Aboriginal Australians and the doomed race theory* (Melbourne: Melbourne University Press, 1997). I thank Alison Holland for a hallway discussion that made me think about the relationship between federation and the disavowal of Aboriginal futures.

[9] This well-known phrase is taken from W.E.H. Stanner's 1968 'Boyer Lecture'. W.E.H. Stanner, *After the dreaming* (Sydney: Australian Broadcasting Commission, 1969), 7.

historical knowledge. Might the geographic loosening of the narrative contract between historians and the nation-state take some of the territorially-possessive venom out of national 'history wars'?[10] Indeed, in recent decades, nationally-bounded historical writing has begun to look methodologically and politically suspect from a number of disciplinary fronts; various national 'history wars', challenges to national exceptionalisms, global frames of vision, and postcolonial critiques of Eurocentric discourses of national self-realisation have all fractured the epistemic accords that contracted historians to the nation-state. In these contexts, tracing transnational circulations of ideas, capital and bodies in the past seems an attractive project.[11] By unmaking the historical inviolability and inevitability of the nation-state, transnational historians make a compelling case for their methodological and political utility and the profession itself is certainly taking on a more transnational temper.

In this chapter I would like to suggest that transnational history's apparent potential to address myriad political and methodological malaises is only made possible by a serious case of disciplinary amnesia. Indeed, the transnational turn has in no small way been energised by repeated critiques of national historiography as a 'toxic' product of Eurocentric nation-making in the 19th century.[12] This turn, I would like

---

[10] Marilyn Lake, for example, suggests that transnational 'thinking' can directly address the ways in which 'Australian history has conscripted the past into the service of the nation'. Marilyn Lake, 'On history and politics', in *The historian's conscience: Australian historians on the ethics of history*, ed. Stuart Macintyre (Melbourne: Melbourne University Publishing, 2004), 96.

[11] Ann Curthoys and Marilyn Lake conduct an insightful discussion of transnational history in their 'Introduction', in *Connected worlds: history in transnational perspective*, eds. Ann Curthoys and Marilyn Lake (Canberra: ANU E Press, 2006).

[12] 'Toxic product' from Patrick J. Geary, *The myth of nations: the medieval origins of Europe* (Princeton: Princeton University Press, 2002), 15. Even Catherine Hall, in her vital project that brings the empire into the birth of English national history in the 19th century, maintains the territorial coherence of the nation-state. Empires and colonialism matter, for Hall, insofar as they made and remade the boundaries between the (national) metropole and the (colonial) periphery. Catherine Hall, 'At home with history', in *At home with the Empire,*

to suggest, relies on an historiographic genealogy that disowns a range of 19th-century trans-territorial historical writings. Indeed, as White Australia was geopolitically made, many historians (both in Britain and the colonies) sought to understand this outpost of whiteness—and its colonial origins—in what now look like transnational terms. Whilst the first edition of the *English Historical Review* might have asserted the centrality of the 'nation' to historical writing, ideas about trans-territorial racial communities and audiences were similarly prominent in the moment of the discipline's birth. Even as the *Review* attempted to centralise the nation, the ways in which imperialism had produced an imagined 'transnational' audience refused to disappear entirely from the frame of vision.[13] We are not the first historians to think transnationally about (white) Australia, and the absence of these early trans-territorial histories from our disciplinary genealogies is worrying.

Beginning with the range of ways in which national historical writing has been challenged in recent decades, I would first like to draw out the historiographic consensus that similarly structures the transnational turn, postcolonial critiques of national historiography, and recent considerations of the 'history wars'. Secondly, I sketch a brief 'counter-history' of historical writing in the second half of the 19th century to suggest that, for many historians at this *fin de siècle*—in sharp contrast to our dominant narratives of disciplinary origin and birth—the nation-state wasn't the only territorial container of historical knowledge. Indeed, for a range of writers across the settler periphery and metropole, modernity was signified by the global circulation of people and ideas; as the *EHR* asserted, the 'whole race' of 'English speaking peoples' had spread across the globe. As we are faced with our own globalising modernity, and the transnational analytic vocabulary seems to solve a series of nationally-produced dilemmas, we might do well to remember a

---

eds. Catherine Hall and Sonya O. Rose (Cambridge: Cambridge University Press, 2006), 32–42.

[13] 'Prefatory note'.

series of historians who understood their own late-19th-century modernity—and the imperial expropriations that underwrote it—in similarly trans-territorial terms.

Disciplinary genealogies and the transformative possibilities of transnational history

Transnational historians suggest that historicising nationally necessarily involves the *retrospective* imposition of contemporaneous national sovereignties with concrete genealogical effects.[14] Importantly, this critique functions on both political and empirical registers; framing the past in national terms involves isolating what are, in fact, empirically interconnected pasts and this imposition grants legitimacy to the territorial demands of nation-states in the present. These critiques offer compelling avenues to understand the political ferocity of nationalism and its historiographic discontents (like the eruption of 'history wars'). Precisely because historical knowledge is a crucial balustrade of national belonging and entitlement, challenges to national historical narratives will necessarily be greeted by an ideological backlash. As numerous historians have subsequently argued, the animating problem in the 'history wars' seemed to be the threat that an emergent professional consensus about colonial exploitation posed to public historical narratives of territorial entitlement and national identity.[15] Transnational history, then, promises to remake the discursive boundaries that made these wars possible (and, perhaps, inevitable). Moreover, a counter-national turn is occurring at multiple historiographic sites—this turn only lends weight to its political and methodological promise.

---

[14] On the emergence of transnational history see Ann Curthoys and Marilyn Lake, eds., *Connected worlds: history in transnational perspective* (Canberra: ANU E Press, 2006).

[15] Martin Krygeir and Robert Van Krichen, 'The character of the nation', in *Whitewash: on Keith Windschuttle's fabrication of Aboriginal history* (Melbourne: Black Inc., 2003). See also Anna Clark, 'History in black and white: a critical analysis of the black armband debate', in *Country: Journal of Australian Studies* 75, ed. Richard Nile (St Lucia: University of Queensland Press, 2002).

Postcolonial scholarship has long pointed out the ways in which national historical writing tends to mobilise both the temporal and territorial logics of colonialism. In western conventions of historical thought, Europe functions as the origin of modernity and non-western cultures are situated as ahistorical predecessors of modern national communities. Dipesh Chakrabarty thus suggests that because the discipline of history in the 20th century 'universalize[d] the nation-state as the most desirable form of political community', histories written about the former colonial periphery tended to assess the acquisition of this political status by colonised people in a metanarrative of liberal progress and national self-realisation.[16] In historical terms, colonised peoples become modern at the moment they 'achieve' liberal nation-statehood.[17]

In settler societies, these temporalising logics take on even more potency.[18] If (post)colonial national history discerns the realisation of national independence as the unshackling of imperial dependence, the acknowledgement of the continuing colonial relationship between white Australia and its Indigenous peoples becomes a narrative impossibility. In this way, the continuing presence of Indigenous peoples haunts the peripheries of national historical consciousness as a destabilising force in narratives of national self-realisation and liberal accomplishment.[19] It's little wonder that most settler societies have been plagued by 'history wars' in the last few decades; Aboriginal political campaigns have, in their very existence, fractured the stubborn temporal and spatial demarcations

---

[16] Dipesh Chakrabarty, 'Postcoloniality and the artifice of history: who speaks for "Indian" pasts?', *Representations* 37 (1992): 19.

[17] Partha Chatterjee, *The nation and its fragments: colonial and postcolonial histories* (Princeton: Princeton University Press, 1993).

[18] This point is made by Bain Attwood in 'The paradox of Australian Aboriginal history', *Thesis Eleven* 38 (1994).

[19] See Chris Healy, *Forgetting Aborigines* (Sydney: UNSW Press, 2008).

of late-20th-century (white) settler national historical knowledge.[20] Perhaps, simply by surviving the onslaught of settler colonialism, Aboriginal Australians destabilise the historico-territorial myths of settler nationhood and 'dispute the moral legitimacy of the nation-state.'[21]

Historicising nationally doesn't only present a problem in former colonial states; for many global historians there are serious implications to the segregation of modern history into national boundaries. In an apparently globalising world, historians have begun to consider the ways in which the global movement of people, ideas, and capital have a much longer history. Indeed, transnational history offers a powerful critique of the ways in which globalisation is frequently exceptionalised as a late-20th-century phenomenon.[22] Debates about the impact (positive or otherwise) of globalisation on local cultures frequently pretend that national borders were virtually impenetrable for much of the 20th (and, indeed, 19th) century.[23] With such ahistorical accounts of previous national inviolability stabilising both violently reactive nationalism and naively hopeful globalism, it's little wonder that historians have attempted to grant globalisation a much longer genealogy. A genealogy of global

---

[20] Patrick Wolfe, *Settler colonialism and the transformation of anthropology: the politics and poetics of an ethnographic event* (London: Cassell, 1999). On the ways in which settler colonialism relies on the maintenance of a clear division (both spatial and temporal) between white settler 'civilisation' and indigenous 'culture' see Rod MacNeil, 'Time after time: temporal frontiers and the boundaries in colonial images of the Australian landscape', in *Colonial frontiers: Indigenous-European encounters in settler societies*, ed. Lynnette Russell (Manchester: Manchester University Press, 2001).

[21] This phrase is taken from A. Dirk Moses, 'Genocide and settler society in Australian history', in *Genocide and settler society: frontier violence and stolen Indigenous children in Australian history*, ed. A. Dirk Moses (New York: Berghahn Books, 2004), 6.

[22] See, for example, Craig Calhoun, Frederick Cooper, and Kevin W. Moore, eds., *Lessons of empire: imperial histories and American power* (New York: New Press, 2006).

[23] David Held and Anthony McGrew, 'Introduction', in *The global transformations reader*, eds. David Held and Anthony McGrew, 2nd ed. (Cambridge: Polity Press, 2003).

exchange, interdependence, and transnationalism productively disrupts the imagined historical inviolability of the nation-state.[24]

In these (and myriad other) ways, national historiography has become the 'bogeyman' of much theoretical debate. This counter-national temper of current historiography relies, moreover, on a common disciplinary genealogy. This genealogy traces how, over the course of the 19th century, professional historical knowledge became knowledge of the nation.[25] For world historians attempting to unmake the autonomy of the nation, the 19th century represents a lamentable narrowing of the historical gaze. Benedickt Stuchtey and Eckhardt Fuchs look to the 'historiographic expression of European' nationalism in the 19th century, which 'encouraged a geographic narrowing of the [discipline's] subject matter.'[26] As the modern nation-state was 'born' in Europe (France, Italy, and Germany), the discipline of history supplied nationalism with the legitimacy of historical inevitability.

World historians are not alone; postcolonial scholars similarly examine the 19th century—as a moment of both high imperialism and disciplinary birth—to find a troubling accord between national historical writing, the temporalising logics of liberalism, and the 'sorting categories' that made colonial expropriation and exploitation possible.[27] In the British (historiographic) world, the writings of 19th-century Whig historians (who discerned the reformist unfolding of liberal Britain as an inviolable island story beginning in the 13th century) bear particular responsibility for the national territorialisation of historical writing. As

---

[24] See, for example, David Christian, 'History and global identity', in *The historian's conscience: Australian historians on the ethics of history*, ed. Stuart Macintyre (Melbourne: Melbourne University Publishing, 2004).

[25] On the 'muddiness' of this emergence, see Ann Curthoys and John Docker, *Is history fiction?* (Sydney: UNSW Press, 2006).

[26] Benedikt Stuchtey and Eckhardt Fuchs, *Writing world history 1800–2000* (Oxford: Oxford University Press, 2003), 15.

[27] Ann Laura Stoler, *Haunted by empire: geographies of intimacy in North American history* (Durham: Duke University Press, 2006), 3.

Uday Mehta argues, a key 'strategy of exclusion' for liberal thinkers who espoused the apparently universalising rights of man lay in the mutual encoding of racial difference, political competence, and historical development. For these thinkers, the right to 'representative government and democracy [was] dependent upon societies having reached a particular historical maturation or level of civilization'.[28] This historical maturation, however, was differentially achieved; it could be endlessly deferred for non-white societies. From the perspective of postcolonial and global historians, then, the containment of historical knowledge within national territorial parameters in the 19th century was directed by the racial encodings of imperial rule (by racially certifying European nation-states at the telos of progressive historical development) and the operation of European nationalism (as modern nation-states were made and remade in the rhetoric of liberal rationality).

Similarly, the birth of Australian History as a modern, professional discipline is frequently represented as a moment when historical consciousness turned inward. In many ways, the progressive births of professional (national) history in Europe, Australian nationalism, and then modern Australian history-writing makes this historiographic narrative even more compelling; national history first became the possession of the European nation-state and was subsequently implemented in the colony soon after federation. Nineteenth century historians in the Australian colonies are thus divorced from the moment of disciplinary birth precisely because they tended to write their histories in imperial and colonial terms.[29] The federation of (white) Australia and

---

[28] Uday Singh Mehta, *Liberalism and empire: a study in nineteenth-century British liberal thought* (Chicago: University of Chicago Press, 1999), 9.

[29] See, for example, Tom Griffiths, *Hunters and collectors: the antiquarian imagination in Australia* (Cambridge: Cambridge University Press, 1996); Stuart Macintyre, 'Rusden, Turner and the lessons of the past', in *The writing of Victoria's history*, ed. Jeff Leeuwenburg (Melbourne: Baillieu Library, 1994). And Elizabeth Kwan, 'G.C. Henderson: advocate of "systematic and scientific" research in Australian history'; and Deryck Schreuder, 'An

the birth of 'national' historical consciousness thus represent both an historiographic break (with colonial historical writings) and a moment of disciplinary origin. So too, discussions of the 'history wars' employ this historiographic narrative to great analytic effect. 'Pre-histories' of this skirmish frequently ignore the formative possibilities of 19th-century historical writings—after all, if the 'history wars' were produced by the alignment of historical knowledge with nationalism, then the beginning of this problem must lie in the birth of national historiography after federation.[30] The problems of (white) national history seem to originate in an alliance between (white) Australian nationalism and the modernisation of the discipline.

Across multiple disciplinary sites, then, the political and methodological worth of our transnational sensibility relies on the certainty that in the late 19th century the destination of liberal history (modernity) looked firmly national. Perhaps, though, in our move to decentre the nation from contemporary historical practice we have employed a genealogy that ignores the constitutive impact(s) of empire on both sovereignty and historical thought in the late 19th century. As Frederick Cooper suggests, in the 19th and early 20th centuries imperial unity and trans-territorial political reach could function as signifiers of modernity.[31] Indeed, the 19th-century globe was geopolitically managed as much by empires as it was by the boundaries of nation-states. So too (as the various campaigns for imperial federation suggest), in the broader

---

unconventional founder', both in *The discovery of Australian history*, eds. Stuart Macintyre and Julian Thomas (Melbourne: Melbourne University Press, 1995).

[30] See, for example Henry Reynolds, who argues that there was no space for violence in national historiography in contrast to imperial historians. Henry Reynolds, *Aboriginal land rights in colonial Australia: a lecture delivered at the National Library of Australia 21 October 1986* (Canberra: National Library of Australia, 1988). 'Prehistory' taken from Lorenzo Veracini, 'A prehistory of Australia's history wars', *Australian Journal of Politics and History* 52.3 (2006): 439.

[31] Frederick Cooper, *Colonialism in question: theory, knowledge, history* (Berkeley: University of California Press, 2005).

imperial world a national geopolitical present and future didn't necessarily mean a departure from empire.[32] Whilst the denial of national independence to non-white colonies such as India relied on the idea of territorial, racial and historical distance between the metropole and periphery, in the settler empire the racial commonality of the settler colony and metropole forged powerful racial and historical connections between Britain the colonies. Andrew Thomson and Duncan Bell have found that the 19th-century empire was often imagined as an historical community of English speaking peoples with global reach.[33] So too, the successful claims on liberal rights by settlers in the mid-19th century forged powerful imaginative connections between reform at 'home' and the liberal experiments in the settler periphery. Perhaps for some 19th-century thinkers, modernity was imperial and global in orientation, and the settler empire and its associated racial congenialities suggested a global territory of liberal governance and history.

Liberal histories and the settler empire: an alternate genealogy

It was precisely this historicised object—namely, the settler empire—that the chair of the Colonial Institute in London employed to frame the organisation's agenda. In his 1869 opening address to what would become the Royal Colonial Institute, John Bury hoped it would be a site where the experiences of empire would coalesce. In the discussion that followed, the complex political relationships within empire were seen as a matter in

---

[32] On the various proposals for imperial federation see: Nicholas Aroney, 'A Commonwealth of Commonwealths? Late nineteenth century conceptions of federalism and their impact on Australian Federation', *Journal of Legal History* 23.3 (2002); and T.N.Harper, 'Empire, diaspora and the languages of globalization, 1850–1914', in *Globalization in world history*, ed. A.G. Hopkins (New York: Norton, 2002).

[33] Andrew S. Thompson, *The empire strikes back? The impact of imperialism on Britain from the mid-nineteenth century* (Harlow: Pearson Longman, 2005); Duncan Bell, *Victorian vision of the global order* (Cambridge: Cambridge University Press, 2008).

need of *historicised* discussion.[34] So too, speakers at the Colonial Institute were, unsurprisingly, keen to distinguish between the colonies peopled by the '*Anglo-Saxon* race' and others such as 'India, [where the task of empire] was very different because we have to respect their idiosyncrasies'.[35] Indeed, the 'great and diversified system of the colonial empire' could be explained by the different racial constituencies in each territory. These 'mixed dependencies comprising masses of weaker or less energetic races' required 'equitable, adaptive and generous government' but weren't historically comparable with the homeland. However, whilst paternal control of the colonies could be justified when this periphery was populated by black bodies, in settler contexts shared racial membership short-circuited the territorial and temporal distinctions between a national metropole and colonial peripheries.[36] Speakers continually asserted that the rise of representative government in the settler periphery placed this empire in the same historical and racial landscape as the metropole. Indeed, a crucial component of the Royal Colonial Institute's discussions would be historical and Bury hoped 'matters relating to the early history of the colonies' would find an audience.

Unsurprisingly, in many British settler colonies in the mid-19th century, local histories were produced that charted this type of progress. In the late 1850s, for example, Victoria had been gripped by its first eruption of historicised discourses that took the colony itself as their subject.[37] The 1850s and 1860s witnessed the publication of the histories of William Westgarth, James Bonwick and Thomas McCombie, and

---

34 John Bury, 'Preliminary proceedings', *Proceedings of the Royal Colonial Institute* 1 (1869): 1–5.

35 William Westgarth, 'The relations of the colonies to the mother country', *Proceedings of the Royal Colonial Institute* 1 (1869): 154.

36 This point is made by Daiva K. Stasiulis and Nira Yuval-Davis, *Unsettling settler societies: articulations of gender, race, ethnicity and class* (London: Sage, 1995).

37 See Griffiths, *Hunters and collectors*.

colonial newspapers and magazines began including articles of historical interest. Like the speakers at the Royal Colonial Institute 20 years later, these historians situated Victoria as part of the trans-territorial history of liberal reform and racial progress. James Bonwick's history of Victoria, 'using old colonial records ... mark[ed] the difficulties of ... progression and indicate[d] the ultimate triumph of freedom'.[38] For many historians of colonial Victoria in the 1850s, 60s and 70s, Victoria was simply another example of the Anglo-Saxon story of unfolding liberty and racialised superiority. William Westgarth similarly drew two conclusions from the history of Victoria; first, that the 'invading progress of the colonists [was an] immutable law of nature and history'; and secondly, that the 'early' granting of full manhood suffrage was, in fact, a comprehensible outcome of the racialised character of the Victorian settler population.[39] So too, Thomas McCombie revealed that 'the old system ha[d] been silently and rapidly passing away and an entirely new order of things ... developing itself. From a perfect despotism ... to the very opposite point of democracy.' Unlike the Indigenous population who 'weren't fit to have a political existence', the responsible and respectable Victorians demonstrated precisely the liberal character of British settler-colonial stock.[40]

The characteristics of these settler-colonial historians also reverberated in metropolitan political and historical debates in the later 19th century. James Bonwick suggested to the Royal Colonial Institute on his visit to London that the history of empire would much more productively draw on the traditions and style of 'Sharon Turner rather

---

[38] Thomas McCombie, *The history of the colony of Victoria from its settlement to the death of Sir Charles Hotham* (Melbourne: Sands and Kenny, 1858), 1–4.

[39] William Westgarth, *The colony of Victoria: its history, commerce and gold mining* (London: Sampson Low, Son, and Marston, 1864), 3, 5–9.

[40] McCombie, *The history of the colony of Victoria*, 1–4.

than Hume or Macaulay'.[41] Citing Turner's *History of the Anglo-Saxons* and *History of England* from the first decades of the 19th century, Bonwick mobilised a tradition of explicitly racialised histories as the framework to comprehend empire—they simply needed to expand Turner's geography. Other settler-colonial speakers suggested that to understand the history of the settler colonies 'one needed to study the mother-land and watch as it emerges from barbarism and note its conduct among the rude shocks of the 15th and 16th centuries'.[42] However, these Anglo-Saxon outposts, whilst mirroring the early development of England, had in many ways leapfrogged ahead towards the telos of liberal development. As Flora Shaw would remark in the 1890s:

> What is to be seen and studied [in Australia] gives us a glimpse into the ... history that is to follow after our time ... its developments carry on the history of the race, she offers the introductory chapter of a new history.[43]

Shaw was not alone; various papers on developments in New Zealand and Canada discussed how these colonies were pursuing political reform at a much faster pace than the homeland.

The pace of reform in the settler periphery, moreover, provided some reforming metropolitan liberals with concrete examples of the destination of British historical change; they functioned as retrospective 'test cases' for liberal reform amongst racially-congenial populations.[44] Whilst the Reform Acts of the 19th century could signify the uniquely liberal competencies of the English nation and the outcome of centuries

---

[41] James Bonwick, 'The writing of colonial history', *Proceedings of the Royal Colonial Institute* 26 (1895): 231.

[42] Earl of Onsnlow, 'State socialism and labor government in Antipodean Britain', *Proceedings of the Royal Colonial Institute* 28 (1893): 98.

[43] Flora Shaw, 'The Australian outlook', *Proceedings of the Royal Colonial Institute* 28 (1893): 112.

[44] Antoinette Burton, 'Introduction: on the inadequacy and the indispensability of the nation', in *After the imperial turn: thinking with and through the nation*, ed. Antoinette Burton (Durham: Duke University Press, 2003).

of historical development, they could also be 'braided together' with the liberal reforms of the settler empire that preceded them to suggest that modern history was global rather than national.[45] At certain moments in 19th-century British liberal thought—which, because of its reforming character was firmly historicist in orientation—the globalising movement of the British race across the settler periphery forged powerful trans-territorial connections between the settler periphery and the metropole.[46]

Indeed, in the collection of *Essays on reform* written in support of the 1867 British Reform Act by university liberals, the Australian democratic experiment provided proof of how liberal extensions to the franchise might be successfully achieved. In James Bryce's chapter on the historical development of democracy in Europe, he argued that any attempt to halt the move towards liberal reform would subvert the historically ordained progress of the British race. Equally significantly, another contributor to the volume argued that British conservatives opposed to the Reform Act should simply read the histories of McCombie and Westgarth for there 'wasn't an offensive page amongst them'.[47]

The liberal political and scholarly career of James Bryce in many ways mirrored the global temper of Anglo-Saxon historical consciousness.[48] Bryce chaired the Oxford branch of the Imperial Federation League in the 1880s, and by 1910 he had visited most of the settler empire, seeking to understand how the institutions of English law

---

[45] The phrase 'braided together' is taken from Tony Ballantyne, *Orientalism and race* (New York: Palgrave, 2006).

[46] Andrew S. Thompson, *The empire strikes back?: the impact of imperialism on Britain from the mid-nineteenth century* (Harlow: Pearson Longman, 2005).

[47] James Bryce 'The historical aspect of democracy' in *Essays on reform* n.e. '(London: MacMillan, 1867), 239–67; Charles Pearson 'On the working of Australian institutions' in *Essays on reform*, 194.

[48] On the connections between Bryce's historical writings and his political career see Keith Robbins, 'History and politics: the career of James Bryce', *Journal of Contemporary History* 7.3 (1972).

and governance were operating in these new locations.[49] As an historian, Bryce spent much of his career historicising the movement of English legal institutions outside British territory. Historians, for Bryce, needed to comprehend historical change within these reterritorialised parameters and racial difference and migration were two of his central analytic concerns. In Bryce's own words in 1900, 'a Teutonic tribe … had extended over much of the globe … in an empire of peaceful settlement and migration in the last three centuries', and this historical process was in need of empirical investigation.[50]

In a series of observations that resonate all too disturbingly with the claims of many a globalisation theorist today, Bryce went on to argue that:

> the world is becoming *one* in an altogether new sense … the European races have gained dominion over nearly the whole of the earth … As the larger human groups absorb or assimilate the smaller, the movements of politics, and of thought in each of its regions becomes more closely interwoven with those of every other. Whatever happens in one part of the globe now has a significance for every other part.

For Bryce, the ultimate logic underpinning these developments was the move towards representative government across the globe. The global spread of liberal governance was an historical inevitability. The spread of Anglo-Saxon law meant that 'world history was becoming one history'.[51] In order to comprehend the global trajectories of empire, then, Bryce reached to the language of Anglo-Saxon exceptionalism and racialised liberal competence. Most importantly, this liberal competence was the unique possession of the 'Anglo-Saxon'. Other races would simply

[49] James Bryce, 'Address on colonial policy', Aberdeen, 21 April 1892, British Library, London.

[50] James Bryce, *Studies in history and jurisprudence* (Oxford: Clarendon Press, 1901), 3.

[51] James Bryce, *University and historical addresses* (London: Macmillan, 1913), 211.

'disappear' as these regions were 'closely interwoven' in a global community of shared racial membership and liberal history.[52]

At this *fin de siècle*, then, shared racial membership functioned as a powerful anodyne to territorial isolation. It should come as no surprise that many contributors to the federation conventions in Australia were deeply familiar with Bryce's work.[53] Moreover, according to Bryce, this was a nation-state that joined a global community of Anglo-Saxon liberal politics at the moment of federation. It was no coincidence that (Ab)original Australians were firmly excluded from the boundaries of Commonwealth citizenship; there was no place for them in this white man's country.[54] In this way, (white) Australia wasn't necessarily only a moment of sovereign birth, it also represented a firm statement of trans-territorial belonging, and thinking in global terms about historical change provided crucial support for this 'transnational' imagined community.

Conclusion

Present-day critiques of modern historical practice that locate the origin of the 'narrative contract' between historians and the nation-state in the geopolitical reconfigurations of Europe ignore the multiple ways in which the expansion of empire mattered for 19th-century historians. Moreover, if nation-states represent a particular ordering of territory and governance alongside an articulation of a population's ethnic and historical coherence, this triad of population, governance and territory was an equation equally managed via the framework of empire well into the 20th century; histories of a 'people', their governance, and territory could and were written about empires. As late-19th-century historians

---

[52] Ibid. 213.

[53] For a discussion of Bryce and Australian federation see Graham Maddox, 'James Bryce: Englishness and federalism in America and Australia', *Publicis* 34.1 (2004).

[54] For a discussion of the 'white man's country' see Marilyn Lake, 'White man's country: the trans-national history of a national project', *Australian Historical Studies* 24.122 (2003).

were implicated in the formation of the modern discipline and its professional and rhetorical conventions, they examined an imperial world where the graduated sovereignties within the settler empire suggested interdependence and racial commonality rather than national exclusivity. For Bryce and a range of metropolitan historical thinkers and settler-colonial historians, modernity was liberal, but, equally importantly, modern history was the story of a globalising population that reformed the spaces of empire with justifiable racial exclusions and territorial expropriations.[55] In sharp contrast to our own narrative of disciplinary birth, for Bryce, and for others, modern history was a narrative in which liberalism was being realised in trans-territorial rather than national terms.

In our own 'globalising' *fin de siècle* we have similarly adopted a transnational vocabulary. In our context this adoption functions as a corrective response to perceived methodological limitations and political violences of historicising nationally. In seeking to understand these 'history wars' as *only* a problem of national historiography, however, we have animated an historiographic genealogy that ignores the trans-territorial and global traditions of historical writing in the 19th century and the expropriate colonial work they performed. I raise these territorially disruptive histories to problematise this commonly evoked disciplinary genealogy, and not only as a project of 'empirical' correction. As the critiques of national historical writing affirm, the stories we tell about 'our' past have concrete political consequences. This disciplinary amnesia might have some worrying consequences.

Given that our own era is characterised by its own narratives of liberal reform that function to deny the sovereignty of racialised Others, we might do well to reconsider the globalising rhetorical company we are keeping, accidentally or otherwise. (I'm thinking here of the cross-

---

[55] Bryce was not alone; we might also consider James Froude and John Seeley who are now usually segregated into 'imperial' history. This segregation, however, might not always have been so secure.

national military and economic interventions frequently justified by the universalising claims of economic and political liberalism.) Moreover, locally, state 'interventions' into remote Indigenous communities and the rolling back of Indigenous rights to self-determination have been similarly justified by declarations of political and cultural incompetence. As the hegemony of liberal politics once again looks global in scope—and with concrete local effects—our historical vocabulary has similarly shifted, and these connections are disconcerting. Reaching for a language of transnationalism, then, doesn't necessarily resolve the epistemological quandaries and violences of liberal modernity.

Perhaps, instead, we need to more carefully historicise the relationship between modern historical consciousness, liberalism, nationalism, and claims to globality. It's possible, moreover, that the nation-state might not be our only historiographic 'problem'. We also need to remember how the universalising claims of liberalism refuse to be contained within national boundaries. The moment of (white) Australia's geopolitical birth, when historians employed a globalising narrative of liberal reform to uphold the legitimacy of settler-colonial territorial expropriation, all too clearly demonstrates the damage transnational thinking can do. The ways in which the globalising histories of Thomas McCombie, James Bonwick and James Bryce swiftly (dis)placed Indigenous peoples from their present should serve as a reminder of the ways in which transnational history isn't without its own strategies of exclusion.

Part 2

Whiteness on Indigenous missions and reserves

4

Colouring (in) virtue? Evangelicalism, work and whiteness on Maloga Mission[1]

Claire McLisky, University of Copenhagen

On 1 April 1885 the Protestant missionary Daniel Matthews, of the Maloga Mission on the Murray River in New South Wales, expressed his views of Aboriginal people's fitness for work in his annual mission report. While he had not, he wrote, witnessed the 'growth of industry' which he had anticipated would accompany Aboriginal people's 'improved life and religious experience' on the mission, this was not altogether surprising, as 'the present race of aborigines [sic]' were 'a degenerate people' lacking in the 'power of endurance, hardihood, and nerve'.[2] Indeed, Matthews continued in the next year's report, the missionaries of Maloga had 'probably expect[ed] too much from a people who for many generations have been strangers to the toil, thrift, and plodding energy, so characteristic of our race'.[3]

In this statement, the missionary pitted one race's vigour and persistence against the absence of these characteristics in the other. And, while his 'admission' that he had 'probably expected too much' of the mission's Aboriginal residents served many immediate purposes—not the

---

[1] This chapter presents work which is further developed in my 'Settlers on a mission: faith, power and subjectivity in the lives of Daniel and Janet Matthews' (PhD thesis, University of Melbourne, 2008).

[2] Daniel Matthews, *Tenth report of the Maloga Aboriginal Mission station* (Echuca: Riverine Herald, 1885), 31 March 1885, 38, Mortlock Library, Adelaide.

[3] Daniel Matthews, *Eleventh report of the Maloga Aboriginal Mission station* (Echuca: Mackay and Foyster, 1886), 1 April 1885, 5.

least of which was to justify the slow progress he had made in making the mission self-sufficient—his observations were grounded in an understanding of race which held sway far beyond the mission field. In this schema whiteness—or the white 'race'—was placed at the apex of an evolutionary hierarchy which was thought to determine a person's ability to perform a range of functions including work, cognition and worship. And for Daniel Matthews, as for many other Protestant missionaries, work was the most important of these. These missionaries' definition of 'whiteness', this chapter contends, was in fact linked inextricably with assumptions about an individual's ability to labour, an attribute which in turn was imbued with significant moral status.

Despite the fact that the idea of racial fixity was not consonant with the evangelical concept of universal salvation, the pages of Matthews' reports, diaries and letters, and those of others like him, were characterised by their uneasy juxtaposition of these parallel discourses of inclusion and exclusion.[4] And, although it was unusual for Matthews to compare the two 'races' explicitly, the comparison was most explicit in his discussions of Aboriginal labour. Aboriginal people, though 'of one blood' with the rest of humanity, were according to Matthews both physically and culturally incapable of hard work.[5] Yet despite the supposed intransigence of their elders, Matthews believed, 'we have everything to encourage us in the young, who are being trained and educated in those

---

[4] Matthews was not unusual in his ability to reconcile evolutionary and evangelical thought. For discussions of evangelical attitudes to racial classification and Darwin's theory of evolution see David N. Livingstone, *Darwin's forgotten defenders: the encounter between evangelical theology and evolutionary thought* (Edinburgh: Scottish Academic Press, 1987); and David N. Livingstone, D.G. Hart and Mark A. Noll, eds., *Evangelicals and science in historical perspective* (New York: Oxford University Press, 1999).

[5] Johnny Phillips, cited in Daniel Matthews, *The fifth report of the Maloga Aboriginal Mission* (Echuca: Riverine Herald, 1880), 22. For further discussion of Matthews' ideas on race, see Claire McLisky, '"All of one blood? ": Race and redemption on Maloga Mission, 1874–1888' in *Historicising whiteness: transnational perspectives on the construction of an identity*, eds. Leigh Boucher, Jane Carey and Katherine Ellinghaus (Melbourne: RMIT Publishers, 2007), 408–15.

qualities which we believe will make them good citizens and industrious members of the community'. With the right instruction in the right environment, it seemed, productivity could be taught regardless of race.[6] However, the promise of change for future generations was in practice rarely, if ever, realised, the discursive constitution of Aboriginal peoples as children in a 'family of man' in reality signalling an 'endless deferral' of their rights.[7]

Taking this observation as its starting point, this chapter uses discussions of work on Maloga Mission as a window into the ways in which whiteness, race, and labour were linked in the minds of Christian missionaries and settler society more broadly in the south east of Australia in the late 19th century. Though disparate and often contradictory, missionaries' observations can tell us much about the material, social, and spiritual economies of Christian missions during this period, while also casting light upon the complicated role of whiteness in determining the position of Aboriginal workers in the settler-colonial economy as a whole. As such, the chapter moves from a general discussion of whiteness and labour in the south east of Australia to the more specific formulations espoused by the missionaries of Maloga Mission.

Whiteness, race and labour in the settler-colonial mission field

In the 19th century, as Angela Woollacott has noted, whiteness was part of 'a racial lexicon forged in multiple colonial sites, especially the

---

[6] Matthews, *Eleventh report*, 5.

[7] Catherine Hall, *Civilising subjects: metropole and colony in the English imagination, 1830–1867* (Oxford: Polity, 2002), 42. See also Ann Laura Stoler, 'Intimidations of empire: predicaments of the tactile and unseen', in *Haunted by empire*, ed. Ann Laura Stoler (Durham: Duke University Press, 2006), 5. On the ideological work done by the infantilisation of Aboriginal people in the mission context, see Nicholas Thomas, 'Colonial conversions: difference, hierarchy and history in early twentieth-century evangelical propaganda', *Comparative Studies in Society and History* 34.2 (April 1992): 366–89.

confrontational and violent sites of settler colonialism.[8] It shaped conceptions of racial hierarchy, and in settler colonies like Australia was used to justify Indigenous dispossession, colonial rule and violence. But while there is a small but growing body of work on whiteness in the settler-colonial context, there is little historical work dealing specifically with whiteness in the complex but critical context of Christian missions.[9] Furthermore, the relationship between whiteness and labour in the mission field has barely been touched upon. This is perhaps surprising, given United States whiteness studies' early grounding in labour relations, represented most famously in David Roediger's 1991 book *The wages of whiteness*.[10] Yet, while clearly ripe for exploration, the question of whiteness and labour in 19th-century missions is not without its pitfalls.

One potential problem with using whiteness as a category of analysis during this period has been identified by Leigh Boucher, who suggests that historical treatments of whiteness have been plagued by a lack of definitional clarity between whiteness as 'the operation of power via racialised exclusions', and whiteness as an explicit empirical designation.[11] This is particularly pertinent to the late 19th century, when 'whiteness', rather than 'British' or 'Anglo-Saxon', was only just beginning to emerge

---

[8] Angela Woollacott, 'Whiteness and "the Imperial turn"', in *Historicising whiteness: transnational perspectives on the construction of an identity*, eds. Leigh Boucher, Jane Carey and Katherine Ellinghaus, (Melbourne: RMIT Publishers, 2007).

[9] This area has begun to be explored. See, for example, Joel Martin, 'Almost white: the ambivalent promise of Christian missions among the Cherokees', in *Religion and the creation of race and ethnicity: an introduction*, ed. Craig R. Prentiss (New York: New York University Press, 2003), 43–60. For Australian case studies see Tracy Spencer, '"We had to give them everything": Adnyamathanha agency in the economy of "whiteness"', in *Historicising whiteness: transnational perspectives on the construction of an identity*, eds. Leigh Boucher, Jane Carey and Katherine Ellinghaus (Melbourne: RMIT Publishing, 2007) 416–26; McLisky, 'All of one blood?', 408–15.

[10] David Roediger, *The wages of whiteness: race and the making of the American working class*, 2nd ed. (New York: Verso, 1999).

[11] Leigh Boucher, '"Whiteness" before "White Australia"?', in *Historicising whiteness: transnational perspectives on the construction of an identity*, eds. Leigh Boucher, Jane Carey and Katherine Ellinghaus (Melbourne: RMIT Publishing, 2007), 16–25.

as a racial category. On Christian missions such as Maloga this was certainly the case, with missionaries—who generally referred to their Aboriginal charges as 'blacks'—only infrequently identifying themselves or other non-Aboriginal people on their mission explicitly as 'white'.[12] For this reason, the moments at which 'whiteness' did emerge specifically as a designation in missionary texts during this period are particularly important, as they suggest shifts and developments in missionaries' awareness of racialised selves in relation to racialised others.

If the idealisation of white labour was one of the economic and ideological foundations of the white Australian settler colony, it was an equally seductive, if more problematic, notion for missionaries whose material investments in settler colonialism sat often uncomfortably alongside their 'higher' spiritual goals. Premised on the notion that the Australian continent before European occupation could be classified as *waste lands*, Australian settler colonialism relied upon the furphy that Aboriginal people lacked the skills and the perseverance to render land productive.[13] Aboriginal 'idleness' enabled them to be discursively proscribed associations with work, despite the fact that their labour, paid and unpaid, was integral to the success of many colonial industries, including Christian missions.[14] In this way, Ann Curthoys and Clive Moore have argued, settler colonialism rendered Indigenous labour simultaneously desirable and undesirable: 'desirable because available and

---

[12] Claire McLisky, 'All of one blood?', 408–15.

[13] Patrick Wolfe, 'Nation and miscegenation: discursive continuity in the post-Mabo era', *Social Analysis* 36 (October 1994): 92–152. See also Deborah Bird Rose, *Hidden histories: black stories from Victoria River Downs, Humbert River and Wave Hill stations* (Canberra: Aboriginal Studies Press 1991), 46.

[14] Julie Evans, Patricia Grimshaw, David Philips and Shurlee Swain, *Equal subjects, unequal rights: Indigenous peoples in British settler colonies, 1830–1910* (Manchester: Manchester University Press, 2003), 4. For a discussion of the role of Aboriginal labour on Christian missions, see Roslyn Kidd, *The way we civilise: Aboriginal affairs— the untold story* (St Lucia: University of Queensland Press, 1997), 64. In the 20th century Christian missions also benefited from stolen Aboriginal wages. See Dawn May, *Aboriginal labour and the cattle industry* (Cambridge: Cambridge University Press, 1994), 73.

exploitable, and undesirable because Indigenous cultural and material life was at odds with the colonisers'.[15] Furthermore, the very presence of Indigenous labourers acted as a reminder of their continuing claims to the land. Perhaps for this reason, white employers continued to insist that Aboriginal people were poor workers, though they used them nonetheless as cheap labour.[16]

From an Aboriginal perspective, labour was seen in quite a different light. Richard Broome has claimed that 'Aboriginal people saw little point in regular daily work, as it was not how their traditional economy operated'. And, though this explanation has less applicability in the late 19th century when many Aboriginal people had already lived for years on missions or pastoral stations and were at least to some extent reliant upon regular work from white employers,[17] Broome's observation that 'Aboriginal workers also placed Aboriginal business before white needs, leaving when it suited them and not their bosses', was a continuing factor in colonial labour relations.[18]

While labour was central to Protestant missionaries' vision for the future of the Aboriginal 'race', there was enormous disagreement between sects, and even between individual missionaries within sects, as to how labour fitted into the 'civilising' project.[19] Whatever their persuasion,

---

[15] Claire Williams and Bill Thorpe, *Beyond industrial sociology* (North Sydney: Allen & Unwin, 1992), 98, cited in Ann Curthoys and Clive Moore, 'Working for the white people: an historiographic essay on Aboriginal and Torres Strait Islander labour', in *Aboriginal workers: special edition of labour history*, eds. Ann McGrath and Kay Saunders, 69 (November 1995): 13. See also Richard Broome, *Aboriginal Australians: black response to white dominance, 1788–1980* (Sydney: George Allen & Unwin, 1982), 86.

[16] Richard Broome, *Aboriginal Victorians: a history since 1800* (Crows Nest: Allen & Unwin, 2005), 62–3.

[17] Broome, *Aboriginal Australians*, 57.

[18] Ibid. 62–3.

[19] Some, such as the Moravian missionary Friedrich Hagenauer of the Victorian mission Ramahyuck, imagined that while 'full-blood' Aboriginal people were inevitably destined to 'die out', those of mixed heritage could—and should—become quickly assimilated into a Christian working class, by any means necessary. For analysis of Hagenauer's views see

however, all Christian missionaries were reliant on Aboriginal labour for the existence of their missions, and when Aboriginal residents resisted work most missionaries showed no reluctance to use compulsion.[20] Because of the comparative lack of external regulation of missions during this period (especially in New South Wales, where the Board for the Protection of the Aborigines was formed only in 1883), mission managers and superintendents exercised an enormous degree of power in allocating, and enforcing, labour regimes. For this reason the sort of labour that was imagined for, and foisted upon, Aboriginal mission residents depended upon arbitrary and shifting factors, including the mission's financial status, the missionary's state of mind, and his or her views on the theoretical 'benefits' of labour to the future of the Aboriginal 'race'. Perhaps most importantly, however, missionaries were themselves personally invested in establishing a link between whiteness and productivity. Convinced of the importance of labour for salvation, they strove to represent themselves as 'God's willing workers', the faithful few battling the Devil amongst a sea of heathen. The backdrop of settler

Felicity Jensz, 'Collecting cultures for God: German Moravian missionaries and the British colony of Victoria, Australia, 1848–1908' (PhD thesis, University of Melbourne, 2007). Others, including the Matthews and their contemporaries John Green of Coranderrk and John Gribble of Warangesda, disagreed. See Heather Goodall, *Invasion to embassy: land in Aboriginal politics in New South Wales, 1770–1972* (St Leonards: Allen & Unwin, 1996; reprinted Sydney: Sydney University Press, 2008). On Coranderrk specifically, see Diane Barwick, *Rebellion at Coranderrk*, eds. Laura E. Barwick and Richard E. Barwick (Canberra: Aboriginal History Inc., 1998). See also Marguerita Stephens, 'White without soap: philanthropy, caste and exclusion in colonial Victoria 1835–1888: a political economy of race' (PhD thesis, University of Melbourne, 2003). On Warangesda see Beverley Gulambali Elphick and Don Elphick, *The camp of mercy: an historical and biographical record of the Warangesda Aboriginal Mission Station, Darlington Point, New South Wales* (Canberra: Gulambali Aboriginal Research, 2004); Tom Mayne, 'John B. Gribble: "The blackfellow's friend"', *Indigenous Leadership* 36 (August 2003): 4–8.
[20] For an example of the erratic behaviour of mission managers regarding Aboriginal work see Penny Brock, *Outback ghettos: Aborigines, institutionalisation and survival* (Melbourne: Cambridge University Press, 1993), 37.

depravity and Indigenous idleness made missionary work appear even more virtuous.

The case of Maloga

Though it existed for only 14 years (between 1874 and 1888), Maloga Mission looms large in the history of 19th-century Australian missions for several reasons. In its time the largest mission to Aboriginal people in Australia, the mission housed over 200 residents during the 1880s, many of whom converted to Christianity in 1883 in what was at that time the largest revival experienced on an Aboriginal mission. Positioned on the border of New South Wales and Victoria, Maloga was also the site of some controversy as local Aboriginal people moved back and forth across the Murray River to escape oppressive regimes in both colonies, and became a refuge for many after the notorious 1886 *Aborigines Protection Act*, which decreed that Aboriginal people of mixed descent could no longer live on Victorian missions.[21] As the first, and largest, 'second-wave' Aboriginal mission in New South Wales, Maloga and its founders Daniel Matthews (a Methodist) and his wife Janet (a Baptist) were chief instigators in the push for the formation of the New South Wales Aborigines Protection Board, an organisation which ironically was eventually responsible for the mission's demise.[22] Even after its closure the legacy of Maloga—where many Aboriginal people learned to read and write, were encouraged and supported materially in their petitions for land, and where young Aboriginal men and women became politicised

---

[21] An Act to Amend an Act Intituled [sic] 'An Act to Provide for the Protection and Management of the Aboriginal Natives of Victoria', Parliament of Victoria, no. 912, 1886. For discussion of the 1886 Act (known colloquially as the 'Half-Caste Separation Act'), see Russell McGregor, *Imagined destinies: Aboriginal Australians and the doomed race theory, 1880–1939* (Carlton: Melbourne University Press, 1997); Wolfe, 'Nation and miscegenation'; John Chesterman and Brian Galligan, *Citizens without rights: Aborigines and Australian citizenship* (Cambridge: Cambridge University Press, 1997); Evans et al., *Equal subjects.*

[22] Nancy Cato, *Mister Maloga* (St Lucia: University of Queensland Press, 1993); Bain Attwood, *Rights for Aborigines* (Sydney: Allen & Unwin, 2003).

through the missionaries' universalist Christian worldviews—continued into the 20th century.[23]

As a privately owned mission run along non-denominational lines, Maloga Mission was both more and less secure than other Church-run missions in the south east. Because the land on which the mission was built was owned by Daniel Matthews and his brother William, the missionaries had relatively better land security than most of their equivalents, who were employed by colonial churches or missionary societies which relied on government land grants to continue operating. Yet for this very reason, their motives for employing Aboriginal labour were the subject of constant speculation amongst the mission's enemies, who claimed that the Matthews were using the mission as a pretext to exploit Aboriginal labour to run their own farm.[24] Indeed, though their wrongdoing was never substantiated, doubts about this issue were cited as the official justification for the New South Wales colonial Government's 1888 decision to move the mission from Maloga to the adjacent Aboriginal reserve, Cummeragunja, hence effectively closing the Matthews' mission.

Over the course of Maloga's existence changes of fortune, and mentality, changed the way in which labour—whether Aboriginal or 'white'—was seen on the mission. As the mission became reliant on public funding during the early years of the 1880s, it became more and more difficult for the missionaries to gainsay either government policy or

---

[23] Wayne Atkinson, 'The schools of human experience', in *The First Australians*, ed. Rachel Perkins (Melbourne: Melbourne University Press, 2008).

[24] This conundrum had been commented upon in a report commissioned by the New South Wales Government in 1883, in which it found that 'great difficulty has been found in obtaining suitable work for those [residents of Maloga] who are willing and competent to labour, as, were Mr. Matthews to employ them on his own property his motives would be liable to misconstruction'. 'Protection of the Aborigines (Minutes of the Colonial Secretary, together with reports)', New South Wales Legislative Assembly, 2 March 1883. Both Nancy Cato and Richard Broome comment on the pressure under which this placed the missionaries. See Cato, *Mister Maloga*; Broome, *Aboriginal Australians*, 80.

private interests. The expansion of agriculture and pastoralism was inescapable—settler society was slowly, but surely, working its way towards an imagined 'end-point' of total settler domination. In this context, all the missionaries could do was ameliorate the condition of those Aboriginal people displaced by colonial expansion, and attempt to mould them into 'good Christian workers'.

In directing and controlling the types of labour that Aboriginal people performed on the mission, the Matthews were attempting to effect a transformation in the work culture of Aboriginal people. Labour they considered redemptive; the Protestant values of faith, work and family formed the core of their mission ideology, and were a key aspect of the message they communicated to Aboriginal converts.[25] The Matthews' ideas about Aboriginal labour were also, however, formulated in a climate of multiple racial and cultural conflicts. For all their professed idealism, the Maloga missionaries needed to sustain the mission as a private enterprise in a secular state, to feed, clothe and shelter mission inmates, and to ensure the continuation of their own roles as missionaries. They relied upon the labour of Aboriginal people to do all these things. Aboriginal labour was deployed in establishing an orchard and vegetable garden, from which the mission was fed and which occasionally brought in a profit. During periods when the mission could not sustain them, Aboriginal men were sent out to work on sheep and cattle stations, the missionaries exhorting them to provide for their families with the wages they earned. It is important to note, however, that productivity was not just a matter of pragmatism for the missionaries. It was also an article of faith, and in this context the mission's failure to become self-sustainable was a particular source of ire to them.

---

[25] The historical and denominational peculiarity of this approach to work was first analysed by Max Weber in his ground-breaking work, *The Protestant ethic and the spirit of capitalism*, first published in German in 1905 but later translated by Talcott Parsons (London: Unwin University Books, 1930).

Mission life was thus organised around labour. During the day the mission's activities were clearly delineated along gender lines, with Aboriginal men working in the garden, building houses, and from 1883 fencing in the Aboriginal Reserve (later to become Cummeragunja), while Aboriginal women cooked, baked, cleaned and sewed. However, the 'work' done on the mission was not just of a material nature. In the evenings mission residents of both sexes gathered for singing and prayer. Weekly Bible lessons were 'much appreciated by some of the men and women'; Matthews took care to make the lessons 'of a special character for those more advanced in intelligence and religious experiences'.[26] These nightly meetings were in fact the most regular and reliable activities on the mission, drawing a considerable crowd even during times of trouble and discord.

By emphasising spiritual training to this degree, Matthews was going against the opinion of the New South Wales Protector of Aborigines George Thornton, who believed that Aboriginal people were incapable of benefiting from religious instruction. Thornton contended that, since Aboriginal people had been proven capable of reading, writing and 'the use of figures', they should be 'taught trades', and made 'useful and sometimes clever mechanics'.[27] The 'females', for their part, 'should be taught how to be useful and valuable as domestic servants'. Thornton did not discuss the reasoning behind these suggestions, but his opinion was ultimately shaped by what he called his 'knowledge of the painful fact' that 'the black aboriginals are fast disappearing—destined soon to be extinct'.[28] It is clear that he envisaged that the Aboriginal people trained on mission stations such as Maloga and Warangesda (run by Matthews' friend John Gribble) would contribute to the lowest sector of the colonial economy. By defying the advice of Thornton and others involved with the

---

[26] Matthews, *Eleventh report*, 16 May 1884, 10.
[27] George Thornton, 'Report, 14 August 1882', New South Wales Legislative Assembly, 30 August 1882, in Norman Family Papers, PRG 422, Mortlock Library, Adelaide.
[28] Ibid.

Aborigines' Protection Association and the Aborigines' Protection Board (both of New South Wales), Matthews adhered to his long-stated belief that Aboriginal people were *not* a dying race. Further, in encouraging men on the mission to become preachers and spiritual teachers to the white shearers and drovers with whom they worked, he demonstrated that his aspirations for Aboriginal people went far beyond their 'usefulness' to colonial society. Rather, Matthews was interested in Aboriginal peoples' usefulness to God, and to his own evangelising project. This vision, of course, was no less an imposition on Aboriginal people than Thornton's vision of a labouring underclass, but it was one which had significantly different outcomes.

The tension between spiritual and menial work on the mission was ironic considering that the very ethic by which the missionaries lived—that of piety, diligence and productivity—had been 'intended to end the false dichotomy between the highly privileged vocation of religious work and the lesser esteemed life of toil in the everyday world'.[29] As Joan Martin has explained, early Protestant reformers such as Martin Luther and John Calvin 'gave Western thought and Christianity the first interpretation of work as a positive social act applicable to all persons in every socio-economic, political, and occupational status'. This interpretation was 'intended to end what the Reformers saw as a false dichotomy between the highly privileged vocation and calling of the religious life and the lesser esteemed life of toil in the everyday world prevalent in Roman Catholic thought'.[30] Yet Protestant missions to Aboriginal people, despite their 'broad church' approach, fostered an unequal relationship between spiritual work—most often done by the 'white' mission residents, or the missionaries—and menial work, assigned to those lacking in 'whiteness'.

---

[29] Joan Martin, *More than chains and toil: a Christian work ethic of enslaved women* (Louisville: Westminster John Knox Press, 2000), 122.
[30] Ibid.

Unsurprisingly, a tension between spiritual and secular work was also evident within the Aboriginal community at Maloga. Once members of the community became involved in proselytisation, those 'chosen' for spiritual work were privileged by the missionaries above others. The gendered nature of mission life, furthermore, meant that some converts had far greater access to the privilege of this kind of 'work' than others.[31] For the Aboriginal men of Maloga, opportunities to teach outside the mission meant greater respect and autonomy within the mission; women on the other hand were generally limited in their proselytisation to within the mission grounds. In April 1884 Matthews reported that even when the Aboriginal men were forced to leave the mission to seek employment such as rabbiting for local squatters, they were 'full of determination to preach the gospel while they are away'.[32] And, though according to the missionary they were 'exposed to fierce temptations, the more so because of their Christian profession', most were reported to return with their Christian honour intact. In this formulation, Matthews represented the 'work' entailed by evangelisation as equally, if not more, important than the physical work undertaken by these men on their travels. In a climate of sin and obduracy on the part of surrounding settlers, Matthews considered maintaining the faith to be *hard work* for the Aboriginal residents; certainly not the easy option.

It was during this period that Matthews first reported the mission's Mauritian-born school teacher, Thomas Shadrach James, taking Aboriginal men with him on Sundays to 'assist in preaching the Gospel of Salvation to the settlers on the Victorian side of the Murray'.[33] For the first time in the mission's history, the Aboriginal people of Maloga—

---

[31] There is much to be said on the gendered nature of work at Maloga Mission, and the degree to which even residents' conversion testimonies seem to have reflected a gendered socialisation around working activities. See Claire McLisky, 'The location of faith? Power, agency and spirituality on Maloga Mission, 1874–1888', paper presented at the Biennial Conference of the Australian Historical Association, Melbourne University, 9 July 2008.

[32] Matthews, *Eleventh report*, 21 April 1884, 7.

[33] Ibid. 2 June 1884, 11.

notably the men—were being given credit for a very different kind of work from the fencing, building, shearing and cropping previously mentioned. Moreover, they appeared to seek and organise this work independently of the white missionaries who were clearly 'in charge' of other forms of work on the mission. In this case, Matthews' comments about the execution and results of their work were overwhelmingly positive. Yet at other times, especially when Matthews was feeling the pressure from Maloga's governing bodies, even his most favoured protégés were pressured to undertake hard physical labour, often resulting in acts of fierce resistance.

The question of authority came to a head when the missionary encountered resistance amongst some Aboriginal men with whom he had made a 'contract' to fence in the recently granted 'Aboriginal Reserve'. Disappointed that 'the men do not take an interest in what is for their welfare', Matthews decided to replace the men with hired white labour.[34] Four days later he reported that the reserve fence was 'going on rapidly, and satisfactorily in the hands of the white men', and could not resist comparing their work to that of the Aboriginal men.[35] He longed, he wrote:

> to see our men work with the same vigour and persistency. Some day I may do so. If they could direct their energies in this way, and go on in the path we indicate, they would soon become a self-supporting and thrifty community. Presuming they were people of this character, they would soon take their place in society, and there would be no need for Mission Stations.[36]

While Matthews here attempted to align himself with what he called 'his men', who in his opinion had nothing to lose in embracing a more vigorous work ethic, he had in effect aligned himself with the white workers whose persistence he so admired. What held the missionary and

---

[34] Ibid. 1 and 21 September 1885, 15.
[35] Ibid. 25 September 1885, 16.
[36] Ibid. 16.

his white workers together, in this discursive construction, was the productivity (understood through the colour) of their working bodies and their commitment to capitalism, which also defined the boundary between coloniser and colonised in the settler colony as a whole.[37]

It is perhaps ironic to note that these workers belonged to the same general class of settler colonists that Matthews often disparaged elsewhere as 'wicked white men', a degenerate influence on the Aboriginal people of the region. In these instances the missionary constructed himself as benevolent white protector battling off the evils of other men who, he implied, also held power over Aboriginal people. In the act of asserting his own managerial right—a right anchored in white Christian virtue and British middle-class culture—over the irreligious working-class whites whom he perceived as a moral and physical danger to potential converts, the missionary in effect broadcast the message that it was whiteness, and white men more specifically, who held the power in colonial society. And power, in this conception, was intrinsically related to productivity. Since the 16th century, as Anne McClintock has observed, idleness had long been associated with corruption and poverty. In this construction responsibility for the condition of Aboriginal people on the mission was easily displaced from the missionaries on to unruly Aboriginal bodies, apparently too undisciplined to take advantages of the opportunities offered them.

Despite these characterisations of Aboriginal people as resistant to work, the lack of industriousness on the mission was often in fact the result of the missionaries' inability to provide workers with labour, tools, or remuneration. Indeed, in April 1885 Matthews wrote in his diary that

---

[37] While the discourse of Aboriginal 'idleness' remained (and continues to remain) a constant across time and geography, it does need to be acknowledged that, especially during the later years of the 19th century, whiteness was not always equated with fitness for work in the north of the continent. For a detailed exposition of this idea see Warwick Anderson, *The cultivation of whiteness: science, health and racial destiny in Australia* (Melbourne: Melbourne University Press, 2002).

the 'industrious men' were 'annoyed & dissatisfied', and wanted to go away to work for money.[38] Unrest on the mission over these issues was not limited to the men; in the same diary entry Matthews reported that Liz Barber had 'threatened to pack up and leave the place "because you don't give us money to buy jam, and extras"'. Matthews' solution to the latter complaint was to enlist the help of Janet—'Mrs M', he wrote in his diary, 'is to make jam'. Procuring work for the men was not so easy, and Matthews was forced to send a letter to two neighbouring pastoralists with whom the missionary had uneasy relationships in order to solve this problem. Never, Matthews wrote, had he experienced 'more care & anxiety in the work than now', observing that Miss Booth, a visitor from Melbourne 'says I'm like Moses'.[39] This was not the first time the missionary had compared himself to a biblical figure.

Ignoring for the moment Matthews' concern with his own trials, the Aboriginal men's expressions of desire *for work* turn on its head the missionary's claim, cited at the beginning of this paper, that he had expected 'too much' from the Aboriginal workers. Rather, it seems, the workers had expected 'too much' from him. When they wanted full-time, challenging work with adequate remuneration, all he could provide them with was odd jobs around the mission, in exchange for rations or occasionally wages if the work was part of a contract.

Conclusion

Writing in the North American context, David Roediger has suggested that idealising white labour was one way for white Americans to make peace with their complicity in the slave labour of African Americans at the same time that it gave them a psychological reassurance that helped to compensate for their own oppression.[40] Racial dynamics in Australia, a settler colony materially reliant upon Aboriginal labour and yet

---

[38] Daniel Matthews, 'Diary', 8 April 1885, Mortlock Library, Adelaide.
[39] Ibid.
[40] Roediger, 13.

discursively reliant upon its denial,[41] developed in a completely different context, with the relationships between settlers and Aboriginal workers differing radically to those which developed between white settlers and African Americans in the United States. Indeed, the position of Australian Aboriginal workers, as Aileen Moreton-Robinson and Patrick Wolfe have suggested, was much more similar to that of Native Americans, although much work remains to be done on any such comparison, particular in the mission context.[42] Yet despite the vast differences between the Australian and North American contexts, Roediger's comment on the psychological function of linking labour with whiteness remains useful. Indeed, while Daniel Matthews could not be said to have 'made peace' with Aboriginal exploitation as such, his attempts to denigrate the abilities of Aboriginal labourers in his *Tenth* and *Eleventh* reports similarly suggest an acute awareness of the need to delineate imagined boundaries between the 'races' in order to protect his own position. It is also possible that the self-designation of virtuous white worker gave missionaries like the Matthews a psychological reassurance which, like that of the white American workers of which Roediger wrote, compensated somewhat for the social ridicule they faced in their own positions as marginalised whites.[43]

In this context, the utility of mission histories in revealing relationships between race, labour and whiteness becomes clear. While missionaries like Matthews invested their own uprightness in their status

---

[41] For an overview see Curthoys and Moore, 'Working for the white people.'

[42] Aileen Moreton-Robinson, 'Writing off Indigenous sovereignty: white possession within the United States' Whiteness Studies literature', paper presented at the Re-Orienting Whiteness Conference, Melbourne University, 3–5 December 2008; Patrick Wolfe, 'Land, labor, and difference: elementary structures of race', *American Historical Review*, 106 (2001): 866–905.

[43] For a discussion of the complexity of liminal whiteness see Matt Wray's *Not quite white: white trash and the boundaries of whiteness* (Durham: Duke University Press, 2006). For a discussion of the specific fragility of missionary claims to white privilege, see Joanna Cruickshank's chapter in this collection.

as 'God's Willing Workers', the settler-colonial missionary enterprise relied implicitly on notions such as 'blackness' and 'whiteness' for its constructions of virtue. Justified by the evangelical imperative to convert souls, missionaries assumed their authority not just on the basis of their race and class, but also on their assumed superior 'productivity'. Indeed, it is possible to argue that for a whole generation of Christian missionaries, race and class were simply *understood* through productivity, a scenario which left little room for the Aboriginal people who found themselves defined as not just unproductive, but also on this basis as incapable of owning land or securing self-determination. Paradoxically, the evangelical emphasis on spiritual labour was malleable enough to give many residents the opportunity to move, and work, outside the mission sphere. This they did in spite, and not because, of the oppressive associations between whiteness and productivity so emphasised by Christian missionaries.

5

'A most lowering thing for a lady': aspiring to respectable whiteness on Ramahyuck Mission, 1885–1900[1]

Joanna Cruickshank, Deakin University

In September 1893, a measles epidemic raged on the Victorian mission of Ramahyuck. At the height of the epidemic, Ellie Hagenauer, the daughter of the missionary managers of Ramahyuck, recorded in her diary how she had visited the homes of the Aboriginal mission residents. 'Poor little Mary Darby' she wrote 'her eyes are very blighted. I washed her face & hands & made her more comfortable. Then washed the Stephens & Moffats. Oh it was dreadful. I think it took a deal of strength from me'.[2]

The missionary imperative, which drove Europeans like Ellie Hagenauer's parents to Christianise Aboriginal people, required and indeed affirmed certain kinds of physical and emotional proximity between missionaries and those they evangelised. On missions such as Ramahyuck, Aboriginal and white people lived side-by-side, shared food and drink, and touched each other. They spoke of each other using language that was familial and often affectionate. Such proximity threatened racial boundaries and hierarchies that were central to

---

[1] Permission to quote from the *Le Souef Family Papers* was kindly given by Marjorie Le Souef. I am also very grateful to Professor Pat Grimshaw for her helpful insights, to Claire McLisky and Jane Carey for their patience during the editing process, and to the anonymous readers of the chapter for their helpful comments.
[2] Diary of Ellie Hagenauer [DEH], 20 September 1893, 4370A/634, *Le Souef Family Papers*, MN 1391, Battye Library, Perth.

respectable white society, at a time when the nature of racial difference was being widely debated. For white people on and around mission stations, this could produce considerable external and internal tensions.

This chapter explores the anxieties around whiteness and respectability on Ramahyuck mission station in the late 19th century. It focuses particularly on the diaries and personal letters of Ellie Hagenauer, read in the context of the experience of the Hagenauer family and their racialised perspective. Ramahyuck was a significant mission and has received attention from a number of historians, but the papers of Ellie Hagenauer provide a different perspective from the reports to church and government officials that form the basis of most other accounts.[3] In their references to whiteness, Ellie's writings also provide new insights into the mission experience, which had enormous significance for many Aboriginal people in colonial Australia.

The Hagenauer family in Victoria

Ellie was the youngest daughter of Friedrich and Louise Hagenuaer, German Moravian missionaries who founded the Ramahyuck mission in Gippsland in 1863. She was born in 1873, the seventh of eight children.[4] The personal writings considered here date largely from the 1890s, when Ellie had completed her final schooling in Melbourne and was living back at the mission. That these papers date from the later years of the Hagenauer family's time in Victoria is significant in understanding Ellie's attitude to both whiteness and respectability.

---

[3] Accounts of Ramahyuck include Bain Attwood, *The making of the Aborigines* (Sydney: Allen & Unwin, 1989); Felicity Jensz, 'Collecting cultures for God: German Moravian missionaries and the British colony of Victoria, Australia, 1848–1908' (PhD Thesis, Melbourne University, 2007); John Harris, *One blood: 200 years of Aboriginal encounter with Christianity: a story of hope* (Sutherland, NSW: Albatross Books, 1990), 200–5, and Robert Kenny, *The lamb enters the dreaming: Nathanael Pepper and the ruptured world* (Melbourne: Scribe, 2007).
[4] Noel Stewart, 'Mrs Ellie Grace Le Souef (1873–1947): she helped to found a zoo', in *As I remember them* (Perth: Artlook Books, 1987), 103.

When the Hagenauers first began their missionary work in Australia their nationality, religious convictions, and association with Aboriginal people meant that they occupied an ambiguous position in settler society. German nationality was not necessarily a barrier to respectability, as of all the non-British migrants to the Australian colonies, Germans appear to have been among the most accepted. They were generally small farmers and labourers of the kind desired by Australian colonial administrations for settlement, they had a reputation for being politically docile and, unlike some European groups such as southern Italians, they seem to have been considered 'white'.[5] From 1849, several large groups of Germans arrived in Victoria, and the *Argus* commented:

> We trust that they may receive a hearty and generous welcome. As the pioneers of a useful and valuable description of people it is in our interest to afford it to them. They will teach us many arts of which we are ignorant, and by their quiet industry and good conduct they will gain here, as they have gained in South Australia, the esteem and friendship of their fellow-colonists.[6]

Given their apparent adaptability to British settler culture, Germans were not the target of widespread racism prior to the tensions created by the Boer War. Nonetheless, many German settlers deliberately maintained their language and cultural practices, creating a subculture within settler society. This could result in hostility and some Germans were ostracised or harassed.[7]

For the Hagenauers, their Moravian convictions created further potential barriers to integration with settler society. The Moravian

---

[5] Charles Meyer, *A history of Germans in Australia 1839–1945* (Caulfield East, Vic. Monash University, 1990), 23–4.

[6] *Argus*, 13 February 1849. Meyer, 24.

[7] Meyer, 24. There was also considerable negative comment in the Australian press about German colonial ambitions in the Pacific Islands during the late 19th century, which presumably impacted upon German communities in Australia. See Peter Overlack, 'Bless the Queen and curse the Colonial Office: Australasian reaction to German consolidation in the Pacific, 1871–99', *Journal of Pacific History* 33.2 (September 1998): 133–52.

movement was part of the groundswell of European pietism which pre-empted the evangelical revival of the 18th century.[8] Moravian missionaries, mainly from working-class backgrounds, valued hard work and practical skills over scholarly prowess and explicitly disavowed involvement in the politics of the states in which they worked. They aspired to personal devotion to Jesus, humility and a rejection of 'the world' and its values. The Moravian missionary handbook claimed:

> The Brethren … demean themselves as loyal and obedient subjects, and strive to act in such a manner, under the difficult relations in which they are often placed, as may evince, that they have no desire to intermeddle with the politics of the country in which they labour, but are solely intent on the fulfilment of their official duties.[9]

Moravian missionaries, therefore, were not expected to seek social advancement or become entangled in the affairs of society.

If such factors as nationality and religious conviction militated against the Hagenauers becoming established members of respectable settler society in Victoria, even more significant was their choice to live and work among Aboriginal people. The first Moravian missionaries in Australia had experienced intense opposition from local settlers to their first mission, established at Lake Boga in 1843, and were forced to close it.[10] Like other missionaries, they competed with settlers for land and they were accused of potentially politicising Indigenous people.[11]

Growing up on the mission, the Hagenauer children lived in close proximity to Aboriginal people. They were nursed by young Aboriginal women and, when they reached the age of school attendance, they joined

---

[8] For an excellent introduction to the Moravian movement see W.R. Ward, *The Protestant evangelical awakening* (Cambridge: Cambridge University Press, 2002), 116–59.

[9] Quoted in Jensz, 'Collecting cultures for God', 275.

[10] For an account of the Moravian mission at Lake Boga, see Kenny, *The lamb enters the dreaming*, 86–99.

[11] Kenny discusses settler opposition to missionaries, including Hagenauer, Ibid. 12–26.

the other mission children at the Ramahyuck school.[12] For several years, this school was taught by an Aboriginal woman named Bessy Flower, though she was replaced by a white male teacher before Ellie was born. Jessie Mitchell has written about the potential for intimacy between missionary children and Aboriginal people, and such potential certainly existed at Ramahyuck.[13] It is difficult to imagine anywhere else in the Australian colonies in the 1870s where Aboriginal and white children were being educated in the same classroom, at one time by an Aboriginal teacher.

In spite of these factors, by the time Ellie Hagenauer began her diary in the 1880s the Hagenauer family had taken significant steps towards integrating with—and even achieving significant status within—settler society. From the outset, missionary work made it impossible for them to remain within a German subculture in Victoria. Physically, their mission was at a distance from the major centres of German settlement. The family had to learn English to deal with colonial officials and to communicate with Aboriginal people. Friedrich Hagenauer had regular contact with representatives of both the Australian Presbyterian and Church of England denominations, who shared oversight of aspects of his missionary work. Though Hagenauer remained a loyal Moravian, in 1869 he was given the full status of an ordained minister by the Presbyterian Church of Victoria.[14]

Friedrich and Louise Hagenauer also went beyond merely pragmatic engagement with colonial society. Moravian missionaries all over the world traditionally sent their children to be educated at Moravian

---

[12] Ellie was nursed by an Aboriginal woman named Emily Stephens, with whom she had a significant relationship for much of her life. See letters from Emily Stephens to Ellie Le Souef, 4370A/713/8/7–14, *Le Souef Family Papers*, Battye Library, Perth.

[13] Jessie Mitchell, 'The nucleus of civilisation: gender, race and childhood in Australian missionary families, 1825–1855', in *Evangelists of empire? Missionaries in colonial history*, ed. Amanda Barry et al. (eScholarship Research Centre, University of Melbourne, 2008), 103–15.

[14] Jensz, 'Collecting cultures for God', 237.

boarding schools in Germany. The Hagenauers followed this practice with their first child, Theo, but he died while away and they chose to educate the rest of their children in Victoria. While the Hagenauer children completed the early years of their education at Ramahyuck mission school alongside the Aboriginal children, for their final years they were sent to boarding school in Melbourne —Presbyterian Ladies College for the girls and Scotch College for the boys.[15] The Hagenauer children, educated in English and with only a small number of German acquaintances, appear to have had mixed feelings about their parents' homeland. In 1898, Ellie wrote with amusement of her younger brother, 'Hen would not sing the National Anthem he is too much of a Deutscher, it was very funny'.[16]

During this same period, Friedrich Hagenauer became increasingly involved in the Victorian government's management of Indigenous affairs. He played a significant role in convincing the Board for Protection of the Aborigines (BPA) to pass the notorious so-called Half-Caste Act, which caused enormous suffering to Aboriginal families forced apart.[17] Hagenauer's active lobbying of the BPA, which will be considered in more detail below, demonstrated his willingness to become involved in the political sphere. This was confirmed when he was appointed Secretary and General Inspector for the BPA in July 1889. In taking on a role within the apparatus of the colonial state, Hagenauer certainly moved well beyond conventional Moravian missionary roles. He also gained a position of some status within settler society.

In the 1880s and 90s, therefore, Ellie Hagenauer was part of a family that was upwardly mobile in social terms. Her years at PLC gave her a significant network among the most respectable members of Victorian settler society. Her diary and letters for this period show that through her father's new responsibilities in Melbourne she and the rest of the family

---

[15] Stewart, 'Mrs Ellie Grace Le Souef', 100–6.
[16] DEH, 20 May 1898, 4370A/638, *Le Souef Family Papers*.
[17] See Jensz, 'Collecting cultures for God'.

were regularly introduced to influential members of Victoria's government and churches.[18] Increased engagement with respectable white society appears to have heightened Ellie's consciousness of her whiteness and the tensions inherent in her own position as a member of the community at Ramahyuck.[19] This added to the already-complicated and often contradictory attitudes to race which are revealed by the way her parents managed Ramahyuck mission and intervened in debates about government policy in relation to Aboriginal missions.

Race at Ramahyuck

Missionaries such as Friedrich and Louise Hagenauer taught that all people were of 'one blood' and equally valuable in the sight of God. Friedrich Hagenauer explicitly criticised those 'pious Christians who confuse Europeanisation with Christianisation'.[20] This belief in the equal spiritual value of human beings was reflected in aspects of life on the mission. Indigenous and non-Indigenous children were educated side-by-side in the Ramahyuck school, which consistently topped the colony in examination results. Indigenous and white Christians worshipped together in the mission church. Of the church at Ramahyuck, Hagenauer wrote:

> On the Lord's day, we have not only all our Black people, but likewise a great many of our white neighbours, which creates a very good feeling in the hearts of the blacks, as they thereby observe that we can worship the

---

[18] For example, see Ellie's detailed accounts of her trip to Melbourne in June 1895 and to Tasmania in October 1896, DEH, 4370A/636 and 4370A/637, *Le Souef Family Papers*.

[19] In addition to the examples of racialised anxieties below, Ellie on several occasions expressed concerns about her family being seen as 'country bumpkins' or 'country cousins' by Melbourne acquaintances. See for example DEH, January 1898, 4370A/638, *Le Souef Family Papers*.

[20] Rev. Hagenauer, *Der Australische Christenbote* 7, 1863, 26, cited in Felicity Jensz, 'The Moravian-run Ebenezer Mission Station in north-western Victoria: A German perspective', (MA Thesis, University of Melbourne, 1999), 77.

same God and enjoy the blessings of salvation without respect of persons or colour.[21]

Like many missionaries, however, the Hagenauers also believed that the Indigenous people of Australia were culturally inferior and in need of civilisation as well as Christianisation.[22] As a result, daily life on the mission was structured in ways that created clear boundaries between Indigenous and non-Indigenous people. In his analysis of the construction of Ramahyuck, Bain Attwood has noted that the mission was physically divided between the Aboriginal mission residents' houses and the 'mission enclave' of mission house, church and dormitory.[23] Other than the women who worked in the house, Aboriginal mission residents were not usually permitted into the missionaries' house.[24] On special occasions, such as when the Hagenauer family gave a concert in their house, Ellie noted that 'the natives' had been allowed into the dining room, or to watch from the verandah.[25] Social contact was also racially determined. Meeting a visitor to the mission, Ellie wrote 'I stretched forth an arm & said "Goodday" thinking he was a halfcaste, I dropped nearly with surprise when I discovered my mistake'.[26] Although the visitor looked 'halfcaste', he was classified as white and so apparently required a different greeting.

The Hagenauers' understanding of race and racial hierarchy came more sharply into focus during debates about government policy towards the missions in the early 1880s. As Felicity Jensz has demonstrated,

[21] F.A. Hagenauer, 'Aboriginal Mission Station Ramahyuck', November 1885, *Proceedings of the General Assembly of the Presbyterian Church of Victoria*, 1885, xix, Uniting Church Archives, Melbourne, cited in Nadia Rhook, 'Inventing other voices: language and power on Moravian missions in colonial Victoria' (Hons. Thesis, University of Melbourne, 2007), 45.

[22] Kenny, *The lamb enters the dreaming*, 316–20.

[23] Attwood, *The making of the Aborigines*, 13–5.

[24] Attwood notes that Hagenauer's study was constructed so that Aboriginal mission residents could enter the study without coming through the house. Ibid. 14.

[25] DEH, 22 January 1892 and 30 July 1892, 4370A/633, *Le Souef Family Papers*.

[26] Ibid. 6 September 1894, 4370A/635.

Friedrich Hagenauer argued strongly for the adoption of legislation which would force 'half-caste' people off the missions.[27] His reasoning reveals an understanding of race as a category that was both self-evident and fluid. In his letters regarding the legislation, Hagenauer expressed his conviction that the few remaining 'full Blacks' at Ramahyuck would eventually die out. The majority of those living on mission stations such as Ramahyuck were, he argued 'half-castes' or 'half-whites'. Many of these were 'nearly totally white people'. Such 'half-whites', Hagenauer believed, desired and deserved an opportunity for self-sufficiency that was not permitted under existing legislation.[28] Hagenauer was critical of the white settlers who fathered illegitimate children with Aboriginal women. Implicit in his argument, however, was the assumption that the white parentage of 'half-whites' had instilled in them new qualities—especially the quality of hard work—which was missing in the 'full Blacks' at Ramahyuck.

The same understanding emerges in a letter Hagenauer wrote in 1882 regarding a young 'half-caste' man who had been brought up on the mission. 'We feel it a great pity', he wrote:

> that so well taught and well behaved a lad as the halfcaste youth Charles Foster should be left among the Blacks, as he could be quite able to earn his living and in fact become a white man in that sense as generally understood. If left among the Blacks of course, ere long he becomes a Blackfellow useless to a very great extent and his good education would also be lost.[29]

Like his arguments to the BPA, this quote reveals Hagenauer's understanding of race as inherited. A 'half-caste' person was innately different from either a 'white' or 'Black' person.

---

[27] Jensz, 'Collecting cultures for God', 259–66.

[28] Friedrich Hagenauer to Br. Connor, 24 March 1884, cited in Jensz, 'Collecting cultures for God', 259–66.

[29] F.A. Hagenauer to Rev. Macdonald, 6 July 1882, 'Letterbooks of F.A. Hagenauer, 1865–1885', MS 3343, National Library of Australia, Canberra.

Such an understanding reflected the broader racial thinking of the late 19th century, in which social Darwinist arguments were marshalled to provide new grounds for the widespread European assumption that 'race', to quote Robert Knox's famous phrase, was 'everything', determining physiology, ability and character.[30] Social evolution or 'developmentalism' was publicly debated in Melbourne in the 1870s, with the evangelical Anglican Bishop of Melbourne, Charles Perry, a supporter of Ramahyuck, arguing against such theories and for racial unity and equality.[31] In addition, Perry questioned the over-emphasis within such theories, on notions of 'civilisation' and 'progress'. Civilisation, he pointed out, was no guarantee of spiritual or moral character.[32] Though Hagenauer shared Perry's evangelical theology, Robert Kenny has argued that as social Darwinist thought became pervasive, Hagenauer became more convinced of the deep-rooted differences between races.[33]

Yet these comments also reveal Hagenauer's assumption that race was fluid and changeable, not simply innate and immutable. Hagenaeur believed that Charles Foster could become a 'white man in that sense as generally understood' or a 'Blackfellow'. Race, then, was a result not simply of innate characteristics, but also of personal choices and the influence of others. Racial identity might be particularly unstable for those of mixed racial heritage, but this understanding of the changeability of racial identity had potential implications for white people living among Aboriginal people, and vice versa.

Hagenauer's arguments to the BPA played a significant role in the eventual adoption of 'An Act to Provide for the Protection and Management of the Aboriginal Natives of Victoria' in 1886. Under this

---

[30] See Nancy Stepan, *The idea of race in science: Great Britain, 1800–1960* (London: Macmillan, 1982), 20–62.

[31] For an overview of social Darwinist views relating to race and their promotion in Victoria see Kenny, *The lamb enters the dreaming,* 288–99.

[32] Ibid. 292.

[33] Ibid. 298–99.

legislation, Aboriginal people identified as 'half-caste' were forced off mission stations if they were under the age of 34. The Act separated families and caused immense suffering and disadvantage. Letters written by Aboriginal residents of Ramahyuck and other Victorian missions to the BPA in the years after the Act was passed provide eloquent testimony to this, as separated families sought permission simply to see each other, or requested the most basic necessities as they struggled to survive in settler society.[34] Ellie Hagenauer's accounts of life on the mission and her own responses to it were written primarily in the years after this Act was passed, as it was gradually implemented. Though she does not mention the Act, the debates over racial identity which accompanied it, and in which her father participated, form the background to her references to whiteness.

Respectable whiteness at Ramahyuck

Ellie's complicated response to her position at Ramahyuck emerges in accounts she wrote of her interactions with both Aboriginal and white people at Ramahyuck. In July 1894, she recorded in her diary an argument with Mr Hasting, a man who had been helping on the mission. During breakfast, she lost her temper and told Mr Hasting to 'be quiet'. 'I shall not put up with his nonsense any longer' she wrote. 'He shall not run down the natives or the Moravians in my presence'.[35]

Ellie's defensiveness about 'Moravians' and 'natives' is evidence of both her sense of identification with these groups and her awareness that such identification was open to criticism. To be a Moravian was to embrace a piety that was conservative by the standards of polite Melbourne society. Ellie did not attend the local races or other local social events so as not to become 'worldly', and noted that the daughter of

---

[34] See Elizabeth Nelson, Sandra Smith and Patricia Grimshaw, eds., *Letters from Aboriginal women in Victoria, 1867-1926* (Melbourne: History Department, University of Melbourne, 2002), especially 123–44 and 239–312.

[35] DEH, 9–10 July, 1894, 4370A/635, *Le Souef Family Papers*.

another Moravian missionary was sent to stay at Ramahyuck 'that she may see that inmates of a Mission house do not go to balls & dances etc'.[36] This conservatism could create embarrassment for Ellie: she noted that while shopping in Melbourne, her father told the shop assistant 'not to put a male & female doll in one box as it was not decent. She thought him a country bumpkin'.[37]

While being a Moravian posed certain social challenges for Ellie, however, being associated with Aboriginal people was far more threatening to respectability. As noted, on the mission, proximity to Aboriginal people was both a pragmatic necessity and a religious duty for the missionaries and their family. Ellie's daily life, as recorded in her diary, could involve theological discussions with Aboriginal Christians, sharing domestic tasks with her former nurse, or having her hair washed by one of the young women on the mission.[38] Physical care of sick mission residents was a regular duty. After visiting one Aboriginal man, Ellie wrote:

> Mother & I went to see old Jack, poor fellow he is very low, barely a sign of life about him. In the afternoon we went over to see him again. Mother did what I could not, she washed his face & changed his clothes & then cleaned the house, it is now a pleasure to visit the old man ... Mother nursed him all day as only she could, my noble Mother![39]

As this quote suggests, Ellie saw a willingness by her mother to physically care for mission residents as a sign of 'nobility'. This perception was not necessarily based on assumptions about racial difference, but her comments demonstrate that such contact was weighted with all kinds of meanings that could and apparently often did have more to do with powerful tropes of maternalism and condescension than of anything like emotional intimacy on an egalitarian footing. Nonetheless, such close

---

[36] Ibid. 17 February 1898 and 23 August 1897, 4370A/638.

[37] Ibid. 12 July 1894, 4370A/635.

[38] Ibid. 15–7 October 1894 and 1 February 1893, 4370A/635, 4370A/634.

[39] Ibid. 22 March, 1893, 4370A/634.

contact between Aboriginal and non-Aboriginal was unusual and Ellie could display a profound sense of internal unease about living so close to the racial boundaries.

This unease is obvious in Ellie's anxieties about the opinions of others as well as her own prejudices. She confided to her diary her anger at a visitor who accused her of eavesdropping. 'I'm savage with Mrs Harm. She thinks evidently I try to listen when she talks to Mr Hardie in the study … I must say I do have some honorable feelings tho' I do live amongst the blacks'.[40] It is not entirely obvious how ironic Ellie was being in this comment, but it clearly communicates her awareness of a common perception that living 'amongst the blacks' could threaten those 'honorable' qualities that respectable white people shared. In judging herself, however, 'native' qualities could also serve for Ellie as a minimum standard against which her own behaviour could be measured. On one occasion, she wrote in her diary 'Tonight I am consumed with remorse for allowing my temper to get the better of me & for not entering into a joke even as well as a native girl'.[41] In both incidents, though whiteness is not mentioned, it is implicitly defined in contrast to the inferior qualities of 'blacks' or 'a native girl'.

This anxiety about preserving the qualities of whiteness while living 'amongst the blacks' emerges not only in comments about Ellie's own behaviour and reputation, but in her concern over the behaviour of those white people associated with her family and the mission. Her brothers, who lived on the mission for part of this time, were subject to scrutiny. She complained of one brother: 'August is not at all sociable but sits playing draughts with the blacks in the old house'.[42] Another brother, Johannes, who was later appointed manager of the mission, also spent significant amounts of time with the Aboriginal men who laboured on the mission. On one occasion, when a fire threatened the mission, Ellie

---

[40] Ibid. 15 February 1895, 4370A/636.
[41] Ibid. 20 March 1896, 4370A/637.
[42] Ibid. 3 March 1897, 4370A/638.

dedicated several diary entries to complaining about 'such laziness as is shewn [sic] by Joh & our native men'. She claimed that 'Mother had a great work to make Joh go—& at last when they did go they sat on our boundary fence & waited for the fire to come ... Such laziness!!!'[43] In this account, Johannes, who associated with the 'native men', was seen to share the quality of laziness, a vice which was repeatedly attributed to Aborigines by settlers, by her father and elsewhere by Ellie.[44]

Most acute, however, was Ellie's concern that proximity between white and Aboriginal people not produce an intimacy that she considered inappropriate. She wrote a very critical note in her diary regarding a neighbour who had visited Ramahyuck:

> Mrs Hooper ... did not leave here till nearly 10 pm & I was so vexed with her, she ought to be with her child at home & not leave the little girl with such a young servant girl (15yrs) for so many hours at night & above all she shd not leave her little servant girl alone there with a black boy.[45]

Though she later added an apologetic note—'Sorry I got scotty and wrote this'—it was clearly the hostility towards Mrs Hooper rather than the principle of guarding against the 'black boy' of which she repented.

Even more explicit, however, were her statements regarding one of the mission schoolteachers, Miss Seymour. Throughout the 1880s and 90s, the mission school was staffed by a series of school teachers employed by the Victorian government. These teachers lived on the mission and had some authority over mission residents, but were not necessarily in sympathy with the missionaries' faith or their methods of managing the mission. Ellie's diaries make it clear that this could produce

---

[43] Ibid. 15 and 16 March 1899, 4370A/638.

[44] For an extended complaint about 'the natives' laziness and incapacity see Ibid. 13 September 1895, 4370A/636.

[45] Ibid. 30 March 1898, 4370A/638.

situations of significant conflict between the missionaries, the school teacher and the mission residents.[46]

In early 1898, Miss Seymour was appointed to the mission school and initially appeared to get on well with the Hagenauers. As the year progressed, however, Ellie made a number of increasingly critical comments in her diary and letters regarding the new teacher. In October 1898, writing to her fiancé in Western Australia, Ellie criticised Miss Seymour for getting involved in 'the blacks' gossip' though 'she means well'.[47] In early November, she wrote in her diary 'Miss Seymour in the miserables. I simply can't understand her at all, allowing herself to get entangled with the blacks'.[48] Three weeks later, these vague references crystallised:

> Mother asked Miss Seymour to resign & I hope she will ... as it is now among the white larrikins in Sale, the laughingstock how the "ladies of Ramahyuck" behave since Miss S allowed her name to be coupled with Haines Cameron & he boasts of his connection with her, a most lowering thing for a lady. I can't understand her a bit.[49]

Haines Cameron was the son of Bessy Flower, the Aboriginal woman who had taught at the Ramahyuck school before Ellie's birth.

Ellie's reaction to the revelation of Miss Seymour's behaviour, and in particular her 'connection' with Cameron, is revealing of her complicated understanding of the relationship between whiteness and respectability. Miss Seymour's actions are criticised not as an offence to religious principles—there is no suggestion that she and Cameron have had sexual relations—but as incompatible with being 'a lady'. Though Ellie interacted

---

[46] Most notably, in 1892, two teachers at the mission school attempted to rally the mission residents against the Hagenauers and, according to Ellie's account, were virtually driven off the mission by the Aboriginal residents, amidst 'loud hurrahs & flying flags'. See Ibid. 11 January–14 March 1892, 4370A/633.

[47] Ellie Hagenauer to Ernest Le Souef, 23 October and 28 October 1898, 4370A/224, 226, *Le Souef Family Papers*, Battye Library, Perth.

[48] DEH, 6 November 1898, 4370A/636, *Le Souef Family Papers*.

[49] Ibid. 27 November 1898, 4370A/636.

with Aboriginal people every day of her life on the mission, she clearly distinguished between such interaction and becoming 'entangled with the blacks'. Intimacy with Aboriginal people, as represented by becoming involved with 'the blacks' gossip' or worse, a romantic relationship, was unacceptable for a respectable white woman, or 'lady'. Miss Seymour's offence was clearly heightened, in Ellie's eyes, by the fact that the unrespectable 'white larrikins' of the local town were using this information to mock the white 'ladies' at Ramahyuck. For Ellie, respectable whiteness was a vulnerable quality. It could be threatened, and thus to some extent was defined, by both unrespectable white people and by those identified as non-white.

Ellie's response to the incident with Miss Seymour makes clear how powerful was her desire to be integrated with respectable white society. This desire existed in conscious tension with her loyalty to her family and religious convictions. As she lamented to her dairy in September 1897:

> It does not do for me to go out to meetings etc. it just makes me long to live among white people & in a white congregation where one can go to meetings and take an interest in church affairs etc. & yet I have such a happy home & so very many blessings for which my heart overflows with gratitude.[50]

Three years later, Ellie's desire to 'live among white people' was granted when she moved to Western Australia with her husband and became a respected member of the upper echelons of settler society in Perth.[51] In keeping with her desire to 'go to meetings and take an interest in church affairs', she was an office-holder in the Women's Service Guild and the Australian Federation of Women Voters, and an active member of Trinity Congregational Church, the League of Nations Union, the YWCA and the boards of a number of state schools.[52] She visited Ramahyuck

---

[50] Ibid. 3 September 1897, 4370A/638.
[51] Stewart, 'Mrs Ellie Grace Le Souef', 104–5.
[52] Ibid. 105.

regularly and maintained an affectionate correspondence with Emily Stephens, the Aboriginal woman who had been her nurse.[53]

Whiteness, Ellie Hagenauer and missions

Reading Ellie Hagenauer's diaries and letters, her personal anxieties about whiteness are obvious. Whiteness was not 'everything' for Ellie, rather it was a central but fraught aspect of her self-understanding, which related in complicated ways to her religious faith, her loyalty to her family, her relationships with individual Indigenous people, and her desire for respectability and sociability. Her proximity to Aboriginal people clearly had the potential to threaten her status as a respectable white woman. However, it also allowed her to construct this status in relation to Aboriginal people, whether through the 'nobility' of nursing Aborigines during sickness, or by defining her own qualities of 'honour' in contrast to the qualities with which she imbued Aboriginal people. Though she was defensive of 'the natives' and had affectionate relationships with a number of Aboriginal people on the mission, she clearly believed that such relationships should involve an emotional distance that echoed the distance separating her family's home from those of Aboriginal mission residents. To violate this principle through inappropriate intimacy was to lower one's status as 'a lady'. Nonetheless, as the incident with Miss Seymour and Haines Cameron demonstrates, both white and Aboriginal people might choose to cross this distance.

Beyond the specific historical experience of Ellie Hagenauer and those who lived at Ramahyuck, can anything broader be gathered from these texts and their context? Ellie's opinions cannot be taken as representative of missionaries as a whole: though she was certainly influenced by her parents, she herself was not a missionary. Focusing on whiteness in her writings does, however, provide some significant new insights into life on missions, where race was defined in ways that had a

---

[53] See letters from Emily Stephen, AC4370A/713/8/7–14, *Le Souef Family Papers*, Battye Library, Perth. Ramahyuck Mission was closed in 1908.

huge impact on Aboriginal residents—whether through the everyday demarcation of racial divisions or through devastating impositions like the Half-Caste Act.[54] In particular, it highlights the diversity of whiteness on and around a mission. Mission histories often focus primarily on the actions of one white man or couple. By contrast, Ellie's writings demonstrate that a variety of white people were involved in mission life at any time, such as an assistant like Mr Hastings, the adult children of missionaries like Ellie and her brothers, visitors to the mission like Mrs Harm or Mrs Hooper and schoolteachers like Miss Seymour. As Ellie's accounts of these people show, different white people on missions related to Aboriginal people in quite different ways, from the apparent contempt of Mr Hastings to the 'entanglement' of Miss Seymour. Such an insight helps guard against the tendency to generalise about all white people on missions as 'missionaries', and then to further generalise about their attitudes to race. On missions, as elsewhere in settler-colonial Australia, whiteness was a diverse construct, though one which uniformly held the potential of power and privilege for those who claimed it.

---

[54] Accounts of the significance of Victorian missions, including Ramahyuck, on the life of Aboriginal individuals and communities are given in Phillip Pepper and Tess de Araugo, *The Kurnai of Gippsland: what did happen to the Aborigines of Victoria* (Melbourne: Hyland House, 1984); and Phillip Pepper, *You are what you make yourself to be: the story of a Victorian Aboriginal family, 1842–1980* (Melbourne: Hyland House, 1980).

6

Calculating colour: whiteness, anthropological research and the Cummeragunja Aboriginal Reserve, May and June 1938

Fiona Davis, University of Melbourne

On a sunny afternoon in late May 1938, two anthropologists, Joseph Birdsell and Norman Tindale, and their wives, Dorothy Tindale and Bee Birdsell, arrived for a short stay at the Cummeragunja Aboriginal Reserve, situated on the banks of the Murray River in southern New South Wales. Through what appeared to be good luck rather than good management, the group drove through the reserve's gates just after the Aborigines Protection Board chief inspector Ernest Smithers who had come from Sydney for what was a big day for the reserve's inhabitants: the commemoration of Empire Day. Their participation, though ironic, appeared at least superficially voluntary. Given indications of some contemporary Aboriginal faith in the residual goodwill of the British Crown, the Cummeragunja people perhaps nurtured some hope that the royal head of the empire would one day prevail over the Australian settler government and offer them rights as Indigenous people.[1] Either way, on

---

[1] For more on these perceptions on Maloga Mission see Claire McLisky, '"The free enjoyment of our possessions": Aboriginal and missionary interests in the Maloga petitions of 1881 and 1887' (Paper presented at the New worlds, new sovereignties: a cross-community interdisciplinary international conference, Melbourne, Australia, 6–9 June 2008). For a more general discussion see Heather Goodall, *Invasion to embassy: land in Aboriginal politics in New South Wales, 1770–1972* (St Leonards: Allen & Unwin, in association with Black Dog Books, 1997; reprinted Sydney; Sydney University Press, 2008), 102.

this day and, apparently, on every 24 May since the late 1880s, residents young and old had donned costumes, decorated their cars and bikes, and paraded through the streets in cheerful spirits. A returned Anzac soldier in full uniform led a colourful parade that included 'Decorated motor floats with streamers and gaily dressed children, black minstrels playing in a gum leaf band and decorated bicycles.'[2] Tindale and Birdsell quickly set up their motion picture camera to capture the event.

The presence of the two scientists at this event highlights the complicated and often conflicting nature of understandings of empire, race and whiteness at this time. Here the Cummeragunja residents are celebrating their inclusion within the British Empire, while on the margins of these festivities are Birdsell and Tindale, their very presence as anthropologists, there to study the 'otherness' of Aboriginal people, undermining to a certain extent this community's claims to inclusion. Using a framework of whiteness I plan to highlight the unacknowledged and often contradictory power of whiteness, hinted at on this day and deeply embedded in Tindale and Birdsell's research trip to the reserve. The use of whiteness studies in this instance is particularly effective, as it helps to highlight the mechanisms of power that underwrote life on the reserve at this time. The records from the expedition, I will demonstrate, reveal that ideas of whiteness, far from being simply an intellectual endeavour, had very real implications for Aboriginal Australians.

My chapter will begin with a discussion of the emerging field of whiteness studies in Australia and the debate regarding research into Aboriginal people. I will then look at the (male) figures highlighted in the records left from the expedition, now kept in the Museum of South Australia, for what they tell us of the working of whiteness, including the notions of superiority and the justification of control over Aboriginal people that this entailed. I will next turn to the response from the

---

[2] Norman B. Tindale, 'Harvard and Adelaide Universities Anthropological Expedition, Australia, 1938–1939, journal and notes', 1938–39, MS AA38/1/15/1, Museum of South Australia, Adelaide, 88.

Cummeragunja people. How did the community react to the expedition's visit? What authority, if any, were they able to hold over this research? The final section of this paper will look at the legacy of this visit today and the question of who now has authority in the expedition records.

The hidden power of whiteness and white privilege has been a growing field of interest for historians over the last decade. In *The cultivation of whiteness* (2002), Warwick Anderson considered the history of medical and scientific conceptions of race in Australia, with a particular focus on shifting ideas of whiteness. Here Anderson wrote that: 'In thus marking whiteness, even within such broad parameters, doctors and scientists gave the national type of body and mentality to which it may aspire'.[3] In the same year, Russell McGregor built on the ideas set out in his 1997 publication *Imagined destinies* in an article which examined the commitment of Australian authorities and scientists to 'breed out' Aboriginal people of mixed descent during the interwar period, in the name of achieving a white Australia.[4] He observed that in these years: 'While the spectre of a "rising tide of colour" inspired administrators to systematise their absorptionist practices, contemporary racial science lent some credibility to their efforts'.[5]

The attempts of white 'experts' to speak for Aboriginal people, particularly, have attracted increasing critique. Within this is the fraught issue of the contingencies of research into Aboriginal people. As Maori scholar Linda Tuhiwai Smith has observed, the 'word itself, "research", is probably one of the dirtiest words in the indigenous world's vocabulary'.[6] Anthropology is a significant offender, as it has, according to Tuhiwai

---

[3] Warwick Anderson, *The cultivation of whiteness: science, health and racial destiny in Australia* (Melbourne: Melbourne University Press, 2002), 245.

[4] Russell McGregor, *Imagined destinies: Aboriginal Australians and the doomed race theory 1880–1939* (Melbourne: Melbourne University Press, 1997).

[5] Russell McGregor, '"Breed out the colour" or the importance of being white', *Australian Historical Studies* 33.120 (2002): 290.

[6] Linda Tuhiwai Smith, *Decolonizing methodologies: research and indigenous people*, 2nd ed. (London: Zed Books, 1999), 1.

Smith, been 'implicated in the worst excesses of colonialism'.[7] Certainly, scientific investigations throughout the 19th century and at least into the first half of the 20th often sought to reinforce notions of Aboriginal inferiority, and necessarily, European superiority.[8] Not surprisingly, then, many academics have described this desire of colonisers to know Indigenous people as 'a fundamental part of the power structures of colonial society'.[9] Anthropology also, however, unsettled some of the prevailing ideas held by colonists while at the same time prompting discussions and highlighting facts that made authorities uncomfortable.[10]

This area has, not surprisingly, stimulated considerable scholarly reflexivity on methodology. Penelope Edmonds, for instance, has criticised what she describes as the 'lack of detailed scholarship that historicises the operations of whiteness in specific times and localities'.[11] She continues: 'If, Homi Bhabha suggests, whiteness is a "strategy of authority" rather than an authentic or essential "identity", it is also observable that whiteness as a "strategy" may be authorised through (constructed) environments and spaces'.[12] My discussion, then, is to be

---

[7] Ibid.

[8] For more on anthropology in Australia see Geoffrey Gray, *A cautious silence: the politics of Australian anthropology* (Canberra: Aboriginal Studies Press, 2007).

[9] For example, Ann Laura Stoler and Frederick Cooper have observed that: 'A large colonial bureaucracy occupied itself, especially from the 1860s, with classifying people and their attributes'. According to Stoler and Cooper, colonial regimes then used this knowledge to 'define the constituents of a certain kind of society' and in turn employ this to demonstrate that their 'cultural knowledge qualified them to govern'. See Stoler and Cooper, 'Between metropole and colony: rethinking a research agenda', in *Tensions of empire: colonial cultures in a bourgeois world*, eds. Frederick Cooper and Ann Laura Stoler (Berkeley: University of California Press, 1997), 11.

[10] Ibid. 14.

[11] Penelope Edmonds, 'White spaces? Racialised geographies, Anglo Saxon exceptionalism and the location of empire in Britain's nineteenth-century pacific rim colonies', in *Historicising whiteness: transnational perspectives on the construction of an identity*, eds. Leigh Boucher, Jane Carey and Katherine Ellinghaus (RMIT Publishing: Melbourne, 2007), 363.

[12] Ibid. 364.

grounded in a specific place—Cummeragunja—at a specific time—May and June 1938—and will clearly reveal the impact of ideas relating to whiteness on this community.

White 'experts'

Particularly from the time the Maloga Mission was established in the early 1870s, Aboriginal people living alongside the Murray River near Echuca had faced considerable pressure to live under white rule.[13] This control was maintained when the New South Wales government established the Cummeragunja Aboriginal Reserve and the bulk of the residents shifted from life under the missionaries Daniel and Janet Matthews to life under an employee of the state. While theoretically residents could move on and off the reserve, they needed the manager's approval to do so. Further, if they found themselves unemployed at any time, as was frequent due to the seasonal nature of work in the region, they were ineligible for government assistance. Many had little option but to live off the meagre rations offered on the reserve, and, accordingly, live under the vagaries of the current manager's rule. Some residents had a brief foray into independence when small blocks of land were allocated for individual farming enterprises. This ended in 1907 when the blocks were revoked for communal farming—later to be leased out to white farmers. The NSW Aborigines Protection Board claimed these blocks were mismanaged, despite significant evidence to the contrary.[14]

The *Aborigines Protection Act* of 1909 gave white authorities the power to remove Aboriginal people of mixed descent from reserves, allowing only 'full bloods' and 'half-castes' over the age of 34 to remain. This control was increased in 1915. It is estimated that by 1921,

---

[13] For more on Maloga Mission see Claire McLisky, 'Settlers on a mission: faith, power and subjectivity in the lives of Daniel and Janet Matthews' (PhD thesis, University of Melbourne, 2008); and Nancy Cato, *Mister Maloga: Daniel Matthews and his Maloga Mission* (St Lucia: Queensland University Press, 1976).

[14] Goodall, 126.

Cummeragunja's population was half what it was in 1908, as the Act was enforced and, effectively, the whitest of the residents were forced to leave.[15] Authorities also removed children in the years that followed, placing them in domestic service, or the Cootamundra Girls Home. Families who had once relied on the forest and the river to provide for their daily food now had to stock their cupboards with adequate bought foodstuffs to prevent white inspectors accusing them of 'neglect' and taking their children.

The idea of a joint Harvard-Adelaide expedition to study the nation's Aboriginal people of mixed descent lay in the collegial contact of Adelaide University's Norman Tindale and E.A. Hooton, an anthropology professor from Harvard University, and his anthropology graduate student, Joseph Birdsell. It was planned that Tindale, who had met with the pair during a visit to the States in 1936, would study the genealogies, while Birdsell conducted measuring.[16] Their approach reflected the scientists' belief that not only did race exist, but that it incorporated both the physical and the social, with 'mental traits, such as an Aboriginal way of thinking or the nomad instinct, [considered] inherited or race specific.'[17] To quote Ian Keen, in this approach: 'Difficulties of social adjustment ... are attributed to the type of cross, not to historical, social and cultural factors.'[18]

---

[15] Ibid. 130.

[16] Anderson, 226–27. For more about the expedition generally see Joseph B. Birdsell, 'Some reflections on fifty years in biological anthropology', *Annual Review of Anthropology* 16 (1987): 1–13; McGregor, 'Breed out the colour'; Jacqueline D'Arcy, '"The same but different": Aborigines, eugenics and the Harvard-Adelaide Universities' Anthropological expedition to Cape Barren Island Reserve, January 1939', *Tasmanian Historical Studies* 12 (2007): 59–90.

[17] D'Arcy, 74.

[18] Ian Keen, 'Norman Tindale and me: anthropology, genealogy, authenticity', in *Connections in native title: genealogies, kinship and groups*, eds. J.D. Finlayson, B. Rigsby and H.J. Bek (Canberra: Centre for Aboriginal Economic Policy Research, Australian National University), 102. For more on the preoccupations of scientific studies of race during the interwar period see Marilyn Lake and Henry Reynolds, *Drawing the global colour line: white*

The plans for the expedition were timely. The 1930s had seen authorities express growing concern over the increasing numbers of Aboriginal people of mixed descent. In 1937 Commonwealth and State Authorities of Aboriginal People decided that the 'destiny' of these people of mixed descent, or this 'half-caste problem' as it was termed, lay 'in their ultimate absorption' into the rest of the population and that 'all efforts [were to] be directed to that end.'[19] With such interest in the topic, then, Tindale and Birdsell appeared assured of the governmental support essential to their 14 month journey, which was to take them across southeast Australia as well as parts of Queensland, Western Australia, and Tasmania. The assistance they needed was not merely financial— although funding was also welcome—rather, they would rely on government representatives to allow them to access their subjects: reserves, for the most part, were not public spaces and they could not be entered without some kind of approval. 'It is agreed', wrote Hooton accordingly before the project began, 'that there should be stressed the capacity of the hybrids for adapting themselves to European civilisation, since this group of the population constitutes a government problem.'[20]

When Birdsell, Tindale and their respective wives, Bee and Dorothy, reached Cummeragunja in late May 1938 it seemed the necessary assistance would, indeed, be forthcoming. Smithers and the reserve's manager, A.J. McQuiggin, greeted the group, as Birdsell noted in his diary: 'Protector Smithers of Sydney gave us a hearty welcome + NSW co-operation seems fully assured.'[21] While McQuiggin's reach may not

---

men's countries and the international challenge of racial equality (Cambridge: Cambridge University Press, 2008).

[19] Aboriginal welfare: initial conference of Commonwealth and state Aboriginal authorities (Canberra: L.F. Johnston, Commonwealth Government Printer, 1937), 2, nla.gov.au/nla.aus-vn118931.

[20] Cited in Russell McGregor, 'Representations of the "half-caste" in the Australian scientific literature of the 1930s', Journal of Australian Studies 17.36 (1993): 56.

[21] Joseph B. Birdsell, Australian daily field journal, 1938–1939, MS AA689/1/1/1, Museum of South Australia, Adelaide, 6.

have been as impressive as that of Smithers, who could coordinate access all over the state, he was able to offer some boys to assist them. 'Set up camps very nicely near the station hall and found the manager most helpful; a team of boys bringing us wood + water + setting up our tents for us', wrote Tindale that evening.[22] Later that night the community held an Empire Day concert and dance, an event for which they had been preparing for months. Not surprisingly, Tindale felt he was a qualified judge on the community's performance, noting somewhat patronisingly in his diary: 'The songs and items were well sung and acted and some of the people showed talent which would not be amiss in any white community'.[23] He and Birdsell both took to the dance floor as the evening wore on, but the real highlight for them was in the research they were able to surreptitiously conduct. While Birdsell took particular note of the physical appearance of the attendees, noting a preponderance of Tasmanians, Tindale asked Smithers about the number of white men present who were either engaged or married to the reserve's women. Smithers, who has been described as 'a professional civil servant' who 'considered himself knowledgeable on Aboriginal conditions, customs and psychology', was apparently all too happy to help.[24] 'These unions', he explained to Tindale, 'do not tend to last'. He remarked that despite this, Aboriginal people sought them out. Smithers would no doubt have been irritated to know that his claim was later contradicted, apparently unknowingly, by one of the Cummeragunja men, who told Tindale that while Smithers supported interracial unions, the type of white people interested in marrying Aboriginal people were 'only … the lowest, the scum of the earth'.[25] Despite the spuriousness of his expertise, Smithers

---

[22] Tindale, 88–91.

[23] Ibid. 91.

[24] Naomi Parry, '"Such a longing": black and white children in welfare in New South Wales and Tasmania, 1880–1940' (PhD thesis, University of New South Wales, 2007), 114.

[25] Norman B. Tindale and Joseph B. Birdsell, 'Cummeragunja sociological data', *Harvard and Adelaide Universities anthropological expedition: sociological, anthropological and ACER data cards*, MS AA 346/4/20, Museum of South Australia, Adelaide.

continued to be of valuable assistance to Tindale. The following morning the pair met to discuss the expedition's route through New South Wales. In between working on genealogies, Tindale made another call on Smithers and his hosts, McQuiggin and his wife, that evening.

Despite this call and, one would assume, other social engagements with McQuiggin, the most influential day-to-day authority on the reserve, neither Birdsell nor Tindale note any of his opinions about Cummeragunja people. Perhaps he refused to participate, although he clearly agreed to allow the men on to the reserve, or maybe the opinions of this man, described by residents later as violent and controlling, held little interest for Tindale and Birdsell. Even when the community speaks out against the reserve, McQuiggin is never mentioned specifically. Their silence is more understandable, however: those who acted against him risked retribution, as events over the following year would demonstrate.

One white man whose opinions were closely noted was the teacher Thomas Austin. Austin had taught at the school for close to a decade when Birdsell and Tindale arrived, and clearly considered himself an expert on not just Cummeragunja people, but Aboriginal people generally. The problem, he told Tindale, was that Aboriginal people developed earlier and this impeded their intellectual growth. He cited two examples to support his case: one was a boy who was sexually active and slow in school; the other, a 12-year-young girl who performed well in her studies and had not yet hit puberty. Austin explained to Tindale that while the station rations did not fulfil dietary requirements, they in fact benefited the children's performance in school as their malnutrition slowed their development. Wrote Tindale after their meeting: 'Undersized native children, partly starved even do better ... for they are late in arriving at maturity and so advance further on the path to educative efficiency'.[26] Disturbingly, the advice Austin doled out to Tindale was not just the confused musings of a local school man, with no

---

[26] Tindale, 99.

reach outside the Cummeragunja school, although this would have been problematic enough. Austin's expertise had, in fact, formed the basis of a recent paper written by Sydney anthropology professor, A.P. Elkin, on that very topic.[27] Austin's advice extended further than just the children, however: he also furnished Tindale with the list of the most intelligent members of the community, including one woman he described as 'most thrifty and honest'.[28] Austin's assistance was particularly important to Tindale in his plans to test the intelligence of children at the school. With Austin's help, Tindale was able to find out more about the 'home environment' and 'previous schooling' of the children, and, using the genealogies already collected, 'to place them in their genetic classes'.[29]

The local doctor, Dr Graham, is the next figure to move from historical obscurity into the limelight during the visit. A picture of malnourishment and ill health emerges in this interview, conducted by Birdsell, in which the doctor complains about the inadequate food on the reserve. Rations were limited to flour, sugar, tea and only occasionally fruit and vegetables, which had led to numerous stomach problems. He suggested to Birdsell that 'the government may tacitly wish these hybrids to die out—at least they [are] doing a good job to help them'.[30] His discussion of disease on Cummeragunja, however, reveals he is not entirely a sympathetic character. He tells Birdsell that one girl infected five men with gonorrhoea, and called for the power to segregate such cases. It is assumed the segregation was to be directed at the girl and not the men involved. The welfare of the girl involved, meanwhile, and the circumstances surrounding her prostitution is not remarked upon. Dr Graham also, according to Birdsell, 'wanted the authority to send

---

[27] Ibid. 97.
[28] Ibid. 113.
[29] Ibid. 107.
[30] Birdsell, 9.

venereal disease and tuberculosis patients to Sydney for segregation', a popular strategy for dealing with such cases over the years.[31]

Community responses

On the one hand, the expedition to Cummeragunja was one of white authority. Here were two white men, who not only had the audacity to measure and calculate the racial status of the Cummeragunja community, but who did so with the permission, and, in most cases, the testimony of the white authorities related to the reserve. On the other hand, however, there is an underlying story which, while it does not overturn this overwhelming authority, does destabilise it. The Cummeragunja people and their forebears had a long history of political activism. This had begun just 25 years after the first settlers arrived in the region and had led to a formal petition for the return of some of their land in the 1880s.[32] Throughout the 1930s, a number of Cummeragunja people joined, or even created, Aboriginal rights movements. William Cooper was one whose efforts took him to Melbourne, and even saw him petition the King, while also writing critical letters to the German and American leaders of the time for their behaviour.[33] The community was aware, at least to a certain extent, of its rights, and was unlikely to allow these two men to measure their bodies and write down their family relationships unquestioningly. Accordingly, just four days in Birdsell noted in his diary that one informant 'indicates station conversation subversive and situation seems to be indicated developing which calls for "Town Meeting"—to explain purpose of study'.[34] Meanwhile, two children whose

---

[31] Ibid.

[32] Rod Hagen, 'Ethnographic information and anthropological interpretations in a Native Title claim: the Yorta Yorta experience', *Aboriginal History* 25 (2001): 217.

[33] For more on William Cooper see Andrew Markus, eds., *Blood for a stone: William Cooper and the Australian Aborigines' League* (Sydney: Allen & Unwin, 1988), and also Bain Attwood and Andrew Markus, *Thinking black: William Cooper and the Australian Aborigines' League* (Canberra: Aboriginal Studies Press, 2004).

[34] Birdsell, 7.

parents had talked 'non cooperation' did not apply themselves in their school tests.[35] Neither of these objections were followed up; no town meeting was held and clearly the children were not exempted from the testing. Ultimately, these white men had the benefit of their white authority: the objections of Aboriginal people did not need to be taken too seriously.

The community's opinions were most clearly expressed when the researchers interviewed them about their health and level of assimilation. In these we hear the views, in many cases taken down verbatim, of the Aboriginal people that did not go on to become famous like William Cooper, or the pastor and footballer Doug Nicholls, but who lived their lives, for the most part, outside of the spotlight. In these interviews, the 'ordinary' Aboriginal people had the rare experience of being questioned by a white authority as to what they thought. Rather than merely discussing the influenza which plagued them from time to time or their love of the Bible, many of these men seized this opportunity to explain to Tindale the many wrongs which had been perpetrated on Cummeragunja people. One man who now read only religious sermons, books by a Dr Tolnodges and the *Christian Herald*, complained that Aboriginal rights to land had been severely curtailed. The bulk of the reserve was leased to a white farmer and his own daughter was 'turned off when fishing and camping there'.[36] Another man pointed to the loss of the farm blocks, remarking there was 'deep resentment among people at this action'. Cummeragunja men, he said, were now forced to work away in Victoria.[37] The failure of white farmers to employ Aboriginal people was pointed to by yet another Cummeragunja resident, who observed: 'Promises given of work in forests have been token'.[38] This reluctance to employ Cummeragunja residents was a particularly painful issue at this

---

[35] Tindale, 107.
[36] Tindale and Birdsell.
[37] Ibid.
[38] Ibid.

time; the reserve had been hit hard by the Depression, its population ballooning as Aboriginal people returned to receive rations, ineligible for any other government assistance under current laws, while local employment had plummeted.[39]

Eight months after Tindale, Birdsell, and their wives departed Cummeragunja tensions came to head on the reserve. Conditions had worsened during 1938 and the highly unpopular manager, McQuiggin, who had been so helpful to Tindale and Birdsell, had not taken kindly to the petition that residents had sent to the Aborigines Protection Board calling for his removal. In February 1939, John Patten, a relative of some of the Cummeragunja people and an activist from Sydney, visited and urged them to take action. Days later, at least 100 residents packed their things and crossed the river to camp at Barmah; many never returned.[40]

Three years after his visit, Tindale drew on some of the problems found at Cummeragunja to support his findings that while Aboriginal people of mixed descent could be assimilated successfully, the reserve system was not the answer. His conclusions appeared to address the concerns of the Aboriginal men who had complained in their health interviews, although they overlooked the very real attachment—and feeling of entitlement—to land, which had underpinned these complaints. Calling for qualified teachers and for vocational training, Tindale cited the example of the farming training given to Aboriginal people on Cummeragunja at the end of the 19th century and the early 20th century: 'although the training itself was ultimately abandoned, the good results are evidence in that some of the older men still find ready employment and good remuneration in the adjoining districts in New

---

[39] Diane Barwick, 'Aunty Ellen: the pastor's wife', in *Fighters and singers: the lives of some Australian Aboriginal women*, eds. Diane Barwick, Isobel White and Betty Meehan (Sydney: George Allen & Unwin, 1985), 188.

[40] Richard Broome, *Aboriginal Australians: black responses to white dominance, 1788-1994*, 3rd ed. (St Leonards: Allen and Unwin, 2001), 172.

South Wales and Victoria'.[41] Tindale appeared to link a subsequent lack of training to the growing dissatisfaction on the reserve: 'It will be remembered that there is increasing unrest and maladjustment at this place, which in former times was one of the most successful experiments in Australia'.[42]

The unrest at Cummeragunja is a frequent theme in Tindale's report. Discussing the role of missions and reserves, he writes that although they may be justified following early contact with Europeans, they mainly provided a site now for full bloods to die out and for the mixed groups to grow. He cited Cummeragunja and Cape Barren Island as examples, writing: 'In such communities there may be even a passive revolt against control and movements away from the area in which the people are retained'.[43] Tindale here highlights an important contradiction in the role of missions and reserve in settler colonies: at the same time as they provided sites where Aboriginal people could be both contained and studied, they were also supposed to be a training ground for assimilation, after which properly trained Indigenous people could join the broader white community. Further, while these institutions attempted to break down traditional community links, Aboriginal people responded by rebuilding and strengthening their communities.

While it may have been too late to stop the revolt on Cummeragunja, the findings of the expedition still had an impact on the community. It may well have spurred on attempts by the Aborigines Welfare Board, the body which replaced the Protection Board, to close down the reserve, attempts that were successfully fought by those residents who stayed or returned after the walk-off. Most notably, the expedition produced an

---

[41] Norman Tindale, 'Results of the Harvard-Adelaide Universities' anthropological expedition, 1938–1939: survey of the half-caste problem in South Australia', *Proceedings of the Royal Geographical Society of Australia, South Australian Branch* 42 (November 1941): 148.
[42] Ibid.
[43] Ibid. 157.

impressive archive of photographs and accounts which are now of value to the reserve's descendants. While these photographs rated little mention in either of the two scientists' diaries, they are now important artefacts for many within the Cummeragunja community. Copies are kept, both communally and individually, on the reserve, and the genealogies are also accessed and discussed, if not always agreed with.[44]

One of the oldest people still living on Cummeragunja remembered the expedition positively when interviewed in 2009. Josie Smith, was 13 years old when Tindale and Birdsell arrived at Cummeragunja. Her picture is there with the others: well dressed in what appears to be a home-made tunic, if judged by the uneven spacing of its buttons, Smith seems to be frowning at the camera. Trying to judge her attitude to the photographer from her expression and body language, I am tempted to conclude that she resented the intrusion in her life. Yet when I interview Smith over 70 years later, my interpretation did not fit with her memories of a tall, friendly man who measured her feet 'to see how much they'd grown'.[45] In Smith's memory Tindale was a welcome guest on the reserve, although she finds it difficult to explain his bizarre attempts to measure her and her siblings, laughing at the ridiculousness of his endeavours. Smith, however, now treasures the photographs left from the visit, although she has less respect for the genealogies, as she says some in the community question their accuracy. Nevertheless, Smith does not recall any opposition at the time to Tindale. She said that she, personally, was happy for him to visit: 'it didn't worry me. I mean, he was a nice man too and he always looked after the Koorie people as well'.[46] Heather Goodall has discussed this importance of photographs to Aboriginal communities, including those Tindale and Birdsell left after their visit to

---

[44] For more on the value of Tindale's photographs to Aboriginal communities see Heather Goodall's account of the Brewarrina community in '"Karroo mates"—communities reclaim their images', *Aboriginal History* 30 (2006): 48–66.

[45] Josie Smith (pseudonym), interview with the author, 23 March 2009, Cummeragunja.

[46] Ibid.

the Brewarrina reserve. She wrote that these images appeared different when seen 'in frames on family walls or carefully placed in albums', than when seen in the archive booklet:

> Certainly the families' own sense of having brought these images back to be among relations has coloured the way they are seen and read, to override the tension between the survey team and their subjects with the closeness of past and present family ties.[47]

Similarly, Gaynor Macdonald has written of the importance of photographs, regardless of the type, to Aboriginal people in confirming genealogies, remarking: 'photos of kin link one to ancestors and to one's children's children when myth and history cannot'.[48]

Speaking to other Cummeragunja people, however, it becomes clear that Smith's memories are more positive than many. One woman claimed the researchers measured the heads of the Cummera people—although the parts of the research cards dedicated to head measurements are blank. Perhaps this memory is more to do with the invasiveness of the visit than cold, hard fact. Other people told me that residents were forced to comply or not receive their rations. Many resent Tindale's genealogies, which were later used in the unsuccessful Yorta Yorta Native Title case in the 1990s.[49] This claim for land was brought forward by the descendants of the Yorta Yorta/Bangerang people who had lived on and around Cummeragunja, and, ultimately, failed because white records were used to prove that, in the words of Justice Olney in his 1998 Federal Court judgement: 'The tide of history has indeed washed away any real acknowledgement of their traditional customs'.[50] Olney's findings were

---

[47] Goodall, 'Karroo', 61–2.

[48] Gaynor Macdonald, 'Photos in Wiradjuri biscuit tins: negotiating relatedness and validating colonial histories', *Oceania* 73.4 (2003): 239. See also Jane Lydon, *Eye contact: photographing Indigenous Australians* (Durham: Duke University Press, 2005).

[49] For more on Tindale's research and the Yorta Yorta Native Title Case see Hagen.

[50] The Members of the Yorta Yorta Aboriginal Community v. the State of Victoria & Ors [1998] FCA (18 December 1998).

later supported when the decision was appealed before a full bench in the Federal Court, and again in 2002 in the High Court. While the 19th-century reminiscences of Edward Curr, a pastoralist and, later, an ethnographer, are widely acknowledged as key to this, important, too, were the records that emerged from Tindale and Birdsell's visit, in particular those relating to tribal boundaries and genealogies.[51] Writing later, anthropologist Rod Hagen, who was involved with the case, observed:

> Indigenous groups, not surprisingly, are highly indignant about having their claims, and the primarily oral traditions on which they are based, judged against the writings of the initial colonisers themselves and on occasion react even more strongly against later 'academic' interpretations of territorial interests, best epitomised perhaps by the work of Norman Tindale.[52]

Conclusion

The power of whiteness embedded in the Harvard-Adelaide expedition's visit to Cummeragunja is not as straightforward as it may at first appear. This research and the thinking that underpinned it had an undeniable impact on the lives of Aboriginal people, both then and now, at local, state and federal levels. The Cummeragunja people came under the scrutiny and, in some cases, the rule of a string of white figures of authority, including those who oversaw the reserve, such as the manager, the teacher, the doctor and the chief inspector, as well as those in scientific circles like Tindale, Birdsell and Hooton. Tindale and Birdsell's diaries reveal that these 'experts' on Aboriginal people used their expertise to legitimise varying levels of authority over Aboriginal Australians at this time. Later, the records were also used to override Aboriginal land claims. Yet the expedition did not simply reinforce white authority. Not only were the researchers ultimately critical of

---

[51] Hagen, 225.
[52] Ibid. 216.

contemporary government policy, but the Cummeragunja people did have a level of agency in this process, at times objecting, and at others trying, as best they could, to direct the research to their own advantage. Moreover, parts of these records are valued by the community today.

Studies which, like this one, critically revisit research into Aboriginal people have the power to destabilise the white authority that they previously stood for. As Gillian Cowlishaw in her book *Rednecks, eggheads and blackfellas* has written, 'by delegitimising the tainted and outworn body of racial knowledge which has been inherited from the past, it might be possible to recognise that local Aborigines, with their particular historical experiences, are the final authorities on their own worlds'.[53] From the calls for a town meeting to the resurrection of the expedition's photos in recent years, an alternate reading of the Harvard-Adelaide records also reveals Aboriginal people defying the profoundly inequitable power relations confronting them and continuing to demonstrate at least some level of authority over their lives and their past.

---

[53] Gillian Cowlishaw, *Rednecks, eggheads and blackfellas* (Ann Arbor: University of Michigan Press, 1999), 303.

Part 3

Writing and performing race: creation and disavowal

7

Theatre or corroboree, what's in a name? Framing Indigenous Australian 19th-century commercial performance practices

Maryrose Casey, Monash University

The reception and framing within histories of practice of Indigenous Australian cultural production in the performing arts has been a problematic and contested field for decades. Though, overtime the terms have changed in line with political and social changes and developments, I argue that these shifts have been limited by continuing *a priori* assumptions about theatre in terms of what it is and the implicit assumptions of European cultural ownership of performances that are discussed under the term. These conjectures continue to have impact on what is included, excluded and defined within Australian theatre historiography.[1]

Aileen Moreton Robinson argues that: 'the white position functions by informing and circulating a coherent set of meanings ... that operate to establish and maintain perspectives and claims of ownership that are understood as ... common'.[2] I argue that this white possessiveness is implicit in Australian theatre historiography and affirmed through the resonances and understandings of the use of terms such as theatre. As I have discussed elsewhere:

---

[1] I would like to thank Aileen Moreton-Robinson, Liza-Mare Syron and the referee for their feedback on this paper.

[2] Aileen Moreton-Robinson, 'The possessive logic of patriarchal white sovereignty: the High Court and the Yorta Yorta decision' *Borderlines ejournal* 3.2, 2004
www.borderlandsejournal.adelaide.edu.au/vol3no2_2004/moreton_possessive.htm.

racialised narratives continue to dominate because the frames of cross cultural reception continue to be locked into a meta-narrative of white normativity; that is, a dominant and normalised vision of what is 'contemporary' in terms of cultural practice and the historical lineage of these practices and who claims cultural ownership of that lineage.[3]

This normalised vision sets the terms in which Indigenous Australians are incorporated into the white Australian imaginary ownership of contemporary practices. This normative vision has tended to operate on the basis that 'theatre' is assumed to be intrinsically and essentially owned by white (implicitly male, heterosexual) practitioners. To apply Moreton-Robinson's arguments about white possession in the context of theatre practice, there is effectively an *a priori* premise that theatre is a 'white' practice, owned from birth by white people. This possessive logic acts as the basic premise for the position/perspective used to judge and categorise work produced by people designated as the 'other'. Practices and performances are labelled from the position of this assumed ownership. 'We gave them theatre' proposed in relation to Indigenous theatre practitioners is still an often uninterrogated and common statement in many contexts from theatre foyers to academic theatre studies conferences. This implicit progress narrative is often most demonstrated through attempts to deal respectfully with non-European derived practices in the use of terms such as 'folk' theatre. Plays by Indigenous Australians such as Kevin Gilbert's *The cherry pickers* (1968) were initially designated as folk theatre.[4] Terminology like 'folk theatre'

---

[3] Maryrose Casey, 'Repositioning the interface for cross cultural reception of Indigenous Australian theatre', *Being there: before, during and after proceedings of the 2006 annual conference of the Australasian Association for Drama, Theatre and Performance Studies (2008)*, ses.library.usyd.edu.au/bitstream/2123/2489/1/ADSA2006_Casey.pdf.

[4] *The writers 3: Kevin Gilbert* (film). Researcher and interviewer James Murdoch, producer Peter Campbell, Australia Council 1992; Gillian Oxford, 'The purple everlasting: Aboriginal cultural heritage in Australia', *Theatre Quarterly* VII.26 (1977): 89. For further discussion of this see Maryrose Casey, *Creating frames: contemporary Indigenous theatre 1967–1997* (St Lucia, UQP, 2004), 3–41.

carries endless resonances that repeat colonising practices placing the cultural production in a secondary place within the traces of 19th-century notions of progress. If everything is folk theatre or theatre on some equal but different basis then the difference is recognised within hierarchies of value. This context makes the act of documenting performances under 'theatre' a fraught act. Yet words such as theatre also carry implicit associations with a type of valorised artistic endeavour that is all too often denied in the discussions of non-European derived practices.

As an expression of the *a priori* premises, what is known as Australian theatre practice is usually presented as beginning when a group of convicts performed *The recruiting officer* in the late-18th century. In this narrative, Indigenous Australian commercial theatre is consistently represented as beginning in the mid-20th century.[5] Yet, within the cross-cultural context in the 19th century, Indigenous entrepreneurs publicly staged performances, advertised in advance in print, with spruikers walking through the towns with a bell prior to performances, booked venues and charged admission. Thus, Indigenous Australian commercial theatrical performance was already in place well before the mid-20th century. These earlier performances were labelled 'corroborees' and have only been discussed under that generic heading.

These corroborees as publicly presented spectacularised events for cross-cultural audiences served multiple functions for Indigenous Australians after colonisation of Australia by Europeans in the 18th century. Including songs, dances and battle displays resonant with culturally specific meanings, the events acted: to claim sovereignty; for political and diplomatic purposes; to provide a means of creating a basis for communication; to educate non-Indigenous settlers about Indigenous cultures; to entertain; and to enable Indigenous Australians to earn money and engage with the settler economy.

---

[5] For example see Geoffrey Milne, *Theatre Australia unlimited* (Sydney: Currency, 2004).

These public performances for a financial consideration developed in part from the pre-contact traditions of welcoming visitors, trading, and from performances for entertainment. Barter and exchange of goods after performances (including the exchange of 'shows') had been a part of traditional inter-community practices. The European practice of giving money or goods to the performers was incorporated into this custom. As dispossession destroyed Indigenous economies and government regulations limited and restricted the ways in which Indigenous Australians could engage with the settler economy, their cultural capital became one of the few options available to Indigenous people as a resource to barter for money, political recognition and economic survival.

Across the 19th century, these performances were organised as towns were built in traditional seasonal and ceremonial camping grounds and Indigenous people were dispossessed of their lands and endeavoured to engage with the settler economy. By the 1850s Indigenous entrepreneurs were attempting to gain access to mainstream European theatres for their performances with limited success.[6] In the late 19th century, many of the largest spectator events were Aboriginal corroborees. In 1885, an estimated crowd of 20,000 turned out to watch the first night of a 'Grand Corroboree', making it possibly the largest spectator event of the 19th century at the Adelaide Oval.[7] Spectacles and theatre companies initiated and controlled by Indigenous Australians operated across the country. For example, a journalist in the *Bulletin* in 1896 noted that:

> An Aboriginal theatrical co., has started operations in Queensland. Some 53 blacks of both sexes are running the show on approved 'white lines', commingling with the corroboree element. The 'co' pitched its tent at

---

[6] *Age*, 2 January 1856; *Argus*, 3 January 1856.
[7] *South Australian Register*, 1885; Bernard Whimpress, *Corroboree: Adelaide Oval 1885* (Kent Town, SA: Whimpress, 2000).

Cooperoo last week, and the whole district turned out to witness the first performance.[8]

Diaries and journals such as that of W.A. Cawthorne, suggest that Aboriginal-organised 'Sunday Corroborees' were a regular part of social life in the mid-19th century.[9] Numerous accounts demonstrate the demand for these performances. Noah Shreeve, a Englishman resident in Adelaide, wrote in 1864 about local Aboriginal people explaining that they held corroborees 'for a pit of fun, the same when you got fiddle', and refusing to 'corrobbery' (sic) on demand, suggesting that he return two days later for the scheduled performance.[10]

Towards the end of the 19th century, corroboree-based public performances were so widespread and successful that there were strong moves by government and church authorities to bring the events under regulated white control.[11] These interventions attempted to restrict Indigenous-controlled corroborees to sanctioned Church or government approved events. Despite this regulation, corroborees continued as local forms of entertainment in rural areas open to all members of the surrounding Indigenous and non-Indigenous communities well into the 20th century. In the late 20th and early 21st century, these displays of dance and song have continued to be part of the repertoire of dance companies and cultural tourist events.

These performances represent an important part of cross-cultural history in 19th-century Australia. However, the terms used to define these performances affect the way in which they are recognised. Concerns about the terminology to describe different cultural practices

---

[8] *Bulletin*, 14 March 1896.

[9] W.A. Cawthorne, *Litterarium Diarium*, 23 March A104, Mitchell Library, Sydney; For further discussion see Michael Parsons, 'The tourist corroboree in South Australia', *Aboriginal History* 2 (1997): 146–69.

[10] Noah Shreeve, *A short history of South Australia* (London: Printed by the Author, 1864): 36.

[11] Whimpress. See Michael Parsons, 'Ah that I could convey a proper idea of this interesting wild play of the natives', *Australian Aboriginal Studies* 2 (2002): 14–26

are not new. One strategy that is used to counter these Eurocentric premises within theatre and performance studies has been to use the word 'performance' as a more neutral term to discuss practices. Though this reframing is useful, I would suggest that the neutrality of this term effectively limits its usefulness as an alternative word to use to discuss the types of performance that come under formal notions of theatre practices. Calling everything performance from the everyday action to formal theatrical events conceals the differences between types of events. At the same time other words such as theatre remain uninterrogated in terms of the meanings, resonances and hierarchies they imply.

The use of generic terms such as performance and theatre to describe practices carry with them resonances of specific European derived cultural practices and notions that do not necessarily serve the theatrical performances from other cultures being discussed. My particular concern at present is the effect of potential ways of framing these previously overlooked Indigenous commercial performances from the 19th century. These performances are generally acknowledged under the term 'corroboree' repeating the blurring between different types of performances that have been practised since European settlement of Australia. Corroboree is a word with common usage that is generally understood to refer to Indigenous performances involving dance, song and music. When discussed in relation to these performances 'corroboree' is often understood as referring to performances such as the re-enactments of dances from the Bomai-Malo ceremonies on Mer (Murray Island) captured on film in 1898 by Alfred Haddon in the Torres Strait Islands.[12] However, it has been and is used to denote a much wider group of types of performances without any differentiation beyond whether the performances are secret and sacred or public. Some early sources suggest that the word corroboree is probably derived from an Aboriginal 'dialect

---

[12] *Dreaming reels: Aboriginal images in Australian silent films 1898–1937*, vol. 1 (1997) Australian Film Archives.

in the early settled districts of New South Wales, and has been carried by the settlers all over Australia.[13] It is generally accepted that the word corroboree is an adaptation of Aboriginal words such as *caribberie*. This word, popularised by the European settlers, has been reclaimed by Aboriginal people. But as anthropologists such as Ronald and Catherine Berndt argue, corroboree is too 'vague a term, lumping sacred and non-sacred together in an undifferentiated way, without adding anything distinctive to compensate for using it.[14] Equally to discuss these events under a general heading of 'performance' does not engage with the specific formal elements of the practice and effectively maintains past practices of locating non-European derived practices in a secondary position.

The historical practice

To further complicate the situation, performances within the cross-cultural context are not the only practices that are effectively erased by the assumptions within the resonances of words such as theatre. Highly developed performance traditions and practices were a central and important element within and across Aboriginal and Torres Straits Islander cultures and life. Performance practices have been an important forum and expression for a vast range of activities from teaching to settling legal disputes. Historically, performance events of song, dance, mime and story can be divided into events associated with ceremonies that are sacred and private, and events associated with entertainment and social negotiations that are public. These performances can be based on the adventures of ancestral beings; magic and power; totemic songs; hunting; dramatic songs and epics; fighting songs; topical events and everyday life. Within Aboriginal cultures, there is no clear division between the sacred and ordinary stories. Rather, sacredness is a matter of

---

[13] A.W. Howitt, *The native tribes of south-east Australia* (London: Macmillan, 1904).

[14] Ronald Berndt and Catherine Berndt, *The world of the First Australians: an introduction to the traditional life of the Australian Aborigines* (Sydney: Ure Smith, 1964), 320.

degree. Within this continuum of connection to the sacred, Indigenous performance can be divided into three major types; ceremony, public performances based on Dreaming stories and performances based on topical issues for entertainment. These latter performances and the ways in which they are documented and discussed are the focus of this paper.

Like the 19th-century performances, these events are not examined within theatre history. One of the reasons for this is undoubtedly the traditional bias within the construction of 'Western theatre' that privileged written performance texts. There are extensive written accounts by witnesses and oral histories that enrich our knowledge of these practices but the performances were not written down as performance texts. This privileging of one type of practice, the written text, has continued despite the changes in contemporary practice that no longer privileges the traditional written 'play' form. The only events usually acknowledged within writings about Indigenous performance are either those related to ceremony or public performances based on Dreamtime stories from within studies of ritual and ethnographic studies of elements of the performance such as song. This focus overlooks a major segment of Indigenous Australian performance.

Corroboree performances based on topical or historical events that are created for entertainment were performed for intra- and inter-community gatherings and for cross-cultural performances.[15] The performances include the alternating of a number of elements within the framework of the performance; these elements include storytelling through narrative, poetry, dance, mime, song, music and visual art. Operating within a paradigm of practice in many ways like European theatre practices, historically, there were performers, musicians, dancers and actors, writers, choreographers, people responsible for body design or costume, props and sets; and a manager responsible for organising the

---

[15] Roger Hardley, 'The social life of Stradbroke Island Aborigines', in *Proceedings of the Royal Society Queensland, Stradbroke Island symposium*, eds. N.C. Stevens and R. Monroe (Brisbane: Brisbane Royal Society of Queensland, 1975), 141–46.

performance.[16] There was a shared aesthetic scale. There were (and are) high expectations about the quality of the performances. Everyone can sing, dance, paint, and tell stories but the audience expects these arts to be performed well and historically an unsuccessful performance has a number of consequences including public criticism and a loss of social and political prestige.

Performances occur in defined and carefully chosen areas. Corroboree grounds were usually marked out and landscaped with a flattened performance space, off-stage areas that were hidden by trees or other physical features, and often built up areas for the audience. The physical environment, including the light and shadows created by the moon and the huge campfires, are used as part of and to enhance the performance. Trees and objects are used as props and sets. These practices all directly parallel western theatre practices both classical and contemporary. The performance space is equivalent to Classical Greek amphitheatres and 20th- and 21st-century practices of using found spaces and site specific venues. Yet implicitly the usual privileging of the European building-based tradition is an important part of excluding Indigenous practices from narratives of theatre. The Indigenous authorial and copyright practices are again both different and equivalent. Topical and historical performances are created and owned by individuals who teach and direct others in the required elements of the performance, song, dance and story.

Historically these performances were toured and were traded between communities. Examples documented since European settlement include many new corroborees created around the interactions between the communities and observations of the European settlers. For example, a European visitor to Australia in 1832 recorded a performance based

---

[16] Catherine J. Ellis, *Aboriginal music, education for living* (St Lucia: University of Queensland Press, 1985), 61.

around observations of the settlers' horses and riding in Tasmania.[17] As well as creating corroborees for entertainment based on their observations of Europeans, Indigenous performers in the 19th century created corroborees around European entertainments that they witnessed. In 1854, a European settler:

> took a party of Jervis Bay and Illawarra blacks to the Sydney theatre, to witness the opera of *Der Freischutz* chiefly with the idea of observing what effect the incantation-scene would have upon them. The scene in the Wolf's Glen riveted their attention. They exhibited great excitement at the circle of skulls in the glen; the mystic casting of the seven bullets; Zamiel, the red man with the long fingers; the toads, and frogs, and other reptiles on the ground; the firing of the gun, and fall of the bird.[18]

Six or seven years later the man returned to Jervis Bay, and witnessed the incorporation of several aspects of the Wolf's Glen scene into:

> one of their moonlight entertainments … They painted their bodies red and various other colours to represent the characters in the opera; with boughs of trees they constructed the glen; guanas [sic], frogs and other animals were supplied by their native forests. The firing of the gun and bringing down the bird, and, in short, all the principal scenic incidents of the opera, were imitated with amusing mimicry.[19]

Based on more informal European performances, in the 1880s, Billy Cassim from Stradbroke Island created a 'Monkey' corroboree after he observed an Italian organ grinder with a trained monkey in Brisbane.[20] Cassim, using a couple of wallaby skins for costume, entertained the communities on the island with his performances based on the monkey's behaviour. There are accounts of these types of corroborees being

---

[17] James Backhouse, *A narrative of a visit to the Australian colonies* (London: Hamilton Adams and Co. 1863, reprinted New York: Astor Lenox and Tilden Foundation, 1967), 82
[18] Roger Therry, *Reminiscences of thirty years' residence in New South Wales and Victoria* (London: 1863), 297.
[19] Ibid.
[20] Thomas Welsby, *The collected works of Thomas Welsby*, vol. II, ed. A.K. Thomson (Brisbane: Jacaranda, 1968), 121.

performed for visitors to the island and touring to communities on the mainland.[21]

Performances were created based on events. Corroborees that have been documented over time and corroborees that continue in the repertoire of different communities vividly evoke the histories of Aboriginal communities offering a series of stories of the past both literal and allegorical. One of the Yolngu peoples in Arnhem Land, have a performance based in song, story and dance that tells of early encounters with Macassan traders, an Indonesian people from the island of Sulawesi. The Macassans had trading arrangements with the Yolngu peoples in Arnhem Land from about 100 years before European settlement in 1788 which continued until it was outlawed in the early 20th century. The performance called the *Jama Jama* (red flag dance) was created after some members of the Nambulwar went travelling with the Macassans in their boats. On their return they created performances based on their adventures.

European colonisation is examined in many stories. A number feature Captain James Cook even in areas where he had never been. These stories use Cook as an iconic representative of European invasion and the abuses of colonialism.[22] Other corroborees focus on specific events. A corroboree performed in 1911 on Bathurst Island recorded in detail the early European settlement in 1824 at Fort Dundas on Melville Island with vivid mimicry of the actions of the crews on the sailing ships as they handled the sails and performed other tasks.[23] Many corroborees focused on finding the humour in the often dire situations Indigenous Australians found themselves in dealing with systemic racism from

---

[21] Hardley, 141–46.

[22] For examples see *Too many Captain Cooks* (video recording) (Canberra: Ronin Films, 1988); Deborah Bird Rose, *Hidden histories: black stories from Victoria River Downs, Humbert River and Wave Hill stations* (Canberra: Aboriginal Studies Press, 1991).

[23] Herbert Basedow, *Notes on the Natives of Bathurst Island North Australia* (London: Royal Anthropological Institute of Great Britain and Ireland, 1913), 308–9.

government authorities and their representatives. The 'Soldier' corroboree, another corroboree created by Cassim around 1884, was a performance based on satirising the military training practices and the soldiers' brutal treatment of Aboriginal people.[24] From Wave Hill in the Northern Territory a corroboree documented in 1944, but with many decades in the repertoire, satirises the treatment of Aboriginal people by the legal system as well as the European attitudes to Indigenous women.

There were a number of corroborees created in northern Australia and the Torres Strait Islands during the Second World War about the impact of the war and in particular aeroplanes. There are corroborees that enact general themes and others that dramatise specific events. For example, hundreds of Allied planes crashed around the Gulf of Carpentaria. The 'Aeroplane corroboree' from Borroloola in the Northern Territory depicts the events around one such incident.[25] On December 1, 1942 a US bomber called Little Eva was returning to base after a bombing raid over New Guinea, hit a tropical storm and crashed at Moonlight Creek in the Southeast corner of the Gulf of Carpentaria. The Yanyuwa people searched for Little Eva and her crew.

The Aeroplane corroboree enacts the story of the missing aircraft, and the events which followed the crash. Songs describe in detail the narrative of the pilot's journey, the storm damaging the airplane, the crash and the searches that followed.[26] Dancers, decorated as Tiger Moths, re-enact the aerial search for Little Eva. Other Yanyuwa

---

[24] Welsby, *The collected works*: 121–23 ; Thomas Welsby, *The discoverers of the Brisbane River* (Brisbane: Diddams, 1913), 116; George Watkins, *Notes on the Aboriginals of Stradbroke and Moreton islands* (Brisbane: Royal Society of Queensland,1891), 141.

[25] See photos at www.abc.net.au/farnorth/stories/s842784.htm. Video at mcarthurriver.wordpress.com/2007/06/25/boys-from-borroloola-performing-the-aeroplane-dance.

[26] See *Ka-wayawayama – Aeroplane Dance* (1993). Producer/Director Trevor Graham. Film Australia; For other descriptions see for example: Rainer Kosok, 'Things as they were, ever changing: the co-existence of continuity and change in Indigenous Australian drama and theatre' (MA thesis, Johann Wolfgang Goethe-Universität, 2005).

performers tell of their ground search for survivors and eventual success. The Yanyuwa aeroplane dance corroboree performance originally extended over a week and was performed when people wished to perform it.

These are stories that are told through multiple art forms for entertainment, education and case—satisfying even the most stringent Australia Council protocols for professional theatre practice. Contemporary European derived theatre has come to take on many forms, often utilising elements such as speech, gesture, music, dance, and spectacle, combining multiple types of performing arts, often with visual arts, into a single artistic form. The Indigenous performances discussed above are formal performance practices with stylised conventions that predate the current rhetoric and practices of European and Euro-derived performance that now explore similar approaches yet they are not examined or acknowledged as clear precursors of current practice on this continent.

Reframing the performances

Writings within theatre and performance studies have been primarily focused on work defined as contemporary, usually text-based theatrical performance work.[27] Performance work labelled corroborees, have been primarily the domain of anthropology. However, even within anthropology, public corroborees, 'although often discussed in passing in the context of other concerns, have received surprisingly little attention.'[28] Over the last decade there has been growing recognition of the gaps in knowledge resulting from the almost exclusive focus on rituals especially

---

[27] For example see: Marc Maufort, 'Listen to them cry out from their Dreaming', *Antipodes* 20.1 (June 2006): 56–62; Brian Crow with Chris Banfield, *An introduction to post-colonial theatre* (Cambridge: Cambridge, 1996); Helen Gilbert, *Sightlines: race, gender and nation in contemporary Australian theatre* (Ann Arbor: Michigan, 1998); Helen Gilbert and Joanne Tompkins, *Post-colonial drama* (London: Routledge, 1996).

[28] Susan Reed quoted in Rosita Henry, 'Dancing into being', *Australian Journal of Anthropology* 11 (2000): 324.

those that are secret and sacred and associated with ceremony within writings on Indigenous performance traditions.[29] An outcome of this shift in focus is that researchers in anthropology and musicology examining Aboriginal and Torres Strait Islander dance and music 'have begun to explore an increasingly disparate range of performance genres put on display for the public gaze.'[30] However, the focus, as with theatre and performance studies, is generally on contemporary practices of song or dance rather than focused on the overall event of the performance or the history of such events.[31] Some attention has been focused on Indigenous controlled performance events within tourist studies. In this field, Michael Parsons has divided corroborees into four main categories, the Peace Corroboree, the Command Performance Corroboree, the Gala Corroboree and what he styles the cultural Tourist Corroboree.[32] His focus has been on the economic exchange within cultural tourism rather than an examination of the performances and their reception. Apart from this, the main contribution to an examination of these performances has been within Aboriginal history studies through examination of specific

---

[29] For examples see: Franca Tamisari, 'Writing close to dance: expression in Yolngu performance', in *Aesthetics and experience in music performance*, eds. Elizabeth MacKinlay, Denis Collins and Samantha Owens (Newcastle, UK: Cambridge Scholars Press, 2005), 165–90; Henry, 'Dancing into Being'; William O Beeman, 'The anthropology of theater and spectacle', *Annual Review of Anthropology* 22 (1993): 369–93.

[30] Fiona McGowan and Karl Neuenfeldt, eds., *Landscapes of Indigenous performance* (Canberra: Aboriginal Studies Press, 2005).

[31] For examples see: Martin Nakata and Karl Neuenfeldt, 'From "Navajo" to "Taba Naba"', *Landscapes of Indigenous performance*, eds. Fiona Magowan and Karl Neuenfeldt (Canberra: Aboriginal Studies Press, 2005), 12–28; Peter Toner, 'Home among the gum trees', in *Landscapes of Indigenous performance*, eds. Fiona Magowan and Karl Neuenfeldt (Canberra: Aboriginal Studies Press, 2005), 29–45.

[32] Michael Parsons, 'Ah that I could convey a proper idea of this interesting wild play of the natives', *Australian Aboriginal Studies* 2 (2002):14–26; Parsons, 'The tourist corroboree'; Michael Parsons, 'Encounters in touriculture' (PhD thesis, Southern Cross University, 1997).

examples in isolation without interrogating the overall framing of these performances.[33]

Other related research includes the growing body of work focused on non-Indigenous controlled exhibitions and tours that often brutally exploited the Indigenous performers. Examples include work such as Roslyn Poignant's *Professional savages: captive lives and western spectacle* (2004) examining the removal of Indigenous Australians by entrepreneurial white recruiters for circuses and exhibitions. In parallel with this research there have been critiques of Indigenous performances of corroborees promoted and managed by non-Indigenous organisations and individuals on the basis of the attribution by white impresarios and managements of 'a savage or exotic otherness to the performers who were packaged into neatly schematised and imperialised glosses for ready consumption by the spectator.'[34]

These hidden histories and critiques are valuable and important. Indigenous people and performers were exploited by circus, theatre and exhibition managements. Indigenous performance has been manipulated to affirm imperial and colonial narratives. However, this is not the whole story. To tell one side of the story without the other is to reify the status of Indigenous performers as victims, and to allow a prescribed idea of Indigenous performance practices to stand unchallenged. In a sense, this erasure repeats the exploitation of Indigenous history that was practised so effectively by white entrepreneurs—this time to reaffirm the received version of theatre history as a gift of white culture to 'our' Indigenous peoples.

---

[33] For example Barry McDonald, 'Evidence of four New England corroboree songs indicating Aboriginal responses to European invasion', *Aboriginal History* 20 (1996): 176–94.

[34] Fiona Magowan, 'Dancing with a difference: reconfiguring the poetic politics of Aboriginal ritual as national spectacle', *Australian Journal of Anthropology* 11 (2000): 308–21.

The point of this discussion though is not just that this work should be included, rather my question is how? What does it mean to look at these public performances as theatre? The Indigenous historical practices are secular performances aimed at entertainment but they maintain a connection through cultural practice to the sacred and the practices related to sacred performance. To just call it theatre risks erasing difference, at the very least erasing links to the sacred, community and place. The use of the term would, in effect, make these performances part of a norm that privileges European practice as originary.

Theatre as a word lays claim to European practices and constructed linear histories that create myths of progression from the classical Greeks to the present. In this normative vision there are metanarratives of theatre that are encapsulated in myths of origin of practice—especially narratives that weave a linear progression that presents a singular 'Western' theatre derived from and/or following the same developmental path as Classical Greek theatre, such as exemplified in the theories of the Cambridge Myth and Ritual School.[35] However contested, these theories continue to be embedded in thinking within theatre history and to express *a priori* assumptions.[36]

The story of Thespis, as drawn from the tale told in Aristotle's *Poetics*, is a prime example.[37] Despite the facts that the earliest recorded theatrical events, as they are generally defined, date back to 2000 BC with the passion plays of ancient Egypt, and that many of the great Classical Greek texts were written under Egyptian influence, notions of what theatre is are all too often constructed within a linear narrative from the imaginary

---

[35] For example see: Jane Ellen Harrison, *Themis: a study of the social origins of Greek religion* (Cambridge: Cambridge University Press, 1927).

[36] For example Gerald Else contested the theories in his 'The origin and early form of Greek tragedy' (MA thesis, Cambridge, 1967. Yet the claims continue, for example see Julie Stone Peters, 'Jane Harrison and the savage Dionysus: archaeological voyages, ritual origins, anthropology and the modern theatre', *Modern Drama* 51.1 (Spring 2008): 3–4.

[37] Stephen Halliwell, ed., *Aristotle's Poetics* (London: Duckworth, 1998).

and highly contested Thespis stepping forward from the chorus to begin the path to Renaissance and contemporary theatre in a progression from collective enterprise to individual artist.[38] This story is then recreated in a parallel linear narratives about European theatre practices as developing from religious rituals.

The notion of Thespis has proven very attractive regardless of the lack of justification because it presents a very particular notion of theatrical performance that locks into the ideas of the individual and progression versus the collective. In effect, Aboriginal theatre, though it has historically been created and presented for tens of thousands of years in ways that contemporary artists within the European traditions have been working towards for the last 100 years, is not recognised or valorised as theatre because they did not make the same journey through text-based 'drama' to contemporary 'physical' theatre.

Perhaps an answer is to claim the terms of the framing of performances by utilising a different word for the general area of formal theatrical performing arts. Theatre, the word and concept, comes from Greek *theatron*, θέατρον, meaning 'place of seeing'; it was the place where people viewed performances. The Classical Greek *theatron* is usually understood as linked to the sacred and the community, as the theatre festivals and religious performances fulfilled a variety of social, cultural and spiritual functions. So perhaps rather than try to change the usage of loaded words, such as theatre and folk theatre, the answer might be to start using a word like *theatron* to denote the field of performances and then use culturally specific names to denote particular forms. In this context theatre in the European tradition would be one more subset within the field rather than the metanarrative that shapes and changes the framing and understanding of other complex performance practices.

---

[38] Scott Scullion offers a provocative and comprehensive critique of Aristotle's claims in "'Nothing to do with Dionysus": tragedy misconceived as ritual', *Classical Quarterly New Series* 52.1 (2002): 102–37.

8

The Wild White Man: 'an event under description'

Maggie Scott, University of Melbourne

William Buckley was one of four convicts who escaped from Sullivan's Bay (Sorrento) in 1803, the original penal colony in the region that was later to become the colonised state of Victoria. He lived with the Wathaurong people and returned to European colonial society in 1835. It is only because William Buckley, a white man, survived his escape into so-called wild, unexplored and highly desirable terrain that so many would be inclined to tell and retell his story.

This chapter is a small part of a much larger research project in which I examined issues of historical truth versus fiction and myth, which I found to be concurrent themes in representations of William Buckley over time.[1] The representations I discuss in my larger research project come from a range of different sources.[2] For this chapter, I am

---

[1] Much of my reading on the debates about fact versus fiction in history centres on Hayden White's comparison of historical writing with literary traditions. See Hayden White, *Tropics of discourse: essays in cultural criticism* (Baltimore: The John Hopkins University Press, 1978); and 'Historical discourse and literary writing', in *Tropes for the past: Hayden White and the history/literature debate* ed. Kuisma Korhonen (Amsterdam: Rodopi, 2006), 25–34. See also Ann Curthoys and John Docker, *Is history fiction?* (Sydney: UNSW Press, 2006); Joyce Appleby, Lynne Hunt and Margaret Jacob, 'Telling the truth about history', in *The postmodern history reader*, ed. Keith Jenkins (London: Routledge, 1997), 209–18.

[2] Representations of Buckley after the 1860s developed into fictionalised, fantastical histories. In more recent times, Indigenous perspectives of Buckley have been uncovered, as well the possibility that he has come to symbolise reconciliation with the past and with Indigenous people. For some examples see Marcus Clarke, 'William Buckley, the "Wild White Man"', in *Old tales of a young country* (Melbourne: Mason, Firth, and McCutcheon,

looking specifically at the period between 1835, when Buckley first returned from the 'wilderness', and the 1860s, after he died in 1856.

Although there is a wealth of primary material about Buckley, it has become apparent that because of his mythological appeal, he is not easy to pin down. During this phase, he has been moulded variously into a John the Baptist figure, an untrustworthy savage, a noble savage, and a captive or castaway. In his earliest incarnations, Buckley is spoken of in colonial journals and diaries, government documents, legal treatises, and missionary reports. Later, in the 1850s, he is also reported in newspapers, examined in colonial histories and anthropologies, and written about in fictions and life stories. I will demonstrate that these early representations of Buckley are often characterised by their contradictions and unspoken anxieties, which are particularly noticeable in the efforts of colonial players to make Buckley serve purposes he did not quite fit.

In the past 50 years, there has been relatively little historical scholarship examining William Buckley's entry back into colonial life and his confusing role as a go-between of colonial and Indigenous cultures. The work that is available has informed my approach to examining how historical fact and fiction are entwined. An exhibition held at Geelong Gallery in 2001, *William Buckley: rediscovered*, generated a catalogue containing a collection of essays in which Buckley is discussed mostly from a literary and artistic perspective.[3] In his useful essay 'Jump up whitefellow: the iconography of William Buckley', art historian Andrew Sayers looks at the changes in artistic images of Buckley over time, and

---

1871); Charles Barrett, *White Blackfellows: the strange adventures of Europeans who lived among savages* (Melbourne: Hallcraft, 1948); Joy Murphy, 'Foreword', in *Buckley's hope: a novel*, ed. Craig Robertson, 2nd ed. (Melbourne: Scribe, 1997); Wathaurong Aboriginal Collective, *William Buckley discovery trail: Victoria* (Bellarine Peninsula: Geelong Otway Tourism Pamphlet, 2000).

[3] See exhibition catalogue, *William Buckley: rediscovered* (Geelong and Mornington Peninsula: Geelong Gallery and Mornington Peninsula Regional Gallery, 2001).

what they might reflect about the period from which they came.[4] Lyn Gallacher's 2004 ABC radio documentary on William Buckley contains historical insights from scholars Tony Birch and Tim Flannery, but mostly incorporates excerpts from professional storyteller Jan Wositzky's one-man play about Buckley.[5] As we can see from these main sources, analyses of Buckley's story are more situated in the realms of fiction and artistic enterprise than in historical fact.

Nonetheless, I have also found many references to Buckley in scholarly articles about colonial history in Port Phillip/Victoria.[6] Although all of these sources are useful in piecing together a contemporary scholarly landscape around Buckley, I found that I needed to draw upon other relevant areas of scholarship in order to ground his story within a more suitable analytic framework. Many of the early sources that I will discuss in this chapter contain fundamental contradictions when observing Buckley's inauthentic 'whiteness' and inherent 'blackness', with all the slippery implications that abound in such descriptions. Hence, Buckley's 'ambivalent' qualities call for a postcolonial analysis in order to discern how issues of power, race, and

---

[4]Andrew Sayers, 'Jump up whitefellow: the iconography of William Buckley', *Voices* 6.4 (1996–97): 14–21.

[5] Lyn Gallacher, William Buckley, *Hindsight*, ABC Radio National, 8 February 2004, www.abc.net.au/rn/history/hindsight/stories/s1014819.htm; Jan Wositzky, Buckley, see www.storytellersguide.com.au/buckleys.htm.

[6] Paul Carter, *Living in a new country: history, travelling and language* (London: Faber and Faber, 1992); Ian D. Clark, '"You have all this place, no good have children …" Derrimut: traitor, saviour or man of his people?', *Journal of the Royal Australian Historical Society* 91.2 (December 2005): 107–32; Carol Cooper, 'Remembering Barak', in *Remembering Barak, exhibition catalogue*, eds. Joy Murphy-Wandin, Judith Ryan and Carol Cooper (Melbourne: National Gallery of Victoria, Ian Potter Centre, 2003), 66–87; Rodney Harrison, 'The magical virtue of sharp things: colonialism, mimesis and knapped bottle glass artefacts in Australia', *Journal of Material Culture* 8.3 (2003): 311–36; Laurie Hergenhan, 'Beautiful lies, ugly truths', *Overland* 187 (Winter 2007): 42–6; Robert Kenny, *The lamb enters the dreaming: Nathanael Pepper and the ruptured world* (Melbourne: Scribe, 2007); Francesco Vitelli, 'Epic memory and dispossession: the Shrine and the memory wars', *Mongrel Publications* 1 (April 2005): 8–21.

land ownership imposed on Indigenous cultures by Europeans functioned.

Over the past 20 years, postcolonial scholars like Homi Bhaba and Robert Young have explored ideas of colonial ambivalence (and about race in particular), seeking to illustrate the instability of the commonly held, normative, empirical colonial narratives.[7] Postcolonial theories provide perspectives which point to the possibilities of resistance to colonialism, the instabilities of colonial power, and the profound problems of colonial nationhood and identity. On ambivalence, Robert Young observes that:

> In occupying two places at once ... the depersonalised, dislocated colonial subject can become an incalculable object, quite literally, difficult to place. The demand of [colonial] authority cannot unify its message nor simply identify its subjects.[8]

The more contemporary field of whiteness studies offers useful scholarship with which to tackle Buckley's problematic appearance as a white/black man.[9] These approaches have assisted me in thinking about the politics of whiteness in representations of Buckley, as well as the way

---

[7] Robert Young, *White mythologies: writing history and the West*, 1st ed. (London: Routledge, 1990). Other important works include: Bill Ashcroft, Gareth Griffiths and Helen Tiffin, *Key concepts in post-colonial studies* (London: Routledge, 1998); Penelope Edmonds, 'Urban frontiers: the racialisation of colonial urban space in Melbourne, Victoria and Victoria, British Columbia 1835–1871' (PhD thesis, University of Melbourne, November 2005); Chris Healy, *Forgetting Aborigines* (Sydney: UNSW Press, 2008); Chris Healy, *From the ruins of colonialism: history as social memory* (Cambridge: Cambridge University Press, 1997); Ania Loomba, *Colonialism/ postcolonialism: the new critical idiom*, 1st and 2nd eds. (London: Routledge, 1998 and 2005); Michael Taussig, *Mimesis and alterity: a particular history of the senses*. (London: Routledge, 1993).

[8] Young, 148.

[9] Jane Carey, Leigh Boucher and Katherine Ellinghaus, 'Historicising whiteness: towards a new research agenda', in *Historicising whiteness: transnational perspectives on the construction of an identity* (Melbourne: RMIT Publishing, 2007), vi–xxiii; Ann Laura Stoler and Frederick Cooper, 'Between metropole and colony: rethinking a research agenda', in *Tensions of empire: colonial cultures in a bourgeois world*, eds. Frederick Cooper and Ann Laura Stoler (Berkeley: University of California Press, 1997), 1–58.

whiteness is constructed in the social world around him. Lynette Russell and Margery Fee, for example, draw upon Homi Bhaba's postcolonial theories to articulate a need to 'think through problems of essentialising binaries and rigid identities' in the highly politicised spheres of 'Aboriginality' and 'Whiteness'.[10] Also relevant to Buckley's problematised position is Sara Ahmed's discussion of the 'Politics of Good Feeling', a hypothesis about how racialised subjects are seen as getting in the way of public happiness because their politicised presence reminds us of the injustices of the social world.[11]

Australian postcolonial scholarship on 'Wild Whites' is also helpful. Buckley was sometimes represented as a *captive* of the Wathaurong, rather than as their guest or as a refugee of colonisation. Kate Darian-Smith's work on captivity narratives has therefore proved extremely useful as a starting point in my analysis of Buckley's colonial ambivalence.[12] Further, Kay Schaffer examines the links between captivity narratives and the idea of nation in her work, and Susan Martin has gone on to identify the significantly different historical contexts between American and Australian captivity narratives, pointing out that many people who lived with Australian Indigenous groups for long periods were never captives, but castaways or escapees from colonies seeking assistance for survival.[13]

---

[10] Margery Fee and Lynette Russell, '"Whiteness" and "Aboriginality" in Canada and Australia: conversations and identities', *Feminist Theory Journal* 8.2 (2007): 187–208.

[11] Sara Ahmed, 'The politics of good feeling', *ACRAWSA e-journal* 4.1 (2008): 1–18.

[12] See Kate Darian-Smith, eds., *Captured lives, Australian captivity narratives: working papers in Australian studies* (London: University of London, Sir Robert Menzies Centre for Australian Studies, 1993)1–13; Kate Darian-Smith, '"Rescuing" Barbara Thompson and other white women: captivity narratives on Australian frontiers', in *Text, theory, space: land, literature and history in South Africa and Australia*, ed. Kate Darian-Smith, Liz Gunner and Sarah Nuttall (London; Routledge, 1996), 99–114.

[13] The captivity narrative is first seen in North America as renditions of the captivities of white men and women by Indians. Hundreds were recorded between the late-17th to the mid-19th centuries, with hundreds more fictionalised versions generated from the 'real' accounts. See Kay Schaffer, 'Captivity narratives and the idea of "Nation"', in *Captured lives,*

We are fascinated by the wild white man, but cannot place him within a stabilising framework characteristic of empirical history. I hope to convey Buckley's ambiguity by discussing how he is a figure who never appears as one image, but as Chris Healy puts it, as a figure that 'does not stand at the centre of a stable narrative but is rather a multiple figure, an "event under description"'.[14]

Buckley's appearance at a camp at Beangala/Indented Head in July 1835 is a repeated representation, and it is this image which has become one of the main 'events' of his life. The first person to record Buckley's 'return' was William Todd, an Irish ex-convict and servant to John Batman, who had been given the task of recording a journal at the camp.[15] In early June 1835, after an 11-day land evaluation at Port Phillip, Batman decided it was right for settlement and made a 'treaty' with 'chiefs' for the land. He left his employees Todd, two other European servants, and five Indigenous men from Sydney at Indented Head to keep up friendly relations with the locals and to assemble a hut and garden.[16] They remained there for approximately two months before John Helder Wedge's arrival in early August and it is clear from the journal that—for

Australian captivity narratives: working papers in Australian studies, ed. Kate Darian-Smith (London: University of London, Sir Robert Menzies Centre for Australian Studies, 1993). Australians were familiar with these narratives of North America and manifested their own 'versions', although Susan Martin notes their significantly different historical contexts. See Susan K. Martin, 'Captivating fictions: Younah!: a Tasmanian Aboriginal romance of Cataract Gorge', in *Body trade: captivity, cannibalism and colonialism in the Pacific*, eds. Barbara Creed and Jeanette Hoorne (New York: Routledge/Pluto Press, 2001), 151–56.

[14] Healy, *From the ruins of colonialism*, 131.

[15] *William Todd, Andrew Alias William Todd (John Batman's Recorder) and His Indented Head Journal 1835* (Chief Illustrator, J.H. Wedge), ed. Phillip L. Brown (Geelong: Geelong Historical Society, 1989).

[16] For Batman's records of this journey, see C.P. Billot, 'The journal', in *John Batman: the story of John Batman and the founding of Melbourne* (Melbourne: Hyland House Publishing, 1979), 79–102. For details and copies of the treaty, see John Batman, 'The greatest landowner in the world', in *The birth of Melbourne*, ed. Tim Flannery (Melbourne: Text Publishing, 2002), 52–8; John Batman, *The Batman deed*, Melbourne, 6 June 1835, Port Phillip Papers Digitisation Project, www.slv.vic.gov.au/portphillip/inter/7315.shtml.

the three white servants at least—there was an atmosphere of both communal living with, and dread of, the Indigenous people. Todd reports his fears of growing numbers of people at the camp and his constant wish that they would leave. The Europeans jealously restricted their food 'rations' to these strangers, but ironically they also agreed to look after all their children at camp while the men, women and 'Sydney Blacks' went to procure food, which would then be bought back to camp and shared with the Europeans in the evenings.

In the diary entry of 6 July 1835, we get a great sense of excitement and relief from Todd when a 'White man came walking up to the Native huts … clad the same as the Natives'.[17] This written appropriation of Buckley narrates an event in which whiteness is recognised, marvelled at and swiftly re-inscribed as European:

> Being a long time with the Natives he has nearly forgot the English language—but the Native Language he can speak fluently. We then brought him to our tent, Clothed him with the best we had—& made him share the same as we.[18]

The speed with which Buckley was snapped up and appropriated in Todd's narrative is very telling. It seems fitting that the three white servants, who never felt entirely comfortable at Indented Head, would latch onto this 'Wild White Man' and suckle some sense of stability and authority from his potential to mediate between the Indigenous people and themselves. Despite this, they also swiftly attempted to erase his appearance of 'savagery' by clothing and shaving him, and giving him bread.

This journal entry is similar to the written appropriation of Barbara Thompson, a shipwreck castaway on the Cape York Peninsula who was

---

[17] Todd, 31. It is very strange that, given Buckley had no English, Todd was able to reiterate so much of his story in this one diary entry on his first day at the camp. Chronological inference seems precarious under such circumstances. For Todd's entries during Buckley's month at the camp before John Helder Wedge's arrival, see pages 31–36.
[18] Ibid.

cared for by an Indigenous community for five years. The 1849 journals of the surveying crew who recorded her appearance reflect similar tropes to Todd's diary entries; the edifying recognition of her whiteness and a swift move to wash, clothe and feed her with proper food. Furthermore, there is an effort to disconnect her from the people who had cared for her. Although the *Rattlesnake* crew all acknowledged that Thompson was well cared for after the shipwreck, the contemporary narratives of the event were framed in the language of her 'escape' from her life in 'captivity' with black men, and her 'liberation' by white men back into the folds of European society.[19]

In 1837—two years after Buckley returned to settler society—missionary George Langhorne took a short dictation from him which strongly suggests that Buckley was not a captive:

> Although opportunities offered, and I sometimes thought of going to the Europeans I had heard were at Western Port I never could make up my mind to leave the party to whom I had become attached. When therefore I heard of the arrival of Mr. Batman and his party it was some time before I would go down as I never supposed I should be comfortable amongst my own countrymen again.[20]

As we will see, constructions of Buckley as a captive serve to reinstall him to a superior civilisation. His contemporaries utilised his 'civilised' whiteness, as well as his 'authentic' Indigenous links to the land.

Whilst Todd and his contemporaries were moved by a need to soothe personal anxieties and fears of coexisting with local inhabitants who may or may not be welcoming, some of the more prominent men of the early

---

[19] Darian-Smith, '"Rescuing" Barbara Thompson', 99–114. A colonial fascination with Buckley's potential sexual escapades is also evident in the sources, and it is worth comparing with Darian-Smith's observations that the construction of captive females always pertained to the titillation of sexual contact between the white woman and the black man.

[20] George Langhorne (with William Buckley), 'Reminiscences of James Buckley who lived for thirty years among the Wallawaro or Watourong tribes at Geelong Port Phillip communicated by him to George Langhorne', in *The life and adventures of William Buckley*, ed. Tim Flannery (Melbourne: Text Publishing, 2002), 199–200.

colonial period in Melbourne actively appropriated Buckley in order to assist their dubious processes of simultaneous possession and dispossession. The Port Phillip Association was made up of 'noteworthy' and influential men from Van Diemen's Land, who planned to colonise Port Phillip against the NSW government's will, hoping the region would be within the jurisdiction of Governor Arthur in Van Diemen's Land, who was a supporter of the Association.[21] One of the members, John Batman, was later to be lionised as a true hero of Port Phillip's colonisation epitomised by his natural bush skills and his supposed ease with the Indigenous people he encountered.[22] However, in his past Batman had an ominous career in Van Diemen's Land as a headhunter when Governor Arthur declared martial law on resistant Indigenous people fighting to keep their lands.[23] The so-called unavoidable violence he committed in the Black Wars was perhaps what caused Batman to attempt the more peaceful approach of 'buying' land from the Kulin peoples in exchange for European material goods. Although Batman's subsequent treaty was likely made in earnest by both parties, it is clear that it was very unlikely to have been recognised by contemporary Indigenous groups as the capitalist wholesale of ancestral country.[24]

It is within the landscape of Batman's precarious entrepreneurial mission that Buckley's image became connected in some way to the operations of power of men from the Association. Both Batman and surveyor John Helder Wedge quickly set about committing Buckley to text, describing his physical presence, his story, his knowledge of the land

---

[21] James Bonwick, *The discovery and settlement of Port Phillip: being a history of the country now called Victoria up to the arrival of Mr Superintendent LaTrobe in October, 1839*, ed. Hugh Anderson (Melbourne: Red Rooster Press, 1999), 30–1.

[22] Ibid. 31–32. James Bonwick is responsible for the early championing of Batman as hero in the 1850s. See also Bonwick's *John Batman, the founder of Victoria* (Melbourne: Samuel Mullen, 1867).

[23] Billot, *John Batman*, 47.

[24] Batman, 'The greatest landowner in the world', 52–8.

and peoples, as well as petitioning for his pardon in writing.[25] This led to a series of political manoeuvrings and skirmishes in which he was utilised as a wager for anticipated wealth and land ownerships in the schemes of Association men and presented to the 'authorities' as both a godsend and as a potential threat, depending on what each player wanted.

John Fawkner is an example of someone who propagated the myth of Buckley as a savage. The son of a convict, Fawkner had travelled as a child with Buckley on the *Calcutta* to Sullivan's Bay in 1803. By mid-1836, he was a prominent and ruthless player in the political organisation of the town that would become Melbourne, acquiring considerable land, along with business, social, and political status.

Fawkner mentions Buckley a few times in his journal of 1835; he appears mostly in passing as a mild presence in the general building of the township, as well as the beneficiary of a yearly wage for his interpretive and policing services.[26] But in his *Reminiscences* of 1862, Fawkner becomes more malignant. Referring to an incident that he had briefly mentioned in his 1830s journal in one line ('The Blacks we learnt intended to murder us for our goods'), Fawkner explains that this isolated sentence actually denoted a plot to massacre the whites.[27] The small settlement was supposedly saved by a young Indigenous man, Derrimut, who warned Fawkner via Buckley's translations: 'The half savage Buckley

---

[25] It must be noted here that Buckley lied about his convict status to Todd and the others left at Indented Head by Batman. He initially gave them the impression that he was in fact a castaway (although this might have been wishful thinking on their part). Nonetheless, whilst Buckley's appearance at the camp may have been motivated by contemporary Indigenous reasons unknowable to us, he might also have been terrified of being convicted again. See Todd's diary for the details of his lies and how the 'truth' emerged. Todd, 31 and 35.

[26] John Pascoe Fawkner, *Melbourne's missing chronicle: being the journal of preparations for departure to and proceedings at Port Phillip by John Pascoe Fawkner*, ed. C.P. Billot (Melbourne: Quartet Books, 1982), 7, 10, 12, 83, 84 and 91.

[27] John Pascoe Fawkner, *Reminiscences*, 1869, MS 8528, State Library of Victoria, Melbourne. I have quoted from excerpts of this document in Billot's *The life and times of John Pascoe Fawkner*.

declared that if he had his will he would spear Derrimut for giving the information'.[28] Despite Buckley's peaceful presence in his 1830s journal, in hindsight Fawkner describes him a worthless, violent mediator who wasn't to be trusted. This contradictory view of Buckley came at a time when Fawkner probably felt the need to re-assert his position in the history of Port Phillip. It is also possible that he resented Buckley's affiliation with the association. Aligned with the association, Buckley was at times framed as an Indigenous white man with connections to the land, essentially allied with the Europeans. According to Fawkner and governors in other states who didn't know him, he was a savage white man, as untrustworthy as the natives, who must be carefully watched. These became prevailing tropes for Buckley.

As we move further from the fledgling settlement of 1835, Buckley's story begins to be used to represent authoritative histories of the Indigenous people of Victoria. Thus his image was utilised in the ensuing catalogues of misconceived knowledge used to describe, confine and mark the so-called decline of the Indigenous population. In 1856 historian James Bonwick describes his efforts to attract the attention of a tight-lipped William Buckley: 'Not being divested of curiosity, we often endeavoured to gain from some one of his acquaintants a little narrative of that savage life, but utterly failed in doing so', Bonwick wrote.[29] Bonwick was clearly covetous of journalist John Morgan's 1852 collaboration with William Buckley, which produced the adventure

---

[28] Fawkner, *Reminiscences*, Wednesday 28 October 1835, cited in Billot, *The life and times of John Pascoe Fawkner*, 115. Derrimut is himself a troubled hybrid figure in a hard place. His role as both assistant and resistor of colonial pressures is explored in Clark, 107–32. This article discusses the possible Indigenous reasons for a massacre and the effect it would have had upon development of the early settlement. Lyn Gallacher's radio documentary about William Buckley points out the contentious possibility that a massacre did take place, except the other way round with Fawkner and his assistants meting out the massacre of Kulin people.

[29] James Bonwick, *William Buckley: The wild white man, and his Port Phillip black friends* (Melbourne: Geo. Nichols, 1856), www.slv.vic.gov.au/vicpamphlets/inter/842440.shtml.

chronicle *The life and adventures of William Buckley, thirty-two years a wanderer amongst the Aborigines of the then unexplored country round Port Phillip, now the Province of Victoria.*[30]

When Buckley died in early 1856,[31] Bonwick was very quick to follow up with *his* version of the 'Blacks as they were than as they are', and the informant he could never procure.[32] This work contributed to his canon on Port Phillip history and reasserted his authority as the foremost historical expert of the region. Bonwick concedes half-heartedly that Morgan's largely apocryphal *Life and adventures* was probably the most accurate source pertaining to the main details and events of Buckley's life, utilising large slabs from the text to support his own more 'authentic' and truthful history.[33] Unlike Morgan, he prefers not to attribute any intelligence whatsoever to Buckley, calling upon distinguished contemporary players of the early Port Phillip landscape to confirm that Buckley was so 'dull and reserved, that it was impossible to get any

---

[30] John Morgan (with William Buckley), 'The life and adventures of William Buckley, thirty-two years a wanderer amongst the Aborigines of the then unexplored country round Port Phillip, now the Province of Victoria', in *The life and adventures of William Buckley*, ed. Tim Flannery (Melbourne: Text Publishing, 2002).

[31] The details of Buckley's death were printed in the following papers: *Argus*, 2 February 1855; *Argus*, 7 March 1856, 7; *Cornwall Chronicle*, 2 February 1856, 3.

[32] The preface to Bonwick's *William Buckley: the wild white man*, reveals a view that Indigenous people were degraded and dying out. His use of Buckley seems intended as the vehicle by which to preserve an authoritative narrative as to 'how they really were'.

[33] Buckley was born in 1780 and grew up in Macclesfield, near Cheshire, England. He was brought up by his grandparents and as a young man was apprenticed as a bricklayer. He joined the military and fought in the Netherlands in wars against Napoleon; then, back in England, was found in possession of stolen goods and transported with a sentence of 14 years to the British colonies in Australia. After escaping in 1803, Buckley was eventually accepted into Wathaurong society, the custodians of the coastal and inland regions ranging from what is now known as Werribee, west through to the Otway Ranges and north as far as Ballarat. After 1835, he then presumably lived between Wathaurong, other Kulin societies, and settlers in and around the nascent establishment of Melbourne. He left for Hobart in 1837, where he lived and worked as a storeman, then as a guard at a women's prison. He remarried in 1840 and was put on a pension in 1850. Morgan, 'The life and adventures of William Buckley'.

connected or reliable information from him'.[34] Despite this, Buckley is also a 'wonderful character' whose very presence in his writing supports Bonwick's authoritative constructions of the 'Port Phillip Blacks'.[35] Thus William Buckley exists in Bonwick's texts as a figure of profound ambivalence. After all, Bonwick's primary aim is not to provide a detailed portrait of Buckley, but to fill the majority of his chapters with his specialist knowledge about the 'primitive days of Port Phillip, and the savage state of the Aborigines'.[36]

This aim is reiterated in the second edition of his history in 1863, when he faithfully tells the truth of Buckley's story, legitimising it 'in the very language of the authorities, at the risk of seeming somewhat dry in detail'.[37] Once again, the opening chapter on Buckley stands in for the remaining 26 chapters discussing the 'Blacks of Victoria' from 'Physical Appearance' to 'Infanticide and Cannibalism' and, finally, their 'Decline'. In addition, he reveals a scathing disdain for a man who did not impart Christianity or civilisation to the Indigenous people with whom he stayed for so many years.[38] Yet, in a fit of further ambivalence, he reveals his own desires when he gives himself licence to transpose a romantic and entirely imagined longing for Victoria's 'primitive' state, mediated via the figure of Buckley:

> Fain would we picture the home life of this 'man of the woods.' Fancy draws him in an alcove retreat, on the flowery banks of a murmuring stream,

---

[34] Bonwick, *William Buckley: the wild white man*, 7. Bonwick's charge of stupidity is contradicted by Wesleyan missionary Reverend Joseph Orton. Although Orton was also motivated by a 'civilising' (religious) mission, in 1836 he found Buckley to be a man of 'thought and shrewdness', but without leadership qualities. Cited in Barrett, 22–6.
[35] Bonwick, *William Buckley: the wild white man*, 7.
[36] Ibid. preface.
[37] James Bonwick, *The wild white man and the blacks of Victoria*, 2nd ed. (Melbourne: Fergusson and Moore, 1863), www.slv.vic.gov.au/vicpamphlets/inter/892794.shtml.
[38] Ibid. 2.

gliding through the rosy hours in companionship with a swarthy Delilah of the forest.[39]

Bonwick's main competition was Tasmanian editor John Morgan, who constructs his version of the 'truth' about Buckley in a fictive history. In his preface to *Life and adventures*, Morgan notes that as a weathered newspaper writer, he was aware that 'all his labours will be scattered to the winds, as old gossip', and that he must therefore engage in a succinct and straightforward writing style.[40] In this manner, he cobbles together his own authentic version. Written in the first person from Buckley's perspective, it is nonetheless difficult to gauge what the extent of Buckley's involvement was; or, indeed, why he chose Morgan as a confidante.

One possibility, openly declared in the preface, is their mutual need for finances.[41] Morgan guarantees the authentic nature of their venture by declaring the existence of a trusteeship from which both would receive equal shares of the financial rewards. Morgan is thus seen to carefully avoid the fate of Daniel Defoe, who was accused of living off the great profits of his fictional history of Robinson Crusoe, which was widely believed to have been pilfered from the diary of a 'real' castaway, Alexander Selkirk.[42] Morgan thus plays on this public desire for the literary genre that writer/historian Tony Birch ironically describes as 'My time amongst the savages'. Further, Birch warns that we should be sceptical about the historical value, and especially the Indigenous ethnographic value, of such narratives, which tended to produce highly embellished tales, were after a strong commercial outcome, and attracted

---

[39] Ibid. 3.

[40] Morgan, 'The life and adventures of William Buckley', 3.

[41] Ibid. 1–7. It is very difficult (if not impossible) to ascertain sales of Morgan's book in order to gauge how popular it was at the time of printing. Morgan's narrative was reprinted by a Melbourne paper upon Buckley's death (*Argus*, 7 March 1856, and its following instalment, 27 March 1856) indicates that the narrative probably received a wide readership a few years after it was first printed.

[42] Ibid. 5.

a populist readership with a desire for risqué and melodramatic material.[43] Nevertheless, Morgan relied on the attraction of the 'true story' of a 'real life' castaway to ensure the saleable authenticity of his text.

This manufacture of Buckley in the mould of the Robinson Crusoe genre is interesting because it depends on the belief Bonwick held so dear: that the role of a castaway in foreign lands was to stay true to European ideals of religion and civilised life, thus proving the eternal strength of such principles, even in isolation.[44] Says Bonwick: 'How he might have signalised himself in the councils of the tribe, and astonished their savage minds with the prowess of civilisation!'[45] Yet, as writer Barry Hill points out, Morgan had to strain to fit his version of Buckley in to this Crusoe mould.[46] There was one major difference between these two figures, says Hill: Buckley was not alone. Unlike Crusoe, Buckley's Other was not a solitary, convenient and pliable Man Friday. He lived within many societies of Others. Says Hill:

> There was no space, literally or metaphysically, for an individual to be 'alone'. Wherever he went … the meanings of the country kept him company: he may not have known all the meanings but [the] social fact was everywhere.

---

[43] Birch's comment is in reply to Tim Flannery's assertion that Morgan's narrative is from a 'real' Indigenous perspective. For more details, see Gallacher.

[44] This style, made popular by Daniel Defoe's *The life and strange surprising adventures of Robinson Crusoe* (1719), emerged in the 1700s and was a strong mixture of 'fact' and 'fiction' which proved palatable to wide, colonial audiences interested in the private lives of colonial 'adventurers' in new worlds. For more about the appeal of 'fictive history' and its influence on the distinctions between history and fiction, see Jill Lepore, 'Just the facts, ma'am', *New Yorker*, 24 March 2008, 79–83. Barry Hill says the prevailing appeal of the Crusoe story model (utilised for Buckley over 100 years after it was released) is as 'founding myth of modern and romantic individualism'. See Barry Hill, 'Buckley, our imagination, hope', in *William Buckley: rediscovered*, exhibition catalogue, ed. Geelong Gallery (Geelong, Mornington Peninsula: Geelong Gallery and Mornington Peninsula Regional Gallery, 2001), 8.

[45] Bonwick, *The wild white man and the blacks of Victoria*, 3.

[46] Hill, 10.

In this sense, Buckley was a threat. He *knew too much* about the real lives, country, cultures and humanity of the inhabitants of this highly sought-after land, and was in danger of articulating what many settlers didn't want to hear. If so, when Morgan and Bonwick took up the story of an 'illiterate' man, they were sure to make it more palatable to European audiences by reiterating the captive theme and by utilising Buckley to substantiate their own constructions of Indigenous life. Representations of Buckley have thus come to illustrate the depths of colonial anxieties and desires, which were projected onto the Indigenous Other. They lent authority to the labelling, categorisation and naming of Indigenous peoples and culture from a white colonial perspective. These were the roots of misconceptions, ignorance and prejudices about Indigenous peoples which still exist today.

9

Perpetuating White Australia: Aboriginal self-representation, white editing and preferred stereotypes

Jennifer Jones, University of Melbourne

Foundational Aboriginal women writers who published in the 1970s often collaborated with white people in order to bring their publishing projects to fruition. These white people were drawn from political, religious and social interest groups; communities of commitment to which the Aboriginal women belonged.[1] As fellow travellers, they shared similar values and willingly acted as facilitators for the publishing project. Aboriginal women faced considerable barriers to their authorial aspirations in this era, including a disinterested general public with a predilection to forget Aboriginal issues,[2] few established Indigenous writers to act as mentors[3] and often a meagre formal education.[4] While alignment with a community of commitment provided tangible benefits, it also required pragmatic compromise. Some of these compromises were textual, reflected in editorial changes that aligned the narrative with the world view of the collaborating party. These changes were often to the

---

[1] Jennifer Jones, 'As long as she got her voice: how cross-cultural collaboration shapes Aboriginal textuality', *Altitude* 5 (2005), www.api-network.com/scgi-bin/altitude21c/fly.cgi?page=Issue5.

[2] Chris Healy, *Forgetting Aborigines* (Sydney: UNSW Press, 2008), 16.

[3] Roberta Sykes, 'While my name is remembered', in *Oodgeroo: a tribute*, ed. A. Shoemaker (St Lucia: University of Queensland Press, 1994), 35.

[4] Aileen Moreton-Robinson, *Talkin' up to the white woman: Aboriginal women and feminism* (St Lucia: University of Queensland Press, 2000).

detriment of Aboriginal cultural priorities.[5] As Gillian Whitlock comments, the textual construction of the autobiographic self, negotiated between editor, author and implied reader, is 'not a place where the desire to speak is liberated unconditionally, but rather a site of multiple constraints and negotiations of meaning.'[6]

For Ella Simon, a Biripi woman from NSW who published her life story *Through my eyes* in 1978, these constraints and negotiations centred on the transformation of her life narrative from an oral to written text.[7] Based upon the re-transcription of Ella Simon's original oral recordings, this chapter examines the white collaborator's engagement with the oral narrative. I argue that the style of emendations and omissions reflect the white collaborator's capacity to accommodate otherness. Although government policy regarding Aboriginal people had moved from assimilation to self-determination when *Through my eyes* was published, public thinking did not necessarily align with official rhetoric. Ella Simon's preferred self-representation was still substantially suppressed during the preparation of her book. The textual suppression of her Indigenous perspective demonstrates the collaborator's prioritisation of the needs of a still-robust ideology of 'white Australia'.

Here 'whiteness' is taken to be a discursive regime in which white and Indigenous Australian subjects are produced.[8] White subjectivity and white privilege is predicated upon the denial of Indigenous sovereignty and ongoing Indigenous dispossession.[9] White privilege also extends to

---

[5] Jennifer Jones, *Black writers and white editors: episodes of collaboration and compromise in Australian publishing history* (Melbourne: Australian Scholarly Publishing, 2009).

[6] Gillian Whitlock, *The intimate empire: reading women's autobiography* (London: Cassell, 2000), 162.

[7] Ella Simon, *Through my eyes* (Adelaide: Rigby, 1978).

[8] Alison Ravenscroft, 'The girl in the picture and the eye of her beholder: Viet Nam, whiteness and the disavowal of Indigeneity', *Continuum* 18.4 (2004): 509–24.

[9] Aileen Moreton-Robinson, '"I still call Australia home": Indigenous belonging and place in white postcolonising society', in *Uprootings/regroundings: questions of home and migration*, eds. Sara Ahmed et al. (Oxford and New York: Berg, 2003), 23–40.

the discursive construction of Aboriginality. As Marcia Langton famously posited, the white Australian majority base their understanding of Aboriginality upon racist stereotypes and mythologies, the 'stories told by former colonists', not upon relationships with actual people.[10] Because these stories are based upon stereotypes and mythologies, the way white Australians think about Aboriginal people does not necessarily keep pace with official government policy, but may instead be rooted in the past.[11] For example, between 1909 and 1940, NSW government policy advocated the 'protection' of Aboriginal people on segregated reserves,[12] 'smooth[ing] the dying pillow' on the mistaken assumption that 'the Aborigines were dying out'.[13] The projected outcomes of 'protection' policy co-operated with the goals of the official White Australia policy, preventing non-whites from entering Australia while non-whites already here conveniently expired.[14] The exposure of the racially-motivated atrocities of the Second World War influenced the adaptation of overtly eugenicist policies, and biological absorption shifted to cultural assimilation.[15] The NSW state government formally adopted a policy of assimilation in 1951. This policy required Aboriginal people to 'live as white Australians do',[16] revealing a continued commitment to cultural

---

[10] Marcia Langton, *Well, I heard it on the radio and I saw it on the television: An essay for the Australian Film Commission on the politics and aesthetics of filmmaking by and about Aboriginal people and things* (North Sydney: Australian Film Commission, 1993), 33.

[11] George Morgan argues persuasively that government practise also rarely aligned with official rhetoric. See George Morgan, 'Assimilation and resistance: housing Indigenous Australians in the 1970s', *Journal of Sociology* 36, (2000): 198–204.

[12] Tim Rowse, 'Introduction', in *Contesting assimilation*, ed. Tim Rowse (Perth: API Network, 2005), 1–24.

[13] James H. Bell, 'Assimilation in New South Wales', in *Aborigines now: new perspectives in the study of Aboriginal communities*, ed. Marie Reay (Sydney: Angus and Robertson, 1964).

[14] Anthony Moran, 'White Australia, settler nationalism and Aboriginal assimilation', *Australian Journal of Politics and History* 51.2 (2005): 172.

[15] Rowse, 'Introduction', 178

[16] Russell McGregor, 'One people: Aboriginal assimilation and the white Australian ideal', *History Australia* 6.1 (2009): 3.6.

homogeneity underpinning the 'white Australia' policy.[17] It was not until 1973 that the NSW government finally repealed all elements of the 1909 *Aborigines Protection Act* and following the Whitlam Labor government, adopted a policy of Aboriginal self-determination.[18] Yet texts like Ella Simon's *Through my eyes*, which carry a history of cross-cultural collaboration, provide an account of the social construction of Aboriginality that suggest the rhetoric of self-determination and cultural plurality was far from a functioning reality.

Ella Simon recorded her oral narrative between May and December 1973, in the founding moments of self-determination; a policy which 'ostensibly gave Aboriginal people some voice and options' in deciding the direction of their own future.[19] Her life story *Through my eyes* was launched five years later, in 1978. Thus the collaborative construction of the narrative between 1973 and 1978 (the transcription, editing and publication processes) offers insight into the negotiations between Aboriginal self-presentation and the stories white Australians expected and accepted about Aboriginality.

Ella Simon was born in 1902 near Taree on the mid-north coast of NSW. She was raised on Purfleet Aboriginal Station by her Aboriginal maternal grandparents. When she gained an exemption from the provisions of the *Aborigines Protection Act* in 1957 she was described as a 'light caste Aborigine' and deemed suitable for assimilation into the white community.[20] Ella Simon became the first Aboriginal Justice of the Peace[21] and was a member of several Christian and women's community organisations, including the Country Women's Association and Quota.

---

[17] Gwenda Tavan, '"Good neighbours": community organisations, migrant assimilation and Australian society and culture, 1950–1961', *Australian Historical Studies* 28.109 (1997): 77–89.

[18] Rowse, 'Introduction', 19.

[19] Tim Rowse, 'The certainties of assimilation', in *Contesting assimilation*, ed. Tim Rowse (Perth: API Network, 2005), 244.

[20] Simon, *Through my eyes*.

[21] Ibid.

She was a matriarch of high standing in her Indigenous community when she decided to record her life story. Ella Simon's social links in the white community provided physical resources and support that enabled her to record her narrative.[22] One white friend drawn from this network, Anne Ruprecht, facilitated the transcription, editing and publication of *Through my eyes*.[23]

Ella Simon's oral recordings consist of five audiotapes that were retained by Ruprecht. In 2008 I had the tapes digitised and then I re-transcribed them. The overall quality of the recording was poor due to the limited microphone sensitivity of the cassette player and Simon's health conditions. The poor quality of the recording undoubtedly impacted upon the original transcription in 1974. Ruprecht used a small grant from the Australia Council to fund the transcription. Budget restrictions prompted her to engage typists who would accept token remuneration. These were 'friends or daughters of friends who needed a part time job and were typists'.[24] Ruprecht was the only one in her circle who had any significant contact with Aboriginal people.[25] The typist's decisions were thus unlikely to have been informed by Aboriginal cultural knowledge. Ruprecht recalls several examples where these typists 'doubt[ed] the truth' of Simon's recollections and felt authorised to change 'whole sections' of the transcript.[26] Upon discovering the most obvious errors, Ruprecht had to 'change back' these sections of the transcript.[27] During this process she and Simon decided that the oral voice didn't 'read properly', so the text was rendered into Standard English:

> When it is spoken into a tape, it's not quite the same when it's transcribed. There were two schools of thought about this ... one school of thought was

---

[22] Including blank tapes, a tape recorder, and assistance with funding applications from the Aboriginal and Torres Strait Islander (ATSI) Arts Board of the Australia Council.

[23] Anne Ruprecht, interview with author, 2004, Sydney.

[24] Ibid.

[25] Simon, *Through my eyes*, 179.

[26] Ibid. 181 and 182.

[27] Ibid. 182.

that the way she spoke was poetic, and to leave it as that. But when I showed her that, she said, 'this doesn't read properly, this doesn't read properly at all'. So then I started to re-write quite a bit of it, just in the language that she wanted, which was just straight forward English.[28]

The standardisation of Ella Simon's Indigenous storytelling style reflects the historical denigration of oral culture as illiterate, incorrect and therefore deficient.[29] Other foundational Aboriginal authors, embarrassed by the rendering of their Aboriginal English into writing, also supported its standardisation.[30] The standardisation of the narrative also reveals the prioritisation of the requirements of the printed form and the comfort of a projected white readership ill-equipped to hear Aboriginal voices. As Ong argues, reading a text involves 'converting it to sound, aloud or in the imagination'.[31] Widespread unfamiliarity with Indigenous Australian culture meant that few mainstream readers would have been able to hear, let alone value, the oral features as they read. This prioritisation of sight over hearing[32] can also be understood as a mask or double mimesis that covers the narrative[33] and presents a socially acceptable biographic face to the audience.

---

[28] Ruprecht.

[29] Ian Adam, 'Oracy and literacy: a post-colonial dilemma?', *Journal of Commonwealth Literature* 31 (Jan 1996): 101; Walter Ong, *Orality and literacy: the technologizing of the word* (London: Routledge, 1982), 11.

[30] Patsy Cohen and Margaret Somerville, 'Reflections on Ingelba', *Westerly* 36 (June 1991): 45–9.

[31] Ong, 8.

[32] Close examination of this inversion of Derridian logocentrism is beyond the scope of this article. The Derridian position (oral primacy and writing an inadequate derivation) is Eurocentric, ignoring the role of writing as a tool of domination in colonised societies (see Adam). The denial of literacy maintained Indigenous subordination. Contemporary examples include the privileging of written accounts over local oral knowledge in native title disputes. See Gillian Cowlishaw, 'On getting it wrong: collateral damage in the history wars', *Australian Historical Studies* 127 (2006): 194.

[33] Kaja Silverman, 'White skin, brown masks: the double mimesis, or with Lawrence in Arabia', *Difference: A Journal of Feminist Cultural Studies* 1.3 (1989): 48.

Once standardised, Ann Ruprecht took the manuscript to the Australia Council, where those concerned assessed the manuscript to be too detailed and still too colloquial: 'When all of this was put together, the Australia Council said, "There is too much detail in this" and they handed it over to somebody, some writer, to edit it'.[34] The contracted editor reportedly adopted a high level, academic register and slashed the number of stories told. One casualty of this revision was the removal of multiple narrations. In oral discourse the orator reiterates important points through repetition or 'copia'.[35] Ella Simon's oral narrative is copious because different versions of the same story are told for different purposes. With repetitions now removed, the manuscript was much shorter, but used highly sophisticated language. Anne recalls the shock of reading the edited manuscript:

> I had to ... start all over again. They went to a different extreme. It was too much of a literary style ... in the opening pages it talked about how 'she opined' and ... other trendy words. And when Ella saw these she said 'I don't know what these words mean!' and I said to her, 'I don't either!' So, we started off again.[36]

To achieve the desired register Anne Ruprecht re-wrote the manuscript again. With her health now rapidly failing, Ella Simon accepted the multiple changes to her narrative as the price of publication:

> She was just pleased to get the book finished and back into a form that was more like what she would have written, and to get it out, because she kept saying to me that she didn't think the book would come out before she died. So she was anxious for it to come out and as long as the main thread of the story was there, she was happy.[37]

Thus the published version of *Through my eyes* preserves 'the main thread' of Ella Simon's experiences, but not as seen through Ella Simon's

---

[34] Ruprecht.

[35] Ong, 39.

[36] Ruprecht.

[37] Ibid.

eyes alone. The process of transcription, editorial emendation and re-writing ensured that the manuscript also reflected the collaborators' vision of Aboriginality. Recalling some of the changes made by the typist, Anne Ruprecht argued that:

> If a project such as this has been subjected to so much of the 'we know better than you' attitude, we have to be very careful with what is recorded and reported—that is if it is really the truth we are seeking and not just confirmation of our own prejudices.[38]

In her role as facilitator Anne Ruprecht contested the corrections imposed by the typist, hoping that her own efforts helped to 'set the record straight ... about Aboriginal history and culture'.[39] However, as the cultural and textual construction of Aboriginality is derived primarily from 'inherited, imagined representations',[40] not the self-presentation of actual Aboriginal people, 'confirmation of our own prejudices' is the most likely outcome.

My comparison of the oral narrative with the published text revealed a total of 228 significant differences. The oral manuscript included 159 narrations focusing upon traditional knowledge, oral history, Indigenous perspectives on current affairs, and cross-racial relations; these were excluded from the published text. There were also 69 instances where narrations were included, but were changed to conform to the collaborator's vision. These included the alteration of Ella Simon's perspective on cross-racial relations and Indigenous knowledge, and the management of issues deemed offensive to white readers. In the remainder of this chapter I will examine three of these amended narrations, focusing upon the representation of Aboriginality.

---

[38] Simon, *Through my eyes*, 182.
[39] Ibid.
[40] Langton, *Well I heard it on the radio*.

Kinship, Aboriginal identity and the 'half-caste problem'

Parallel sections of the oral manuscript and the published text offer very different understandings of Aboriginal kinship and cultural survival. The example below centres upon the mixed racial descent of Ella Simon's maternal grandmother, Granny Russell. Miscegenation was a confounding issue for assimilationists because it reflected badly upon white Australians, the purported models of progressivism and racial hygiene. The published text looks for a solution to the problem of miscegenation by highlighting the rejection of so-called half-castes by the 'full-blood' tribal people:

> My grandmother was half-caste herself. In those days, the old Aboriginal tribes wouldn't have anything to do with half-caste children ... If there was any lightness there, the baby would be killed or left to die ... That's what happened to her. The mother was of the opossum clan of the Biripi tribe. Her father was Irish. Her mother died when she was an infant and the tribe simply abandoned her.[41]

Biological absorption posited that 'breeding out the colour' and eventually subsuming the Aboriginal race would safeguard white Australia. By emphasising the rejection of people of mixed descent by the remnant 'full-bloods', white Australians could imagine that these 'half-castes' did not retain their Aboriginal culture.[42] It was argued that although 'part-Aborigines' problematically retained an Aboriginal social identity, their racial and geographic proximity to white people made them amenable to shedding this identity and 'merg[ing] socially with the general European community'.[43] It was believed that they would eventually 'metamorphose into white Australians'.[44]

---

[41] Simon, *Through my eyes*, 22.

[42] See for example James H. Bell, 'The Part-Aborigines of New South Wales', in *Aboriginal man in Australia: essays in honour of Emeritus Professor A.P. Elkin*, eds. Ronald M. Berndt and Catherine H. Berndt (Sydney: Angus and Robertson, 1965), 396.

[43] Ibid.

[44] McGregor, 'One people', 292.

The published text has it that Ella's grandmother was 'simply abandoned' when her mother died, but the story is not so simple. In the oral manuscript this narrative of abandonment is contextualised by other layers of specificity. The published text deletes the identity of the white father and his interest in his baby and elides the ongoing negotiation of Indigenous identity over time. By contrast, the manuscript reads:

> My grandmother had an Irish father and she was half, she had an Aboriginal mother. She was left under a bush at a place called Burrell Creek. The Aboriginals were travelling with her mother, and they left the baby behind when the mother died ... There are two classes of Aboriginal people; the coast tribe and the hillside. These people are very big-boned people, tall—they call them the *Winmurra's*. The women are very possessive, they keep their men. It is often stated that they would way-lay a man whom they desired and would just take him along to her camp ... The grandmother was this type of woman that came from the bush, but the grandmother's father was an Irishman. He lived in the Monkerai, his name was McGrill. It was told that the mother would steal the baby away from this place, where he tried to keep it at home.[45]

According to Ella's oral narrative, her grandmother held a specific cultural identity into which she was acculturated, regardless of her earlier abandonment or 'half-caste' status. She was a revered and powerful Winmurra woman. She is also identified as the daughter of McGrill from Monkerai district, not simply an anonymous 'Irishman' as in the published version. This account highlights conflicting dimensions of absorption ideology. Although rural people were anxious to have the embarrassing and apparently culturally-bereft 'half-castes' merge and disappear, miscegenation remained a 'shameful colonial secret that many did not want exposed to public scrutiny'.[46] Therefore the identity of Granny Russell's father is obscured. Similarly, his attempts 'to keep [her]

---

[45] Ella Simon, *Through my eyes: oral narrative*, Private collection of the author, tape 3A, 11, n.d.
[46] Moran, 176.

at home', indications of love and acknowledgement of paternal responsibility, are also deleted.

Significantly, this is a section that Anne Ruprecht recalls as having been altered by the typist:

> A well-meaning typist changed what was on the tape to make it sound 'correct'. She had typed that Ella's grandfather had lived 'in a monastery' [but] there were no monasteries in those parts. She said, when I found it on the tape, that he'd lived 'at the Monkerai', which happens to be a small district south of Gloucester in NSW! If the typist had kept to what the old lady had actually said, it would have taken me less time to work out than her 'correction'.[47]

Anne Ruprecht suggests, by implication, that she had repatriated this kinship detail, only to have it removed again by the editor. Such 'corrections' to Ella Simon's manuscript removed evidence of the complex negotiation of Aboriginality in rural Australia, achieving a generalised account of Indigenous history.

Imposing a non-indigenous perspective on Indigenous knowledge: Charlie and the goanna

Assimilation rhetoric, in the broad sweep, required Aboriginal people to repudiate their culture in order to be socially and morally uplifted.[48] Ella Simon's attitude towards traditional culture therefore posed a problem to the editor of her narrative, as it did not align with her supposed status as an assimilated 'light-caste' woman. In this example gathering bush tucker becomes the focus for textual correction. Ella Simon's oral narrative provides fond and detailed descriptions of food gathering and

---

[47] Simon, *Through my eyes*, 182.

[48] The meaning and application of assimilation was hotly contested in the era. The diversity of opinion is exemplified by prominent advocates such as A.P. Elkin, who believed Aboriginal identity could be maintained and modernised, and Paul Hasluck, who believed individuals had to abandon Aboriginality in order to be assimilated. See Russell McGregor, 'Wards, words and citizens: A.P. Elkin and Paul Hasluck on assimilation', *Oceania* 69.4(1999): 243–59.

preparation, and emphasises important knowledge through repetition and shared recollection:

> There was an old Aboriginal, Old Big-eye Charlie we called him. He came to our home a lot, and I saw him catch a goanna; just climbing up a tree. He caught it by the tail and he cracked it like a whip, and the goanna broke its neck. Also, a black snake, just getting into its hole as fast as it could, he just grabbed the snake by the tail and the same crack broke the old snakes' neck. They cooked the animals and often offered us some of the things to eat. There was a sweet yam; the *downg* and the *wombi*. They'd bruise them before they'd put them into the ashes, and cover them until they were cooked. That would serve the family, even cold ... There is also the witchetty grubs and the wasps; they used to half cook them and there was a milky substance that came out of them. We used to watch this old lady do this. Then they would eat the young bees in the comb; that is a milky substance too. They would have their little coolamons, half full of honey, and they would dip this honeycomb with the young bees in it, and they would suck at it. They would then have milk and honey! ... They would enjoy this real milk and honey diet.[49]

Simon concludes the section on traditional diet with a biblical metaphor; that of the Promised Land flowing with milk and honey. This biblical reference reveals the high value she placed upon the quality and taste of bush tucker. The opposite effect, however, is achieved in the parallel version found in the published text. Here the consumption of bush tucker is denigrated:

> There was one old Aboriginal we used to call Charlie. I saw him catch a goanna by just climbing up a tree after it and grabbing it by the tail. Then he broke its back by cracking it around his head like a whip. I saw him do the same thing to a black snake. It was sliding into its hole as fast as it could go, when he grabbed it by the tail and cracked its back in the same way. The old people would often cook things like this that they would catch and offer some to us. We didn't often take up the invitations![50]

---

[49] Simon, *Through my eyes: oral narrative*, Tape 3A, 9.
[50] Simon, *Through my eyes*, 121.

The turn of phrase, 'we didn't often take up the invitations!' replaces the lengthy description of bush tucker and suggests that Simon and her age-mates spurned the food they were offered. This perspective is not supported by the oral narrative, which dwells at length upon bush tucker practices. Nor is it supported by the Indigenous cultural value of respect for elders. Upon hearing this example, family members argued that Ella wouldn't contradict the instructions of an elder of Charlie Bugg's stature.[51] Another oral version of this story, a conversation with her cousin Maude, confirms this view:

> Ella: I remember Fred's father, Charlie Bugg, Charlie used to call in. He used to take us out and get animals, let us have a little taste of it. Oh, he'd give us carpet snake, and they cooked it and gave me a little taste of it; gave all the little kids a little taste of it. He'd give you a little tiny bit; just to taste it.
>
> Maude: Taste it, mmm.
>
> Ella: Mmm, he'd give you a taste of anything; witchetty grubs or anything. If you didn't like it, well.
>
> Maude: You didn't have to have it if you didn't like it.[52]

Maude and Ella concur that trying bush tucker or 'having a little taste' was standard protocol, whilst eating more was optional. As Maude says, 'You didn't have to have it if you didn't like it'. Ella Simon's concentration upon the collection, preparation and taste of bush tucker in three other lengthy manuscript sections also suggests its importance. The editorial treatment of these manuscript sections reflect non-Indigenous perspectives on bush food as being irksome and strange, and supports assimilation ideology by placing cultural distance between Ella Simon's generation and their elders.

The other major change is the amalgamation of the two oral versions and the complete deletion of Maude's voice. As Aileen Moreton-Robinson

---

[51] Jeremy Saunders, Pamela Saunders and Russell Saunders, Conversation, Taree, 14 October 2008.

[52] Simon, *Through my eyes: oral narrative*, Tape 4A, 18.

argues, Aboriginal women's autobiographies are relational; they include the views and voices of the group.[53] Ella Simon attempted to include multiple voices in her foundational life story; before the autobiographical genre, as understood by the collaborators, was capacious enough to accept it. Thus the Indigenised 'yarning' approach, with its cues, repetitions and distinctive language was stripped from the narrative, aligning it with the western convention of a single triumphant protagonist.[54]

Minimising potential offence to white readers

If Aboriginal people of mixed racial descent were divorced from Aboriginal culture and poised to merge into the white community, why was assimilation so difficult to achieve in practice? When this question was posed by scholars in the 1960s,[55] their answers concentrated upon the personal flaws of those who 'failed' to be assimilated, not the flaws of the wider society who failed to receive them.[56] As Maureen Perkins argues, white culture asserts that a coloured person who passes as white 'can be unmasked, as not really belonging, by various non-white behaviours.'[57] Blaming Aboriginal people for their own failure to 'advance' was one strategy used to distract attention from the appalling conditions faced by Aboriginal people on segregated reserves and the recalcitrant

---

[53] Moreton-Robinson, *Talkin' up*, 16.

[54] Marcia Langton, cited in Greg Lehman, 'Telling us true', in *Whitewash: on Keith Windshuttle's fabrication of Aboriginal history*, ed. Robert Manne (Melbourne: Black Inc., 2003).

[55] James H. Bell, 'Assimilation in New South Wales', in *Aborigines now*, ed. Marie Reay (Sydney: Angus and Robertson, 1964), 59–71.

[56] Rowse, 'The certainties of assimilation'.

[57] Maureen Perkins, 'False whiteness: "passing" and the Stolen Generations', in *Whitening race: essays in social and cultural criticism*, ed. A. Moreton-Robinson (Canberra: Aboriginal Studies Press, 2004), 166.

white majority who resisted Aboriginal assimilation, particularly in rural areas.[58]

Ella Simon, a frank and forthright person, didn't hesitate to allocate appropriate blame for Aboriginal disadvantage. The example from the published text below reveals that the collaborators altered potentially offensive narrative sections, in this instance regarding Indigenous education.

> Education comes to mind now ... Teachers ringing up because kiddies are away from school and all that. As I said before, these same children have parents who went to school for years without being taught anything. They came out of school after all those years scarcely able to read.

> I saw it happen in my own family. They all went to school for about ten years and could scarcely spell their own names! No wonder older people weren't interested in their children going to school. What did it matter if the kid missed a day or two here or there? What had education to do with attending school? Whether you had an education or not, you still lived the same; you still just got by like everyone else.[59]

The disinterest of Aboriginal parents is explained by their own poor performance at school, 'They all went to school for about ten years and could scarcely spell their own names! No wonder older people weren't interested in their children going to school'. This infers that Indigenous people themselves are responsible for their own social stagnation, 'Whether you had an education or not, you still lived the same; you still just got by like everyone else'. The manuscript version takes a different view. Ella Simon insists that the failure of Indigenous students reflects the substandard level of education delivered by poorly trained teachers:

> They allowed these missionaries to become government teachers without diplomas or anything, you know. They went there and started teaching. I

[58] Jennifer Jones, 'More than tea and scones? Cross-racial collaboration in the Country Women's Association of New South Wales and the ethos of countrymindedness', *History Australia* 6.2 (forthcoming 2009): 41.1–41.9.

[59] Simon, *Through my eyes*, 162.

knew one woman that came to Purfleet; she was there for 17 years ... She was teaching them children, but them children can't spell their own name. They couldn't read hardly, or write because she wasn't educated. Now they are the parents that you people are dealing with at Purfleet. I tell them, ... 'These Purfleet people ... they are the ones that had a government teacher for more than 17 years, [she] was a missionary, she wasn't a qualified teacher'. She didn't know what she was teaching ... These people say, 'Why don't they send [their children] to school' and I said, 'Because they wasn't educated themselves, and they got on alright' ... and They say, 'Why do you know so much? Who taught you?' I said, 'Don't you ask me that question, because I might be related to you' and that shuts them up![60]

Ella is emphatic that low levels of interest in education amongst the Purfleet community reflect the failings of the long-standing teacher at Purfleet and the racist government policies that enabled her retention. Unlike the published text, which asserts that educated and uneducated Aboriginal people alike 'just got by', the manuscript version acknowledges that people 'got on alright' despite the discrimination they faced. Thus the published version focuses on the failure of the Aboriginal people, while the manuscript focuses upon their resilience and survival against the odds. This position has clearly upset white people in the past, because Ella raises the moot objection, 'They say, "Why do you know so much? Who taught you?"' to which she responds 'Don't you ask me that question, because I might be related to you'. Clearly accustomed to attempted denigration, Ella silences her critics by raising the spectre of her own mixed racial heritage and illegitimacy. She had inside knowledge of the longstanding hypocrisy of white people who attempted to maintain social distance from Aboriginal people in the context of geographic proximity and shared history.

These examples of emendations made to the oral manuscript reveal what the white collaborators saw when they read Ella Simon's life narrative: a perspective on cultural survival that contradicted socially

---

[60] Simon, *Through my eyes: oral narrative*, Tape 5b, 9.

preferred stereotypes and opinions that shamed white Australians. In response, Ella Simon's narrative was changed to more suitably reflect white representations of Aboriginality. The perspective that dominates key aspects of the published version of *Through my eyes* is the perspective of the non-Indigenous collaborators. The imposition of non-Indigenous perspectives on Indigenous knowledge deprives Indigenous readers of important sources of cultural information and perpetuates cross-cultural misunderstanding. Standardising Ella Simon's Indigenous voice and oral storytelling style into 'straight forward English' depletes the cultural integrity of the narrative. Removing the communal oral narration aligns the text with white western autobiographical tradition, which prefers a triumphant, individualistic birth-to-success trajectory. The oral narrative is thickly woven with opinions and responses, recollections of people, places, language and traditions. Unfortunately, the white collaborators transformed this highly detailed oral narrative into a rather threadbare and conformist autobiography.

Part 4

Gender and whiteness

10

A word of evidence: shared tales about infanticide and 'others not us' in colonial Victoria

Marguerita Stephens, University of Melbourne

What constitutes evidence in history? Or, rather, what constitutes enough evidence? In rejecting an established 'fact' of history, how much doubt has to be marshalled against the grain to undermine that fact? The established fact under challenge here is that infanticide was a practice so common amongst Australian Aboriginal peoples in both the pre-and post-contacts eras as to be deemed customary. For much of the 19th century the practice of infanticide stood as a key marker of Aboriginal savagery, primitiveness, and evolutionary ripeness for extinction; or alternately, it identified first nation Australians—and their children—as objects for colonial salvation and recuperation. An alternate version of the narrative is that infanticide was adopted by the *Australians* in the wake of the white invasion as a way of disposing of infants of mixed descent, and that so much killing occurred that it was a direct cause of the demise of many clans.[1]

---

[1] Until the late 1880s, the term 'Australians' was used in ethnographies as a generic term for the Indigenous people of the Australian continent. For example, Edward M. Curr's four-volume *The Australian race* (1886), or Samuel George Morton's 'Hybridity in animals considered in reference to the question of the unity of the human species', published in *The American Journal of Science and Arts* (3 May 1847) and read before The Academy of Natural Sciences of Philadelphia, November, 1846, where Morton said: 'Perhaps no two human races are more remote from each other than the European and Australian'. As debates about Federation took hold, the term became associated with immigrant 'Australians'.

Against what have recently again reissued as 'facts' about Australian infanticide in its various manifestations, I want to suggest, as have others, that the idea that Aboriginal parents (mostly women, less often men) were prone to killing their infants is essentially a projection about the habits of imagined others. I want to argue, further, that the idea took wing, somewhat ironically, because it was a projection about others shared by Aboriginal people and Europeans. Colonial power relations ensured that this shared projection about the habits of 'others not us' would become transformed into a 'fact of history', with enormous implications for Aboriginal people.

That infants were sometimes killed is likely: it is a universal fact of history that infanticides occur in most societies. What is at issue here is the frequency of the practice. In short, was it so commonly practised by first nation Australians as to be rightly considered as a custom in either the pre- or post-contact era, or is it more correctly identified as an occasional and circumstantial event, a 'custom' existing only in imagination yet enabling a range of colonial interventions, including the removal of Aboriginal children from their kin? I want to cast doubt on the veracity of the trope by drawing attention to a series of textual slippages that illustrate the way infanticide became embedded in European myths about the Australians. In particular, I want to draw attention to the impact that one erased word has had on the development of the trope.

Recent contributions to the debate about the extent and circumstances of infanticides amongst Aboriginal clans have come from both sides of the political divide in Australia. In 1997, Pauline Hanson republished Daisy Bates' testimony about infanticide and maternal cannibalism despite it being long discredited.[2] Two years later Justice O'Loughlin of the Federal Court rejected evidence led by the

---

[2] *Age*, 22 April 1997. Richard Hall, 'Fantasies in the desert: the unhappy life of Daisy Bates', in *Black armband days* (Sydney: Vintage Books, 1998), 147–70.

Commonwealth in the Stolen Generations test case that the child Peter Gunner had been rescued by authorities in the 1950s after his mother had attempted to kill him by putting him down a rabbit burrow.[3] As the court sat, a former Commonwealth Minister for Aboriginal Affairs, Peter Howson (1971–72) publicly argued that as late as the 1960s, 'part-European babies had not been allowed to live', and that some thousands of children had been rescued by government welfare officers, not stolen.[4]

As anthropologist Annette Hamilton argued in the early 1980s, 'infanticide is a subject that catches the imagination … To this day many white Australians suppose that Aborigines simply killed off any babies they did not want'.[5] Hamilton found to the contrary that late-19th- and early-20th-century mission records from northern Australia revealed 'a rising number of part-Aboriginal children around stations and settlements' whose ready placement within family genealogies undermined the logic of claims that children of mixed descent were routinely killed in the early contact era.[6] She concluded that infanticide was 'exceptional rather than typical' amongst first nation Australians.[7]

Despite these findings, the issue persists and has come to some prominence again of late in two significant texts that position infanticide as an act of agency, to varying degrees, and as an expression of cultural continuity. In 2007, Lynette Russell argued that 'one of the many ways Aboriginal women involved in the sealing industry … demonstrated

---

[3] Justice O'Loughlin, *Judgement Summary, Lorna Cubillo and Peter Gunner v. Commonwealth of Australia* (Action 14 and 21 of 1996), Federal Court of Australia, 11 August 2000, paragraphs 58 and 821, judgements.fedcourt.gov/2000/1001084.doc.htm.

[4] Peter Howson, 'Rescued from a rabbit burrow: understanding the "Stolen Generation"', *Quadrant* (June 1999): 11–12.

[5] Annette Hamilton, *Nature and nurture: Aboriginal child-rearing in north-central Arnhem Land* (Canberra: Australian Institute of Aboriginal Studies, 1981), 123.

[6] Annette Hamilton, 'Bond-slaves of satan: Aboriginal women and the mission dilemma', in *Family and gender in the Pacific*, eds. Margaret Jolly and Martha MacIntyre (Cambridge, Melbourne: Cambridge University Press, 1989), 236–58.

[7] Hamilton, *Nature and nurture*, 25 and 123.

their considerable agency was in the practice of infanticide.[8] Russell argues that 'although infanticide might be unpalatable today' and that many of the reports may be exaggerated and based on 'projection and transference', nevertheless 'its practice is a matter of historical fact.'[9] Against Protector George Augustus Robinson's reports that Aboriginal sealing women were compelled to kill newborns by the European males who held them as captives or 'slaves' on Bass Strait Islands,[10] Russell argues that 'this oversimplifies the issue and denies the woman autonomy of action.'[11] Russell argues that 'the practice could be considered a form of cultural continuity' and that in killing infants, women exercised some degree of resistance, agency, or power over their own bodies, and over the men—Aboriginal or European—who attempted to control their lives.[12] Russell also suggests that while:

> such actions might well have emerged from desperation, we should be vigilant in acknowledging the possibility that the reporting of it was exaggerated and that such exaggeration might have begun with the women themselves.[13]

Russell's argument that Bass Strait infanticides—admitted to Robinson by Aboriginal women and their European partners—may have been an expression of women's agency, however limited, and of cultural continuity, draws on the work of anthropologist Gillian Cowlishaw.[14] In the late 1970s, Cowlishaw undertook fieldwork in Arnhem Land. Finding

---

[8] Lynette Russell, '"Dirty domestics and worse cooks": Aboriginal women's agency and domestic frontiers, Southern Australia, 1800–1850', *Frontiers* 28.1–2 (2007): 18–46.

[9] Ibid. 32.

[10] N.J.B. Plomley, ed., *Friendly mission: the Tasmanian journals and papers of George Augustus Robinson 1829–1834* (Tasmania: Tasmanian Historical Research Association, 1966), 82 (10 October 1829) and 300 (25 December 1830).

[11] Russell, 33.

[12] Ibid. 33–4.

[13] Ibid. 32.

[14] Russell, 33. Gillian Cowlishaw, 'Infanticide in Aboriginal Australia", *Oceania* 48.4 (June 1978): 262–82.

'almost no reliable contemporary evidence' about Aboriginal abortion and infanticide practices, and reticence on the part of women to speak on those subjects, Cowlishaw turned to 'early' sources to uncover pre- and post-contact practices.[15] She surveyed around 30 testaments from late-19th-and early-20th-century missionaries, explorers, government officials and settlers. All but one source fell into the date range 1874 to the 1970s. While the reports were of variable credibility, they were nonetheless, she argued, so ubiquitous as to warrant a conclusion that a 'high level of infanticide' was once widely practised across the continent.[16]

Cowlishaw grouped the explanations given for the practice in these sources under six headings: that infants born too close to the previous child were killed because women could not suckle and/or carry more than one child at a time (the most common explanation); that twins, deformed, or illegitimate newborns (including post-invasion infants of 'caste') were killed; that girls were killed; that first-borns were always/often killed; that a younger child was killed and eaten to preserve the life of a weak or sickly older child; and that a child would be killed if it caused its mother pain before or at birth.[17] Cowlishaw's survey included contributions from Taplin (in 1874 and 1880), Stanbridge (1876), Howitt (1880 and 1904), Dawson (1881), Palmer (1884), Gason (1886), Curr (1886), Spencer and Gillen (1899, 1904, 1914 and 1927), Roth (1903 and 1906), Mathews (1904), and Goodale (1971). Crediting these explanations to varying degrees, Cowlishaw advanced a further explanation: that infanticide was an expression of resentment by women and girls over their exchange between men, that led them 'to deny their male kin, especially husbands and brothers, their infants'.[18] 'By killing her

---

[15] Ibid. 263 and 271.
[16] Ibid. 281.
[17] Ibid. 264–7.
[18] Ibid. 281.

infant', argued Cowlishaw, a woman denied her husband 'her reproductive powers'.[19] It was, then, a contumacious act of agency.

As Cowlishaw rightly identified, the *belief* that infanticide was customary and frequent amongst pre- and post-contact Aborigines across the continent was an established orthodoxy amongst settlers by the later decades of the 19th century and it persisted into the 20th. But what is the quality of the evidence in these texts? Take Taplin's 1874 account from South Australia, for example. A missionary to the Narrinyeri people of South Australia from 1858 to 1873, Taplin wrote that infanticide was 'very prevalent among the Aborigines before the commencement of this colony' with as many as one-third to half of all infants being killed. Those killed included deformed infants, one of twins, children of 'caste' (of whom there can have been few before the commencement of the colony), 'illegitimate' children, and, most commonly, 'every child … born before the one which preceded it could walk was destroyed, because the mother was regarded as incapable of carrying two.'[20] Indeed, he wrote, somewhat credulously, (for his informant was surely a woman speaking back to power, and perhaps, as Russell suggests, exaggerating for reasons that are now not clear):

> One intelligent woman said she thought that if the Europeans had waited a few more years they would have found the country without inhabitants.[21]

'[T]he most horrible cruelty' was deployed in killing the newborns, wrote Taplin, with the usual method involving the insertion of 'a red hot ember' into each ear of the infant. Yet in his own years amongst the Narrinyeri, he counted only one 'murder' of a child, a deficit which he attributed to deliberate concealment: his testimony therefore spoke of things unseen.[22]

---

[19] Ibid. 279.

[20] George Taplin, *The Narrinyeri: an account of the tribes of South Australian Aborigines inhabiting the country around the Lakes Alexandrina, Albert and Coorong and the lower part of the River Murray* (Adelaide: J.T. Shawyer, 1874), 10–2.

[21] Ibid.

[22] Ibid.

In Gippsland in the 1870s, Alfred Howitt's Kurnai informants assured him that 'they never knew an instance of parents killing their children, but only of *leaving behind* new-born infants'. Howitt concluded that those left behind were necessarily left to die—rather than being taken up by kin, for example—and declared that the Kurnai 'undoubtedly, were guilty of infanticide'.[23] Howitt's assertion became a key point of evidence in the public debate between British and American social evolutionists, J.F. McLennan and L.H. Morgan, over the origins of human culture, a debate in which infanticide was deemed a fundamental marker of primitiveness.[24] Towards the end of the century Howitt circulated an ethnological questionnaire. The relatively few replies to his question on infanticide practices were laced with reticulated 'common knowledge' and included one from a South Australian correspondent who '*inferred* from the remarkable gap that appeared in the ages of children' amongst the Kaura of the Adelaide region, that in 'hard summers the new-born children were all eaten'.[25] It was upon such flimsy evidence that the discourse moved into the 20th century.

The origins of the discourse

Infanticide had been a marker of 'barbarism' since at least the 1780s with respect to India, where it was paired in British thinking about India with the practice of sati.[26] In 1823 Thomas Buxton called for the accumulated

---

[23] Lorimer Fison and A.W. Howitt, *Kamilaroi and Kurnai: group-marriage and relationship, and marriage by elopement, drawn chiefly from the usage of the Australian Aborigines: also the Kurnai Tribe, their customs in peace and war* (Melbourne: George Robertson, 1880), 190.

[24] John Ferguson McLennan, *Primitive marriage* (London: 1876); L.H. Morgan, *Ancient Society*, (London: Macmillan, 1877). See also Morgan's foreword to Fison and Howitt.

[25] Alfred W. Howitt, *The native tribes of south-east Australia* (Canberra: Aboriginal Studies Press 1996[1904]), 749; Howitt Papers, Museum of Victoria, Melbourne. Howitt's transcriptions of returns relating to infanticide are on four handwritten foolscap sheets in these unindexed papers.

[26] Correspondence on Hindu infanticide and *Proceedings of Indian government with regard to practice, 1789–1820*, British Parliamentary Papers, no. 426, 1824; Interrogatories by Governor General in Bengal, 1801, Papers on Police, Missionaries, Hindu Religion and

despatches on Indian infanticide from 1789 to 1820 to be tabled in the House of Commons, signalling renewed interest in the practice by metropolitan moral reformers. However, as Satadru Sen argues, it was in the 1830s that female infanticide in India was 'rediscovered'. 'It was', she argues, a discovery 'viewed as ... a trophy of empire, and a major marker of racial/cultural difference' in which female children became part of the:

> terrain on which British and Indian elite males could confront each other, and on which the colonizing mission could be justified, extended and contested. This was not so much a conversation about children's lives, as it was about the legitimacy of the interventionist state.[27]

Its discovery enabled 'an elaborate regime of surveillance and policing, with certain castes and communities being defined as 'infanticidal' and aberrant.[28]

In the Australian colonies, the development of a popular discourse about Aboriginal infanticide followed a similar chronology. It was set running in 1798 by David Collins (Judge Advocate at Sydney Cove from 1788 to 1796) with a description of the killing of an infant at Sydney Cove. The child's mother had died 'of a consumption' in the wake of the devastating smallpox epidemic that had all but annihilated the clans in the immediate vicinity of Sydney Cove. The suckling infant, clearly dying of the same disease, was stoned and buried with its mother, the father having been unable to find a wet nurse for the child. 'We have every reason to suppose the custom always prevails among them' wrote Collins.[29] The assertion was immediately reiterated by population theorist

---

Infanticide, British Parliamentary Papers, no. 264, 1812–13; Satandu Sen, 'The savage family: colonialism and female infanticide in nineteenth century India', *Journal of Women's History* 14.3 (Autumn 2002): 53–81.

[27] Sen, 55.

[28] Ibid. 53 and 58.

[29] David Collins, *An account of the English Colony in New South Wales (etc)*, vol. I (London: Cadell and Davies, 1798), Appendix XI, 607–8. See also Inga Clendinnen, *Dancing with strangers* (Melbourne: Text Publishing, 2003).

Thomas Malthus who theorised about 'the difficulty of rearing children in savage life'. He wrote:

> Women obliged by their habits of living to a constant change of place and compelled to an unremitting drudgery for their husbands, appear to be absolutely incapable of bringing up two or three children nearly of the same age. If another child be born before the one above it can shift for itself, and follow its mother on foot, one of the two must almost necessarily perish for want of care.[30]

As in India, the trope of the 'infanticidal' native was rediscovered in the Australian colonies in the 1830s. On the edge of the settled districts of New South Wales in May 1830, a European stockman told the explorer Charles Sturt that two Aboriginal men camped nearby had killed and eaten a child just prior to Sturt's arrival. Sturt questioned the accused 'as well as I could'. Admitting that he had no 'corroborating' evidence, he nevertheless recounted the tale, concluding that 'the very mention of such a thing among these people goes to prove that they are capable of such an enormity'.[31] Sturt's looseness with the quality of evidence, his failure to admit the limitations of translation, and the willingness with which this anecdote was admitted into his published narrative speaks of more than naivety: it speaks of an imperial will to power in the rendering of the inhuman and expendable 'other'.

By the mid-1830s similarly unsupported accusations featured in testimony to the long-running British Select Committee on the Condition of Aborigines in British Colonies. Despite speculation by witnesses and commissioners that infanticide was a major cause of the decline of the Australian clans of New South Wales, only one actual killing of a newborn was unearthed and that by a white convict stock keeper motivated by fear that the evidence of his illicit dealings with

---

[30] Thomas Malthus, *An essay on the principle of population* (J.M. Dent & Sons, London, 1973 [1798]), 24.

[31] Charles Sturt, *Two expeditions into the interior of southern Australia during the years 1828, 1829, 1830, and 1831* vols. 1 and 2 (London: Smith, Elder & Co., 1834), 89–90 and 222–23.

Aboriginal women would see him returned to incarceration.[32] At Port Phillip in March 1840, European men accused of abducting young girls from the clans claimed that they were rescuing those 'who would otherwise have fallen victim to the tomahawk of the unfeeling savage'.[33]

The discourse received a particular fillip when, around 1842 or 1843, a circular questionnaire from the British Association for the Advancement of Science was received in the Australian colonies, prompting the Chief Protector of Aborigines at Port Phillip, George Augustus Robinson, to request his Assistant Protectors to seek out information about the practice of infanticide. Entitled 'Queries respecting the human race', the circular was composed between 1839 and 1841 by a committee that included the young Darwin and the venerable philologist J.C. Pritchard, whose four volumes had traced the dispersion of the varieties of mankind across the globe. 'Querie' XVIII of the circular requested colonists, mariners and travellers to ascertain whether 'infanticide occur[s] to any considerable extent [amongst indigenous peoples], and if it does, to what causes is it to be referred, want of affection, deficient subsistence, or superstition?'[34] The Queries were directed, with some urgency, particularly to settlers in lands where the extinction of Indigenous peoples was anticipated. It was at the behest of Robinson that Assistant Protector William Thomas spoke with Billibellary, the *ngurungaeta* or senior man and speaker of the Wurundjeri, in October 1843 about the practice of infanticide. Thomas'

---

[32] Excerpts from journal of missionary William Watson, 6–13 December 1832, in House of Commons, 'Report from the Select Committee on Aborigines (British Settlements) with Minutes of Evidence', British Parliamentary Papers, 1836, 488–89. Reprinted in Irish University Press Series of British Parliamentary Papers vol. 1 (Shannon: Irish University Press, 1968–69).

[33] *Port Phillip Gazette*, 4 March 1840 and 7 March 1840.

[34] British Association for the Advancement of Science, 'Varieties of human race: queries respecting the human race, to be addressed to travellers and others ...', *Report of the Eleventh Meeting of the British Association for the Advancement of Science held at Plymouth*, 1841 (1842), 332–39.

record of this conversation with Billibellary stands out as the single most significant exception to the array of hearsay reports about infanticide in the records of settlers in south-eastern Australia. It is upon this record of conversation that historian Richard Broome recently based his conclusion that the colonial occupation had brought such despair to first nation Australians that women took to killing a large proportion of their infants.[35]

By 1843 so few infants survived that Thomas had, indeed, come to fear that the clans near Melbourne would die out. Yet Broome's assertion that infanticide was a significant contributor to their demise and that women drew on traditional practices that warranted the killing of infants 'when children were born too close together, as the younger could not be carried while the older was still unweaned and lacked mobility' rests on the perceived logic of an explanation first proposed by Malthus and repeated across two centuries.[36] The traction of the explanation lies in the largely unchallenged fiction that 'hunters and gatherers' existed in an unremitting state of displacement, rather than as people who moved in extended family communities in a prescribed seasonal round, carefully cultivating the bounty of their ancestral lands.

The case of the Kulin

By the late 1830s the political influence of the British evangelicals was on the wane. One of the last acts of the faction that had legislated the

---

[35] Richard Broome, *Aboriginal Victorians: a history since 1800* (Crows Nest: Allen & Unwin, 2005), 32.

[36] Broome's *Aboriginal Victorians* is only the most recent. See also Howitt and Fison, 190; Howitt, *The native tribes of south-east Australia*, 750; Frank J. Gillen, 'Notes on some manners and customs of the Aborigines of the McDonnell Ranges belonging to the Arunta Tribe' in E.C. Stirling ed., *Report on the work of the Horn Scientific Expedition to Central Australia, part IV, anthropology*, ed. Walter Baldwin Spencer (London: Dutton and Co.; Melbourne: Melville, Mullen and Slade, 1896), 161; Walter Baldwin Spencer and F.J. Gillen, *The native tribes of Central Australia* (London: Macmillan, 1899), 61; George Taplin, 10–2; J.H. Wedge, *Field notebook, 1835*, in John Batman Papers, State Library of Victoria, Melbourne.

abolition of slavery in 1833 was to establish an Aboriginal Protectorate in the newly occupied Australian colony of Port Phillip. When the Protectors arrived at Port Phillip early in 1839 flush with hopes of redeeming their 'sable brothers', they met not only a barrage of opposition from settlers but indifference from their wards. The clans eagerly accepted the rations and tools of the newcomers, but saw little reason to abandon their own life ways. In the face of disappointment, wrote Manning Clark, these 'high-minded men of goodwill … [soon] became the men with a sorrowful countenance'.[37] In a sense, the furrows on their sorrowful countenances iterate the line that they, and others, came to draw between Europeans and 'others' as their hopeful commitment to universal brotherhood transformed into a demarcating paternalism.

Since early 1839 Protector Thomas had faithfully counted the number of births and deaths amongst 'his' two clans—the Wurundjeri (or Woiwurung) of the Yarra valley and the Boonwurrung of the eastern arm of Port Phillip Bay. Each quarter he reported the numbers to the Chief Protector in a quarterly report. By 1843, Thomas was aware, as was Billibellary, that deaths outnumber births 'at least eight deaths to a birth',[38] and there were almost no young infants in the two clans now; even when the women fell pregnant, they mostly returned after birthing without offspring. In his journal of May 1839 Thomas had vehemently rejected 'a lie' put about by 'that Sydney Journal who has asserted that the Aborigines of Australia are less than the brutes in the scale of Existence void of natural affection, destroying their own offspring to save them the trouble of rearing them'.[39]

---

[37] Manning Clark, *A discovery of Australia: 1976 Boyer lectures* (Sydney: Australian Broadcasting Commission, 1976), 23.

[38] William Thomas, Reply to Circular, 'Report from the Select Committee on the Condition of the Aborigines', New South Wales Legislative Council, 1845, 55.

[39] William Thomas, Journal, 19 May 1839, William Thomas Papers, Mf 5883, CY 2604 reel 1, Matheson Library, Monash University, Melbourne.

As the medical lists of Thomas' clans record, men and women, youths of both sexes, small children, and infants were infected with syphilis, 'the loathsome disease' that arrived with the invaders.[40] It was a disease known to destroy fecundity and infant viability; yet by October 1843 Thomas had suspended his disbelief about the accusations of widespread infanticides, and he too admitted the possibility that the women were deliberately killing their newborns. It was in that context, and under direction from Robinson, that Thomas sat down to talk with the Wurundjeri clan leader, Billibellary on the 7 October 1843. In his Quarterly Report to the Chief Protector of December 1843, Thomas wrote:

> I had a long conversation with Billibellary, Chief of the Yarra tribe on the belief that the Blacks killed their infants. He acknowledged that they did so and named who had had children since I had been among them, 8 in number (two only are now living). He said they had two ways of doing so, one by twisting a cord several times round their necks, the other by putting a karnya (opossum rug) over their heads. He said that the [women] made away with them. The Blackfellows all about say 'that no good have them pickanniney, no country for Blackfellow like long time ago'. I pointed out to him how wicked it was and that God when they died would ask them where those pickannineys were they had killed. I told him that there was country enough for Black and White people if they would but stop in one place. He said if Yarra Blackfellows had a country on the Yarra that they would stop on it and cultivate the ground. He told me that there were three [women] who would soon have pickannineys and he would see that they did not kill them.[41]

---

[40] See for example, Medical Report of Cases Treated by H.G. Jones, Medical Dispenser, to the Aboriginal Natives Melbourne or Western Port District from 1st to the 31st May 1842, VPRS 12 Box, Folder 13, Victorian Public Records Office, Melbourne. Those infected with 'pseudo syphilis' included infants.

[41] Thomas to Chief Protector Robinson, *Quarterly report*, 1 December 1843, VPRS 4467, 1840–49, Victorian Aboriginal Protector Returns, Victorian Public Records Office, Melbourne; Broome, 32–3.

This would seem to be an irrefutable 'confession' as Thomas called it. But this quarterly report was not Thomas's first version of this conversation with Billibellary. Thomas' original journal entry of the conversation has one minor, but significant, difference from the quarterly report he delivered to the Chief Protector in December 1843. Thomas' original journal entry of 7 October 1843 concluded with these words:

> Billibellary promised that he would endeavour to make them let their children live—he said that there were 3 who would soon have pickaninys, Murry, I spend this day with the Blks at the creek.[42]

This original entry suggests, therefore, that it was to three women of a visiting clan from the Murray River, not to women of his own clan, that Billibellary promised to speak, in his role as *ngurungaeta*, in an endeavour to convince them to let their infants live.

Once Melbourne became the most intense site of colonisation in the region, the presence of non-Kulin clans at the nearby Merri Creek was not uncommon. On Sunday the 3 September 1843, a month prior to the conversation, Thomas recorded that '[t]he Blacks are beginning to come in [to the Merri Creek] Billibellary & others a few days since—Now the Murrys & part of Yarra'. Six months earlier, in March 1843, a party of 200 'perfect strangers' from the 'Australian Alps' had arrived at the Merri Creek and the *Tanderrum* ceremony had been performed by the Wurundjeri, in welcome.[43] The 'Murry' clans had perhaps come to Melbourne late in 1843—into country not their own—in response to an invitation from Superintendent La Trobe, delivered by the Wesleyan missionary, Francis Tuckfield, who, in May 1842, had travelled along the Murray River seeking an alternate location for the failed Buntingdale mission. On his return, Tuckfield informed La Trobe that the northern clans, who had limited contact with Europeans, had an 'unusually large

---

[42] Thomas, Journal, 7 October 1843.
[43] Ibid.

proportion of children' and were 'entirely free' from the venereal diseases that had taken such a toll in the occupied districts.[44]

The contrast between the number of children and infants amongst the federated Kulin clans at the Merri Creek, within sight of the town of Melbourne, and the numbers amongst the distant clans still largely unsullied by the impacts of colonialism, could not have been more stark; nor could the cause of the barrenness amongst the former have been more apparent. In recording his conversation with Billibellary, Thomas noted that they had, together, counted only eight infants born to the Wurundjeri and Boonwurrung since Thomas arrived amongst them five years earlier; one only now survived.[45] Given that tragic decline of fertility, how unlikely is it that there would have been three women 'who would soon have' babes in October 1843 when the conversation took place? It is a reasonable conclusion, therefore, that when Billibellary spoke of women killing their infants, he, like Thomas, was speculating about the unseemly habits of others.

Aboriginal people frequently disparaged or expressed fears about 'wild blacks'—a covering term in translation for foreign, and often near-neighbouring, clans. Wesleyan missionary Joseph Orton noted the suspicions of Aboriginal people he met at Port Phillip that those beyond their own country were murderers or sorcerers who would strike in the night. They were 'dreadfully afraid lest we take them among "wild blackfellows" as they call them', wrote Orton. Thomas too recorded that the man Gellibrand had told him 'that if wild Black fellow … got that hair he [Gellibrand] should die'.[46] Protector Edward Parker also inadvertently alluded to one source of the European imaginary of Aboriginal savagery

---

[44] Francis Tuckfield to Charles Joseph La Trobe, 20 May 1842, 'Aborigines (Australian Colonies): despatches of Governors of Australian Colonies, illustrative of conditions of Aborigines', British Parliamentary Papers, 1844, no. 627 (enclosed in Schedule no. 55, Gipps to Stanley).

[45] Thomas, Journal, 7 October 1843.

[46] Joseph Orton, Journal, 14 May 1839, in N.M. Orton Papers, State Library of Victoria, Melbourne; Thomas, Journal, 24 March 1839.

when, in 1845, he told a parliamentary enquiry into the condition of the Aborigines of New South Wales, that there were 'great differences ... observable among the different tribes', with reference to the 'painful subject' of infanticide. 'The Pangurang natives on the lower Goulburn country', he wrote, '*even by the acknowledgement of their enemies*, are free from this crime'. Yet he accepted his own clan's accusations that their Kulin neighbours and enemies, the Daungwurrung of the upper Goulburn River, were 'addicted' to the practice, so much so that they now had only a 'small portion of children'.[47] Parker's evidence suggests how closely the fears and accusations of settlers articulated with the fears and accusations made by Aboriginal clans against people they each regarded as beyond the pale.

Like Thomas' quarterly report of December, the journal entry of October 1843 also recorded Billibellary's despair at the loss of the up-coming generation of his clan, but in different words. According to Thomas:

> he [Billibellary] said that Black [women] say now no good children, Black fellow say no country now for them, very good [one word illegible] & no more come up Pickaniny.

There is, arguably, significant slippage from the meaning of the words 'now no good children' and 'no more come up pickanniny' in the original journal entry, to Thomas's reworked statement in the quarterly report that the women 'made away with them'. The first, in passive voice, offer the possibility of an understanding that since their world had been turned upside down they were no longer to be blessed with viable newborns; the second channels meaning towards the more active intervention of infanticide.

What we have in the exchange between Protector and *ngurungaeta*, I suggest, is two cultured men, jointly speculating about the uncouth habits

---

[47] Edward Parker, Reply to circular, 'Report from the Select Committee on the condition of the Aborigines', New South Wales Legislative Council, 1845, 52–54.

of outsiders. Billibellary may well have been surprised, had he read Thomas' report to the Chief Protector, to realise that Thomas had interpreted their conversation about the habits of 'others' as a confession about the practices of his own clan. Instead of two men mutually looking outwards, Billibellary, and the women of his clan, now became objects of surveillance and sometimes of repugnance. In quite literal terms, this moment represents a 're-orientation' of the Protector from being a partner in a mutual project of protecting the clans in concert with the Wurundjeri leader, to being a principal agent in a white project of objectification, surveillance, and soon, of 'rescuing' and incarcerating Aboriginal children.

Thomas similarly collapsed cause and effect two years later when he told a New South Wales parliamentary enquiry that, from his own observation, the few infants born to his Wurundjeri and Boonwurrung clans were usually 'rotten with disease' and mostly died before they were a month old—a characteristic of infants born with congenital syphilis—and his statement to the same enquiry that 'should there be a birth the infant is artfully put out of the way' because 'as they state, "of having no country they can call their own".[48] In each case, the space between the two versions allows for a devastating wave of infant deaths that came from forces other than wilful, even despairing, maternal intervention.

By the time the conversation between the two men took place at the Merri Creek there was considerable pressure on Thomas and others—fed materially by the British Association's ethnological circular—to discern the practice of infanticide. Aboriginal denials, on the other hand, fell on deaf ears. An Aboriginal man, Mahroot, closely questioned about infanticide practices by the New South Wales enquiry of 1845, vehemently denied that the dearth of children amongst his southern Cadigal clan was due to infanticide.[49] His voice was overborne by that of

---

[48] Thomas, Reply to circular, 55.
[49] Evidence of Mahroot, Minutes of evidence, 'Report from the Select Committee on the condition of the Aborigines', New South Wales Legislative Council, 1845, 4.

John Bede Polding, Catholic Archbishop of Sydney, who, with humanitarian intent, testified that the Aborigines no longer had a 'desire to have their children to survive them' because of 'a deep sorrow prevailing in consequence of a rapid ... destruction talking place amongst them'. Polding admitted that he had not spoken with Aboriginal people on the subject and that his opinion was reached through 'making myself a black, putting myself in that position'.[50]

While correspondents to that enquiry reported local hearsay about infanticides in approximately equal numbers to those who reported no instances in their district,[51] authoritative knowledge about the Australians now increasingly categorised them as infanticidal. Increasingly, reiteration alone stood as evidence and ethnographic description gave way to ethnographic prescription that placed the Australians amongst the lesser varieties of humankind with habits appropriate to their station. With all the authority of Chief Protector and with a high degree of credulousness, Robinson also reiterated cases he had heard second hand to the enquiry. It was Robinson who linked the purported threat of mass infanticides with the project of rounding up the children of the Aborigines of Port Phillip. 'Half-castes', he told the committee, were 'invariably its victim', and 'it would be exceedingly desirable could this fine race be removed to an asylum for protection and instruction'.[52]

In 1858, testifying before a Victorian parliamentary enquiry, the ageing William Thomas again told the committee that the Boonwurrung and the Wurundjeri clans 'made away with' their children and that they now had 'few, if any, births to fill up the ranks of the dead'.[53] He baulked

<hr/>

[50] Evidence of Polding, Minutes of evidence, 'Report from the Select Committee on the condition of the Aborigines' New South Wales Legislative Council, 1845, 6–8.

[51] Replies to circular, Question 17, 'Report from the Select Committee on the condition of the Aborigines', New South Wales Legislative Council, 1845, 22–59.

[52] George Augustus Robinson, Reply to circular, 'Report from the Select Committee on the condition of the Aborigines', New South Wales Legislative Council, 1845, 48.

[53] William Thomas, Minutes of evidence, Select Committee of the Legislative Council of Victoria on the Aborigines, 1858–59, Victorian Parliamentary Papers, 1858–59, 3; William

at separating children from their kin, but, he argued, 'nothing short of removing them a considerable distance from their tribe can ... avert ... the extinction of the aboriginal race'.[54] He warned however, that the people would not consent to part from their children without 'great bribery' or kidnapping.[55] Like Thomas, the authoritative Anglican Missionary Committee recommended 'a central establishment for the reception of the native children from all the tribes' where 'the young ... may become estranged from their own customs'. While some on the Anglican committee initially doubted the justice of the plan, their reticence dissolved when 'one important fact' was impressed upon them by a leading member, G.W. Rusden: namely 'that half-caste male children, borne by aboriginal women, are usually destroyed'.[56] That intelligence was at odds with Rusden's own reply to the committee's circular (which essentially duplicated the British Association *Queries* of 1841) in which he reported that 'the blacks allege that it [infanticide] was uncommon' and that 'many of them are too affectionate to think of it for a moment in the case of their own children'.[57] And so, despite the doubt surrounding such accusations, the practice of 'rescuing' Aboriginal children from their kin and incarcerating them in training institutions began in earnest in Victoria with the establishment of a central children's asylum at the heart of the government Aboriginal station Coranderrk at Healesville in 1863.

That infanticide was one of a range of family-size limitation methods amongst the Australians (along with abortion, polygamous marriage, and

---

Thomas, Evidence to the Select Committee of the Legislative Council of Victoria on the Aborigines, 1858–59, in Thomas, Reply to Circular, 40.

[54] Thomas, Reply to Circular, 40.

[55] Thomas, Minutes of evidence, 3; Thomas, Reply to circular, 51.

[56] Anglican Committee Report [untitled], Select Committee of the Legislative Council of Victoria on the Aborigines, 1858–59, Victorian Parliamentary Papers, 1858–59, in Reply to Circular, 40.

[57] George W. Rusden, Evidence to Select Committee of the Legislative Council of Victoria on the Aborigines, 1858–59, Victorian Parliamentary Papers, 1858–59; Reply to Circular, 51.

strict customary sexual regulation, for example) is likely; that some women resorted to killing infants or children as an act of 'desperate agency' in either the pre- or post-contact periods is also likely; that it was customary and prevalent is not supported by the balance of evidence. What was, in all likelihood, an exceptional and incidental practice amongst Aboriginal people, rather than a matter of common custom, was raised up by the interaction of European and Aboriginal fears of the other into a morally and racially defining trope that marked whole communities as 'infanticidal', and as people whose common rights could be morally suspended. For more than 200 years this discourse has done an inordinate amount of work in constructing the Australians as a people ripe for colonisation and dispossession. From the mid-19th century, it underwrote the institutionalisation of generations of 'rescued' Aboriginal children. With that project of incarceration, Aboriginality became anathema to social inclusion and citizenship in the radically democratic and radically White colonies of Australia.

11

White anxieties and the articulation of race: the women's movement and the making of White Australia, 1910s–1930s

Jane Carey, Monash University

> At the present time the most pressing question for Australia is Immigration. To keep to the 'White Australia' policy, the flow of people from the Old Country must be steady and suitable.
>
> *The Dawn*, 15 December 1924, 4.

> In this country the question of infant life is a most vital one, and should be of deep concern to the whole community, for we have need of all our children. Babies are the best immigrants.
>
> School For Mothers Institute: Its Aims and Objects (Adelaide, 1909).

This chapter examines the racial anxieties at work in the Australian women's movement in the early 1900s, focussing on campaigns and organisations aimed at increasing and 'improving' the white population on the one hand and discussions of the 'Aboriginal problem' on the other. It particularly examines the activities of the National Council of Women, the largest women's group of this period, and the Australian Federation of Women Voters, a smaller but highly influential organisation, as well as local groups which emerged to further these causes. Specifically, it explores efforts to promote immigration from Britain, which went alongside eugenic measures to exclude 'unfit' white migrants as well, and various schemes aimed at producing 'well born' white children. As I hope to show, these seemingly disparate activities were informed by a single racial imperative. The racial interests of the movement coalesced around anxieties about the need for a large and healthy white population to secure the nation's future. Indeed, their racially based reforming campaigns revolved almost entirely around anxieties internal to whiteness. While the women's movement showed remarkably little interest in the 'Aboriginal problem', or the 'peril' of Asian immigration, their vigorous campaigns around improving the quality and quantity of the white population reveal how racialised thinking in fact permeated the movement and animated many of its endeavours. And women's work was presented as essential to implementing these vital racial programs.

The 'racial' history of Australia has been extensively explored in terms of the treatment and experiences of Indigenous people and the fears of 'Asian invasion' which gave rise to the nation's founding doctrine of the White Australia Policy in 1901.[1] But these histories have rarely been linked, in Australia or elsewhere, to the concurrent obsessions with white racial fitness. Similarly, the significant body of scholarship on the racial dimensions of the western women's movement has largely focused on white women's constructions of themselves in relation to racial 'others' —how this could be used to bolster white women's status, and the 'civilising' impulse of the western women's movement in relation to those perceived as racially inferior.[2] Both of these tendencies were certainly

---

[1] See for example, Henry Reynolds, *The other side of the frontier: Aboriginal resistance to the European invasion of Australia* (Melbourne: Penguin, 1982); Bain Attwood, *Telling the truth about Aboriginal history* (Sydney: Allen & Unwin, 2005); Andrew Markus, *Australian race relations, 1788–1993* (Sydney: Allen & Unwin, 1994); David Walker, *Anxious nation: Australia and the rise of Asia 1850–1939* (Brisbane: University of Queensland Press, 1999); Gwenda Tavan, *The long, slow death of White Australia* (Melbourne: Scribe Publications, 2005).

[2] Antoinette Burton, *Burdens of history: British feminists, Indian women, and Imperial culture, 1865–1915* (Chapel Hill: University of North Carolina Press, 1994); Clare Midgley, ed., *Gender and imperialism* (Manchester: Manchester University Press, 1998), and *Feminism and Empire: women activists in Imperial Britain, 1790–1865* (London: Routledge, 2007); Patricia Grimshaw, 'Settler anxieties, Indigenous peoples, and women's suffrage in the colonies of Australia, New Zealand and Hawaii, 1888 to 1902', *Pacific Historical Review* 69.4 (2000): 553–72.

evident in Australia. However, the voluminous discussions of white racial fitness, evident in the Australian women's movement from at least the early 1900s, have not, to date, received much attention.[3]

This chapter is drawn from a much larger project examining ideas about race and whiteness in the Australian women's movement from the 1880s to the 1930s. In this work, I have particularly argued that it is not sufficient to look only to 'others' to explain the operations of 'race'. Following Aileen Moreton-Robinson's proposition that whiteness is 'central to the racial formation of Australian society',[4] I suggest that we need to pay far greater attention to the extensive discussions of whiteness that circulated from the late 19th to the mid-20th centuries as a major domain in which ideas about race were being articulated. Such an approach also reveals the direct connections between Australia's racially restrictive immigration regimes and the policies adopted towards Indigenous peoples—issues which have usually been treated separately

---

[3] The majority of whiteness scholarship is based in the United States. For some of the key works see: David Roediger, *The wages of whiteness: race and the making of the American working class* (London: Verso, 1991); Toni Morrison, *Playing in the dark: whiteness and the literary imagination* (New York: Vintage: Random House, 1992); bell hooks, 'Representations of whiteness in the literary imagination', in *Black looks: race and representation* (Boston: South End Press, 1992); Cheryl I. Harris, 'Whiteness as property', *Harvard Law Review* 106.8 (June 1993): 1707–91; Ruth Frankenburg, *White women, race matters: the social construction of whiteness* (Minneapolis: University of Minnesota Press, 1993). There is also a small but growing body of Australian historical work on whiteness: Warwick Anderson, *The cultivation of whiteness: science, health and racial destiny in Australia* (Melbourne: Melbourne University Press, 2002); Marilyn Lake, 'White man's country: the trans-national history of a national project', *Australian Historical Studies* 35.122 (2003): 346–63; Leigh Boucher, Jane Carey and Katherine Ellinghaus, eds., *Historicising whiteness: transnational perspectives on the construction of an identity* (Melbourne: RMIT Publishing, 2007); Marilyn Lake and Henry Reynolds, *Drawing the global colour line: white men's countries and the question of racial equality* (Melbourne: Melbourne University Press, 2008); .

[4] Aileen Moreton-Robinson 'Preface', in *Whitening race: essays in social and cultural criticism* ed. Aileen Moreton-Robinson (Canberra: Aboriginal Studies Press, 2004), ix.

within surprisingly discrete historiographies.[5] These twin pillars of Australia's racial past both had their foundations in protecting the privileges of whiteness and patrolling its boundaries.[6]

This chapter thus asks questions about the nature and location of racial discourses and their relationship to the national project of White Australia. The campaigns discussed below highlight how racial thinking inspired reforming agendas and supported white women's agency. Beyond this, these activities provide new insights into, in Patrick Wolfe's words, the 'organizing grammar of race', which Ann Stoler suggests was 'a central colonial sorting technique'.[7]

Good white immigrants

I have discussed elsewhere the women's movement's intense activism against the 'menace of mental deficiency' and its racially damaging effects as one key example of how the racial discourses at work in the movement could revolve entirely around whiteness.[8] The campaigns around immigration reveal this racial focus even more starkly. From the 1910s to the 1930s the women's movement took a strong interest in immigration issues, but not, perhaps, in the way we might expect. Their activities did not focus on the need to exclude 'Asian' or 'other' migrants. They assumed

---

[5] On this point see Ann Curthoys, 'An uneasy conversation: the multicultural and the Indigenous', in *Race, colour and identity in Australia and New Zealand*, eds. John Docker and Gerhard Fischer (Sydney: UNSW Press, 2000).

[6] I am drawing here on Matt Wray, *Not quite white: white trash and the boundaries of whiteness* (Durham, NC: Duke University Press, 2006).

[7] Patrick Wolfe, 'Settler colonialism and the elimination of the Native', *Journal of Genocide Research* 8.4 (2006): 387; Ann Laura Stoler, 'Intimidations of Empire: predicaments of the tactile and unseen', in *Haunted by Empire: geographies of intimacy in North American history*, ed. Ann Laura Stoler (Durham: Duke University Press, 2006), 4.

[8] Jane Carey, '"Women's objective—a perfect race": whiteness, eugenics and the articulation of race', in *Re-Orienting whiteness: transnational perspectives on the history of an identity*, eds. Leigh Boucher, Jane Carey and Katherine Ellinghaus (New York: Palgrave, 2009); Jane Carey, '"Wanted—a real white Australia": the women's movement, whiteness and the settler-colonial project', in *Studies in settler colonialism*, eds. Fiona Bateman and Lionel Pilkington (New York: Palgrave, forthcoming).

the White Australia Policy was working effectively to prevent this (as indeed it was). Rather, their activism focused the need for increased migration from Britain, but also, and even more predominantly, on the need for rigorous screening and medical testing to ensure only high quality white migrants were admitted.

To understand the basis of this activism, it is useful to review the provisions of the *Immigration Restriction Act* (1901), the central plank of the White Australia policy. We are all familiar with the first and most notorious provision of the Act, which was designed as a bar to 'non-white' immigration. This prohibited the immigration of: 'Any person who when asked to do so by an officer fails to write out at dictation and sign in the presence of the officer a passage of fifty words in length in an European language directed by the officer'. What is less well known, is that five of the Act's other six provisions were actually directed at excluding categories of white migrants who were deemed racially undesirable. Specifically, section 3 denied entry to:

> (a) any person likely in the opinion of the Minister or of an officer to become a charge upon the public or upon any public or charitable institution;
>
> (b) any idiot or insane person;
>
> (c) any person suffering from an infectious or contagious disease of a loathsome or dangerous character;
>
> (d) any person who has within three years been convicted of an offence, not being a mere political offence, and has been sentenced to imprisonment for one year or longer therefore, and has not received a pardon;
>
> (e) any prostitute or person living on the prostitution of others;

The Act was clearly designed to allow for a careful screening of potential white immigrants. The campaigns of Australia's largest women's organisation, the National Council of Women, around the issue of immigration reveal they were keenly aware of this, and their activism revolved almost entirely around these issues.

From the early 1900s its various state branches established special committees on immigration which reflected the desires for both quantity and quality. Naturally, they had a strong interest in encouraging and providing support, 'protection', and opportunities for women migrants. They also insisted that the selection and supervision of women migrants needed to be carried by Australian women themselves. Thus the Emigration and Immigration Committee established by the Queensland National Council of Women in 1910 concerned itself particularly with the welfare of British immigrant girls coming out as domestic servants. They were keen to encourage such migrants, since the shortage of 'good help' was a constant source of irritation for middle-class women at this time, but they were equally concerned that such immigrants should be properly selected and supervised. What was wanted, they argued, was 'well trained domestics rather than the haphazard ones who were constantly arriving'.[9] The committee aimed to get in touch with bodies which would 'recommend girls of good character and capacity', and to ensure 'proper protection' on the journey and suitable positions when they arrived.[10] The following year they considered sending 'a band of women to England to choose suitable girls as emigrants'.[11] At around the same time the New South Wales Council formed a similar committee which also expressed the view that 'the women selected to be sent out here were not wisely chosen'. And they thus passed resolutions that a committee including women members be formed in London to select immigrants, that 'all women emigrants be passed by a woman doctor',

[9] Minutes, 30 May 1910, National Council of Women of Queensland Records (hereafter NCW of Queensland Minutes), Fryer Library, University of Queensland, Brisbane. This committee was formed in response to the fact that the International Council of Women had established a standing Committee on Immigration, and it was expected that national member organisations would follow suit: NCW of Queensland Minutes, 7 March 1910.
[10] NCW of Queensland Minutes, 10 June 1910.
[11] NCW of Queensland Minutes, 7 August 1911.

and that a matron be appointed to supervise women migrants during their journey to Australia.[12]

Both committees pursued these agendas even more vigorously in the years after the First World War, and both became closely involved with the New Settlers League, formed in the early 1920s, which sought to assist new migrants after their arrival in Australia. Other groups also emerged to support the cause. In South Australia, it was concerns over immigration which led to the reformulation of the National Council of Women in 1921, when Lady Hackett, the lady mayoress, convened a meeting 'to discuss Australian conditions as affecting the immigration of British war service women.'[13] The immigration of girls and women from Britain remained a major focus for the South Australian Council. The Women's Service Guilds of Western Australia, the state branch of the Australian Federation of Women Voters, also took a keen interest in immigration. In the early 1920s, some of its members formed the Women's Immigration Auxiliary Council, which sought to assist new migrants, both in practical terms and by providing entertainment and social events at the hostel provided for them.[14]

These committees dealt almost exclusively with British immigration. The question of non-white migration arose only rarely, and was treated separately. In 1924 one of the topics proposed for discussion at the Australian national conference was 'That there should be a full, unbiased and scientific international investigation of the problems arising from contact between Eastern and Western peoples with special reference to migration.'[15] And in 1925 the South Australian Council passed a resolution protesting 'against the number of undesirable immigrants

---

[12] Minutes, 2 March 1911, National Council of Women of New South Wales Records, MLMSS 3739 (hereafter NCW of NSW Minutes), box MLK 3009, Mitchell Library, Sydney.
[13] 'Report of the National Council of Women of South Australia, September 1921', (Adelaide: The Council, 1921), np.
[14] *Dawn*, 14 June 1924, 5.
[15] National Council of Women of New South Wales, Biennial Reports for 1925–26 (Sydney: Fred W. White Printer, 1926), 11.

coming to Aust. from S. Europe'.[16] But the main concern was with increasing the numbers of British migrants coming to the country. In Western Australia, the formation of the Women's Immigration Auxiliary Council was motivated by the understanding that, 'To the Commonwealth, the greatest problem is that of population, and the danger to her empty areas is a menace which makes it imperative that she should make an effort to people them with migrants from the Motherland'.[17] In 1924, the NSW Committee reported its opinion that: 'immigration, so far as New South Wales is concerned, is at a low ebb and we hope that the dribble will grow into a rushing stream in the coming year'.[18] The following year, they noted that about 12,000 migrants had come to the state over the past two years, 80 per cent of whom were British. And that, while few Scandinavians were coming to the state, 'a number of Northern Italians come, who have been subjected to medical inspection previous to embarking'.[19]

Naturally, these groups remained particularly concerned with increasing the number of women migrants. In 1926 the New South Wales Committee advocated 'a united effort on the part of women of Australia, to attract women of the United Kingdom here'.[20] By 1927 the South Australian Immigration Committee was most pleased to report that girls who were willing to do domestic work were now being given free passages (these had previously only been available to male migrants). Thus the committee hoped that these reforms would mean 'the stream of suitable women migrants to our shores may be greatly increased'.[21] They also continued to argue that women themselves needed to be involved in

---

[16] NCW of Queensland Minutes, 18 May 1925.

[17] *Dawn*, 16 February 1927, 11.

[18] National Council of Women of New South Wales, Biennial Reports for 1923–24 (Sydney: 1924), 23.

[19] National Council of Women of New South Wales, Biennial Reports for 1925–26, 20.

[20] Ibid. 6.

[21] The National Council of Women of South Australia: Report for 1927 (Adelaide: The Council, 1927), 18.

the selection process. In 1923 the New South Wales Council again urged that the selection of women migration should be undertaken 'by Australian women paid for the purpose'.[22] The Queensland Council also resolved in 1923 that 'there should be proper selection by competent persons in Great Britain of the girls to be sent to Australia such persons to be preferably Australian women appointed for the purpose'.[23] This was an issue pursued by all of the councils across the country into the 1930s. A resolution passed at the 1938 national conference urged that the Commonwealth government should 'employ a responsible woman officer overseas to encourage and recommend women immigrants of a good type for Australia'.[24]

But it was child migrants who were seen as particularly desirable. In 1924 the New South Wales Council's Immigration Committee reported its opinion that 'boy and girl migrants are the best for Australia. The Dreadnought scheme holds pride of place so far, having brought out over 4000 boys of a very fine type'.[25] In 1926 they repeated their opinion that 'boy and girl migrants were the best for Australia, for they are adaptable and absorb the conditions of the new country, and become useful members of the community', and reported with satisfaction again on the schemes in place.[26] In Western Australia The Women's Immigration Auxiliary Council also strongly promoted child migration schemes, praising the work done in this area at the Fairbridge Farm cottages. An

---

[22] National Council of Women of New South Wales, Biennial Reports for 1923–24, 23.

[23] NCW of Queensland Minutes, 20 August 1923. In the same year, the South Australian Immigration Committee presented virtually identical resolutions at a meeting with the Minister for Immigration: The National Council of Women of South Australia: Report for 1923 (Adelaide: The Council, 1923), np.

[24] Minutes of Annual Meeting, 15 September 1938, National Council of Women of Australia Records (hereafter NCW of Australia Minutes), MS 7583, box 12, Australian Manuscripts Collection, National Library of Australia, Canberra.

[25] National Council of Women of New South Wales, Biennial Reports for 1923–24, 23.

[26] National Council of Women of New South Wales, Biennial Reports for 1925–26, 20.

article in the *Dawn*, the journal of the Australian Federation of Women Voters, in 1924 reported their opinion that:

> no scheme has been so successful, or promises to be such a triumphant success … [who] could not fail to be inspired by the movement which has enabled these little citizens to be transplanted from the crowded areas of the Motherland to the vast open spaces of Western Australia.[27]

At the time Fairbridge housed some two hundred children.

Alongside the desire to increase the white population through immigration, however, was the fear that, as in the convict era, Australia might become a dumping ground for the lowest elements of British society. Calls for the appointment of women doctors and immigration officers went hand-in-hand with arguments for more stringent medical and other examinations to weed out undesirable migrants. Thus the New South Wales Council in 1921 proposed the need for 'a stricter examination of women immigrants, this examination to be conducted by women doctors, and a special stress be laid upon the necessity for excluding tubercular and venereal cases'.[28] As the president of the National Council of Women of South Australia expressed it in her annual address in 1926:

> People of weak physique and mentality are not likely to be able to adapt themselves readily in a strange land … for this reason it is a responsibility we owe to ourselves as well as to those who desire to settle successfully in Australia that a definite standard of heath and mentality should be required.[29]

In line with the women's movement's broader engagement with eugenics, and reflecting the explicit provisions of the *Immigration Restriction Act*, there was an increasing emphasis on the need to guard against the racial menace of 'mentally deficient' migrants. In 1921 the South Australian

---

[27] *Dawn*, 15 December 1924, 4.

[28] NCW of NSW Minutes, 22 August 1921.

[29] The National Council of Women of South Australia: Report for 1926 (Adelaide: The Council, 1926), 7.

Council's Immigration Committee urged that the medical examination of prospective immigrants 'should include mental and moral fitness'.[30] In 1929 the New South Wales Council wrote to the government to ascertain the number of immigrants who were currently housed in the state's mental asylums, and the type of insanity they suffered from.[31] They were most pleased to discover that these statistics were already contained in the department's annual reports. In 1932 they passed a resolution requesting that 'more stringent examinations on mental, physical and general suitability to Aust[ralian] conditions to be made'.[32] The Western Australian Women's Service Guilds had earlier argued in 1925 that there was a need for 'more supervision over mental defectives',[33] and strongly advocated in 1927 that 'to prevent mentally unfit girls being sent out stricter medical attention was necessary'.[34]

Healthy white babies

Although there was strong support for immigration, it was white babies who were viewed as the best new additions to the Australian population. This was a recurrent theme in discussions both of migration and of the broad arena of maternity and child rearing. The Adelaide School for Mothers, founded in 1909 with the motto 'Babies are the best immigrants', provides a striking example of this major arena of racial work. The school provided medical care and classes for new and prospective mothers, and also health checks for their babies. Its third annual report in 1912 reflected on the hope that the School would be 'of real value to our city by helping the mothers to rear healthier citizens'.[35] And it concluded with an appeal for funds which outlined that 'the work of the School is a national one, having for its object the saving of the

---

[30] 'Report of the National Council of Women of South Australia, September 1921'.

[31] NCW of NSW Minutes, 5 September 1929.

[32] NCW of NSW Minutes, 1 September 1932.

[33] *Dawn*, 15 January 1926, 9.

[34] *Dawn*, 15 March 1927, 9.

[35] *Annual report: Adelaide School for Mothers* (Adelaide: The School, 1912), 3.

babies, and the improvement of the physique of the nation'.[36] This need was heightened during the First World War, as a pamphlet describing the school's work observed:

> The war is depleting our country of her finest and most vigorous manhood. This will weaken her not only in the present, but in future generations. The soundest and healthiest men are needed for the battlefield while the less fit are spared to be fathers of the coming race.[37]

The 1917 report appealed urgently for funds to support them in this cause, which again linked the issues of immigration and reproduction: 'the waste of War must be repaired, which gives an enhanced value to every child born. Therefore we make an urgent appeal for more support from all who have Australia's future welfare at heart. It is cheaper to save the babies than to bring out immigrants'.[38]

By 1923 the School had expanded its work considerably, reflecting the degree of support they had garnered. By this stage, they were operating 30 Baby Health Centres and employed 11 nurses and seven honorary medical staff. It was claimed that the total attendance at these centres was 22,372, and in addition their nurses had made 19,700 home visits.[39] In 1930 this increased to an attendance of 70,706 and 38,471 home visits.[40] And by 1935 it was claimed that the association had made contact with almost every baby born in the state that year.[41] Its primary stated aim in 1924 was 'to bring about a reduction in the Infant Mortality and to build up a healthier and stronger race'.[42] This aim was expanded on the following year when the association's report observed:

---

[36] *Annual report of the School for Mothers' Institute* (Adelaide: The School, 1924), 5.

[37] *School for Mothers Institute: Its aims and objects* (Adelaide: The School, [1916]).

[38] *Annual report of the School for Mothers' Institute* (Adelaide: The School, 1917), 7.

[39] *Annual report of the School for Mothers' Institute and Baby Health Centre* (Adelaide: The School, 1923), 2–3.

[40] *Annual report: Mothers and Babies' Health Association* (Adelaide: The School, 1930), 3.

[41] *Annual report: Mothers and Babies' Health Association* (Adelaide: The School, 1935), 3.

[42] *Annual report of the School for Mothers' Institute and Baby Health Centre* (Adelaide: The School, 1924), 5.

The work of helping mothers to keep themselves and their babies well is of the greatest importance to the State. It reduces the infant mortality, the number of inmates in Hospitals, Home for the Blind, Deaf and Dumb, etc., and helps to build up a stronger and healthier race.[43]

Fulfilling this ambition would require enormous work, as the medical officer Dr Helen Mayo explained in 1935, 'The aim of this Association is to reach as many mothers and babies as possible; to advise the mothers in matters of infant care and management and to keep the babies under constant observation, so that a healthier generation may grow up'.[44]

This group was clearly highly concerned about the 'quality' of the new Australians being produced. The *Parents' book* it published went into at least 16 editions, and indicates the continuing centrality of eugenic ideals to its agenda, and the degree of surveillance and medical intervention which was required to realise this critical national mission.[45] As the opening paragraph of the 1940 edition read:

The proper care of the infant should begin long before it is born, since to produce healthy children the parents must themselves be healthy. It is said that every infant has the right be 'well born.' Up to the present, however, that only means that an infant has the moral right to be born in a reasonable environment, and of parents free from certain diseases or defects, which may be communicated to it before or immediately after birth … It is the object of this little book to give parents information in a simple form which will help them in the task of bringing up young Australians to be healthy men and women and good citizens of our Commonwealth.

---

[43] *Annual report of the School for Mothers' Institute and Baby Health Centre* (Adelaide: The School, 1925), 2.

[44] *Annual report: Mothers and Babies' Health Association* (Adelaide: The School, 1935), 19.

[45] On this issue see also Kereen Reiger, *The disenchantment of the home: modernizing the Australian family, 1880–1940* (Oxford University Press, Melbourne, 1985); Lisa Featherstone, '"The value of the Victorian infant": whiteness and the emergence of paediatrics in Late Colonial Australia', in *Historicising whiteness: transnational perspectives on the construction of an identity*, eds. Leigh Boucher, Jane Carey and Katherine Ellinghaus (Melbourne: RMIT Publishing 2007).

Good citizenship was linked to good health. Its author, Dr Margaret Harper, a physician at the royal Alexandra Hospital for Children and Honorary Medical Director of the Tresillian Mothercraft Training School, went on to advise that 'there is nothing to be dreaded in the fulfilment of the natural destiny of the human race'. But a mother's ability to cope with pregnancy 'cannot be adequate or normal unless she herself is an efficient normal human being'.[46]

An earlier publication, *The Australian mothercraft book*, produced in 1938, included chapters from leading health professionals from both Australia and Britain. Its foreword noted that 'The care and welfare of the mother and her children is of supreme importance for the happiness of her home and the future of the State'.[47] The introduction, written by Helen Mayo, one of the key founding figures of the association and chairman of the editorial committee, opened thus: 'This book is intended for the instruction of women in the art of mothercraft, so that by a popular extension of the knowledge gained by scientific research a healthier generation may arise'. She outlined recent decreases in maternal and infant mortality rates, but said there was still 'room for improvement':

> This improvement will be brought about when mothers learn how to prepare for their children and how to manage them during the difficult years of infancy ... To help parents bring healthy babies into the world and keep them sound in body and mind is a work of national importance, and if this little book furthers that end it will have attained its object.[48]

Its chapters contained covered topics from 'supervision during pregnancy' to 'Kidney and bladder conditions' to 'varicose veins', breastfeeding to the importance of sunlight, cleanliness to care of the eyes

---

[46] Margaret Harper, *The parents' book*, published under the auspices of the Royal Society for the Welfare of Mothers and Babies (Sydney: Angus & Robertson, 1940), 2 & 9.

[47] *The Australian mothercraft book*, published for the Mothers and Babies Health Association of South Australia (Adelaide: Rigby, 1938), 3.

[48] Helen Mayo, 'Introduction' in *The Australian mothercraft book*, 5. Mayo was a leading figure of the women's movement in South Australia, and one of the state's first woman doctors.

and skin. There was a considerable emphasis on the psychology of child rearing, and how to deal with 'problems' such as thumb sucking and masturbation. The first chapter, on 'The expectant mother', advised that only three things were needed to 'ensure the birth of a healthy child. *Healthy parents*, suitable and *healthy surroundings* and *proper medical care and attention* during pregnancy and at the time of birth'.[49]

The interest in increasing the quality of Australian babies was widely shared, as reports in the *Dawn* reveal. In 1928 the journal reported on a lecture by a visiting British doctor, Haden Guest, at the Feminist Club in Sydney:

> You are interested in the question of migration. I would suggest the improvement of the general standard of 'migrants by birth' in this country. Real politics in the future will deal with two fundamental questions—the improvement of the health of the children and education. In these two matters, women will have first call.

His audience were presumably most gratified by his concluding remark that 'There yet remains a very great field of work to be done, which must and can be done only by women'.[50] Later the same year, the *Dawn* reported the remarkably similar opinions expressed by Dr P.K. Roest of Holland in a lecture to the Theosophical Society in Sydney on 'Modern motherhood'. Dr Roest argued that women needed to take a greater role in public life and in politics to complement their influence in the raising of children. He argued that:

> The whole field of positive eugenics is waiting exploration ... Nothing less than radiant, exuberant health for the nation's children can content women who bring the hearts of mothers to the task of nation building ... women legislators, backed by the intelligent opinion of Australian women, [will] give precedence to those things which mean the re-creation of humanity in the likeness of a nobler and more beautiful type.

---

[49] *The Australian mothercraft book*, 9. Emphasis in original.
[50] *Dawn*, 15 February 1928, 6–7.

And he concluded that: '[this] field awaits the labourer and the sooner Australian women realise their destiny the better for the nation.'[51]

A major plank of the women's movement's activities in this area revolved around campaigns for child endowment. This was seen as having far-reaching significance. As the New South Wales branch of the Australian Federation of Women Voters framed the issue at their annual meeting in 1928, child endowment would result in 'increased production; decrease in maternal mortality ... greater efficiency', and more broadly 'the promotion of a healthier race'.[52] In 1929, an article in the *Dawn* linked the women's movement's campaigns on motherhood, child endowment, maternal and infant mortality, world peace, widows pensions, and the nationality of married women as vital issues for the forthcoming elections, and urged readers to 'return candidates who are with the women of Australia in the great fight for the preservation and betterment of the race'.[53]

Locating race

Amidst all this racial fervour, however, there was remarkably little discussion of the 'Aboriginal problem' of the day. The question was not entirely ignored. Both the Australian Federation of Women Voters and, to a lesser extent, the National Council of Women, supported various initiatives relating to Aboriginal welfare, particularly the appointment of white women 'protectors'. These discussions have attracted considerable scholarly attention.[54] While some scholarship has thus characterised the

---

[51] *Dawn*, 19 June 1928, 10–1.

[52] *Dawn*, 22 May 1928.

[53] *Dawn*, 25 September 1929, 2.

[54] Fiona Paisley, *Loving protection? Australian feminism and Aboriginal women's rights, 1919–1939* (Melbourne: Melbourne University Press, 2000), and 'No back streets in the bush: 1920s and 1930s pro-Aboriginal white women's activism and the trans-Australia railway', *Australian Feminist Studies* 12.25 (1997): 119–37; Marilyn Lake, 'Childbearers as rights-bearers: feminist discourse on the rights of Aboriginal and non-Aboriginal mothers in Australia, 1920–1950', *Women's History Review* 8.2 (1999): 347–63.

women's movement of this period as 'pro-Aboriginal', the highly racialised frames within which such issues were discussed mean they must be read with caution. Moreover, as Alison Holland has suggested 'one of the primary reasons for women protectors was to act as guardians of the white race: to stop miscegenation and prevent the growth of a 'half-caste' community'.[55] Certainly this was evident in the National Council of Women's discussions of such issues, which largely reflected the desire to prevent 'miscegenation' by banning contact between white men and Aboriginal women. The 1926 national conference passed four motions urging restrictions on the marriages and movements of Aboriginal peoples towards this end.[56]

The Australian Federation of Women Voters was certainly radical in its demands for more funding for welfare and education, and that land be reserved to 'preserve' and 'protect' the remaining Indigenous population. Nevertheless, they envisaged a large degree of surveillance and control, and certainly did not view the majority of Aboriginal people as ready for the 'privilege' of full citizenship rights. They also generally supported the policy of removing 'half-caste' children from their families. As a long article in the *Dawn* in 1936 argued:

> The suggestion of the Australian Aborigines' Amelioration Association and other bodies, that those people should be drafted into settlements where they might be trained to be self-supporting, and later to be raised to a standard which would permit of their absorption into the white community, has been repeatedly ignored ... These children should be given a training equal to that of white children and taught from the beginning that their destiny is absorption in the white community. There is certainly a need for them to be removed from native camps and their degenerating

---

[55] Alison Holland, 'The campaign for women protectors: gender, race and frontier between the wars', *Australian Feminist Studies* 16.34 (2001): 31. See also Alison Holland, 'Wives and mothers like ourselves: exploring white women's intervention in the politics of race, 1920s–1940s', *Australian Historical Studies* 32.117 (2001): 292–310.

[56] NCW of Australia Minutes, 26 July 1926, box 12.

influence and to be cared for in clean, health-giving, uplifting surroundings.[57]

Indeed, most white women 'pro-Aboriginal' activists largely shared the racial beliefs of those they were opposing, even if they disagreed about what this should mean in terms of racial policy. Even Constance Cooke, one of the most radical of these campaigners, subscribed to prevailing beliefs about Aboriginal primitivism. In an address to the Anti-Slavery and Aborigines Protection Society in London in July 1927 she began by observing that:

> Australian aborigines [were] living representatives of the Stone Age, and also our distant forebears, their blood grouping being the same as that of the Caucasian races, quite distant from that of the negro.

She repeated the opinion of some anthropologists that: 'the gap between their civilisation and ours was too wide to be bridged, and that segregation was their only chance'. In a Model Aboriginal State, overseen by a small number of white government officials, 'they could evolve slowly from the hunting to the pastoral stage of culture'. They could be taught agricultural and other skills and eventually 'they would be competent to govern themselves'.[58]

Nevertheless, discussions of Aboriginal issues were extremely limited. This neglect might be considered surprising given this is widely understood as the most pressing racial concern of the period. In reality this activism was sustained by a very small number of women who developed an intense interest in this area. Far more time and energy was devoted to securing the future of white Australia. There was a wide field of important work for women to do here, not only in the vital production of healthy white babies but also in public health, education, and other forms of 'expert' and professional employment. If we are to appreciate the extent to which racial consciousness pervaded the women's movement,

---

[57] *Dawn*, 16 December 1936, 8.
[58] *Dawn*, 15 February 1928, 12.

and indeed white Australian society at large, we must turn to their extensive anxieties about whiteness. These discussions formed a major domain in which the 'grammars of race' were being articulated and sustained. They thus provide significant new insights into white imaginings of the ideal national population, which were at the foundation of Australia's repressive racial structures.

12

Whiteness, maternal feminism and the working mother, 1900–1960

Shurlee Swain, Australian Catholic University
Patricia Grimshaw, University of Melbourne
Ellen Warne, Australian Catholic University

In the decades immediately following the granting of the suffrage, middle- and working-class women, campaigning through separate organisations to claim citizenship rights, were able to construct a maternalist politics, drawing on their shared identities as actual or potential mothers.[1] Broadly defined, feminist scholars have used the notion of maternalism to characterise policies that associated women with the interests of home and family, built on the assumption that women's nurturing work could be equated with male labour, their contribution to the nation being to raise its future citizens.[2] Drawing on their knowledge of existing earning capacities, and the difficulties facing women who attempted to combine motherhood with waged work, most argued that women with children would be far better served by the payment of an allowance to mothers that recognised their contribution as

---

[1] Marilyn Lake, *Getting equal: the history of Australian feminism* (Sydney: Allen & Unwin, 1999), 56.

[2] Linda Gordon, *Pitied but not entitled: single mothers and the history of welfare 1890–1935* (New York: The Free Press, 1994), 55; Molly Ladd-Taylor, *Mother-work: women, child welfare, and the state, 1890–1930* (Urbana and Chicago: University of Illinois Press, 1994), 3. Joanne Goodwin, *Gender and the politics of welfare reform: mothers' pensions in Chicago, 1911–29* (Chicago and London: University of Chicago Press, 1997), 9.

child rearers and child bearers.[3] Although the goal of a mother's wage was never realised, such maternalist feminist campaigns re-shaped the notion of ideal motherhood and were influential in the introduction of payments and services which made it easier for women to devote themselves fully to the maternal role.

It was a campaign grounded in a mostly disguised racial discourse. Whiteness, Cheryl Harris has argued, needs to be understood as 'an active property' that has been 'used and enjoyed'.[4] And as Ruth Frankenberg has pointed out, a focus on whiteness draws attention to the fact that all systems of differentiation shape the privileged as well as the oppressed.[5] Our investigations into the historical debates on women's right to work, or not to work, stand to benefit from a firmer emphasis on the privileges whiteness affords those who are designated white. This is so even where the main players are protagonists for others in need, and indeed for progressive state intervention that led to the welfare state. This chapter focuses on maternalist feminist campaigns in the first half of the 20th century about married women's work and the privileging of the status of the citizen mother, arguing that their focus on disabilities of gender disguised untested assumptions about the privileges of race. Feminists who sustained a watching brief on women's labour issues could exclude quite unthinkingly Indigenous women and migrant women of colour from their conceptual frame.[6] These activists could ignore, also, working women of southern and eastern European origin whom they regarded as 'not quite white' or 'probationary white', in the terms of

---

[3] For a discussion of the mother's allowance, see Lake, *Getting equal*; Patricia Grimshaw, Shurlee Swain and Ellen Warne, 'Constructing the working mother: Australian perspectives 1920 to 1970', *Hecate* 31.2 (December 2005): 18–30.

[4] Cheryl Harris, 'Whiteness as property', in *Critical race theory: key writings that formed a movement*, eds. Kimberle Crenshaw et al. (New York: New Press, 1997), 282.

[5] Ruth Frankenberg, *White women, race matters: the social construction of whiteness* (Minneapolis: University of Minnesota Press, 1993), 1.

[6] For a critique see Aileen Moreton-Robinson, 'Troubling business: difference and whiteness within feminism', *Australian Feminist Studies* 15.33 (2000): 344–45.

critical race theorists.[7] This was so because such migrants differed in appearance, language, religion and expectations of family from mainstream Australians. The women who were prominent in liberal and labour groups of the women's movement from the turn of the century were shaped as much by their race as by their gender and class affiliations. They therefore situated their arguments for women in the new nation within an uninterrogated assumption of its white destiny. In this the category woman was implicitly designated as white.[8]

Activists' opposition to colonial practices

Activists of the 20th-century women's movement set their faces against practices of the colonial era, when government assistance to families was minimal, and the charities that administered emergency relief recognised no right to support. In good times and bad, families were expected to make the decisions about workforce participation that would ensure their economic independence. Given the lower wages available to females, and the labour required to maintain a home and care for the children, the mother was the least profitable family member to put into the workforce, but women with absent or inadequate breadwinners, and without children of working age, had little choice. In a society that abhorred dependence, such poor women were seen primarily as workers rather than mothers. While, occasionally, there were voices regretting the strain such labour placed on mothers, the necessity itself was seldom questioned.[9]

---

[7] See Matthew Frye Jacobsen, *Whiteness of a different colour: European immigrants and the alchemy of race* (Cambridge: Harvard University Press, 1998); David Roediger, *The wages of whiteness: race and the making of the American working class*, rev. ed. (London: Verso, 1999); Vron Ware, *Beyond the pale: white women, race, and history,* (London/New York: Verso, 1992).

[8] Moreton-Robinson, 346.

[9] The centrality of married women's wages and the structural constraints on their ability to work are discussed in Desley Deacon, *Managing gender: the state, the new middle class and women workers 1830–1930* (Melbourne: Oxford University Press, 1989), 144–50; Anne O'Brien, *Poverty's prison: the poor in New South Wales 1880–1918* (Melbourne: Melbourne

'Is the mother in a position to support the child you referred to?' NSW child rescuer, George Ardill, was asked as he discussed the case of a child of eight, begging 'under the pretext of selling newspapers', before the NSW Select Committee on the Children's Protection Bill in 1891. His response, that 'Yes, she is able to get sufficient work … Laundry work and needle work', served only to condemn her further, not because she was neglecting her child through working but because she was not working hard enough to keep him safely at home.[10] If such mothers struggled with their dual role, charity workers and policy makers believed that they should sacrifice their children rather than their employment.[11] Fairer wages, and better conditions, particularly in areas where work could be done at home, were advanced as solutions to the poor working mother's plight, but if all else failed the children should be removed.[12] 'They will not part with their children; they would sooner die,' J.P. Grant, the Chief Inspector for the Benevolent Society of NSW, lamented.[13] Yet removal

---

University Press, 1988), 89–91. The international literature makes a similar observation. See Jane Lewis, ed., *Woman's welfare, women's rights* (London: Croom Helm, 1983), 8; Mary Kinnear, *A female economy: women's work in a Prairie Province, 1870–1970* (Montreal and Kingston: McGill-Queen's University Press, 1998), 6; and Wendy Gambler, *The female economy: The millinery and dressmaking trades, 1860-1930* (Urbana and Chicago: University of Illinois Press, 1997), 46–7.

[10] *Report of the Select Committee on the Children's Protection Bill and the Infants' Protection Bill*, Votes and Proceedings of the New South Wales Legislative Council, 1891–92, vol. 49 pt.1, 1085.

[11] New South Wales Parliamentary Debates (First Series), vol. LXXXIV (Sydney: William Applegate Gullick, Government Printer, 1896), 2099.

[12] Report of the Chief Inspector of Factories on the 'Sweating System' in Connexion with the Clothing Trade in the Colony of Victoria, Votes and Proceedings of the Victorian Legislative Assembly, 1890, vol. 3, 1241; 'Report of the Shops and Factories Commission, Together with Minutes of Proceedings, Evidences and Appendices' (Adelaide: 1892), New South Wales Parliamentary Debates, 1896, 2742; 'The Population Question', *Woman's Sphere* 10 May 1890; *Royal Commission on Charitable Institutions*, Votes and Proceedings of the Victorian Legislative Assembly, 1892–93, vol. 4, 529.

[13] Royal Commission on Public Charities, 'Minutes of Evidence', Votes and Proceedings of the New South Wales Legislative Council, 1898, vol. 58 pt. 1, 68.

was the only solution that charity could offer. As the superintendent of a Victorian orphanage commented:

> a poor woman who has perhaps to go out washing or into service, cannot do both; she cannot keep the children in the home and go to service, and it is a great charity to take the children from the mother, and get her to give some of her earnings towards the maintenance of the institution.[14]

The policies developed by the various Aborigines' Protection Boards were based on a similar premise. In many states, whether on reserves or attempting to survive as free people, women were sent to work in order to be able to support themselves.[15] If that meant that they were unable to provide for their children then the children would be removed, or kept on reserves or missions.

In the early-20th-century concern for the declining white birth rate led to a re-evaluation of white women's role, resulting in changes in social policy designed to free some poor white mothers from the necessity to earn a living. The system of arbitration, introduced by the new Commonwealth, had institutionalised a male breadwinner model, paying all men a family wage, while limiting women, irrespective of their family circumstances, to between 50 and 60 per cent of the male wage.[16] While feminists continued to argue for fair wages for women they increasingly paired this with a claim much more amenable to male labour activists: the duty of the state to support the citizen mother to stay in the home.[17] Labour women, who held few illusions about the often desperate lives of mothers working in order to provide support for their children, joined with middle-class feminists in the hope that by privileging the mother's

---

[14] Royal Commission on Charitable Institutions, 746.

[15] New South Wales Aborigines Protection Board, *Report for the Year 1900* (Sydney: Government Printer, 1901), 5.

[16] Diane Kirkby, 'Arbitration and the fight for economic justice', in *Foundations of arbitration: the origins and effects of state compulsory arbitration 1890–1914*, eds. Stuart Macintyre and Richard Mitchell (Melbourne: Oxford University Press, 1989).

[17] *Woman Voter*, 27 April 1915. For a discussion of the concept of the citizen mother in Australia see Lake, *Getting equal.*

right to support they would eliminate their need to undertake waged work.[18] While the solution to the problems arising from women's dependence on men lay in equal pay, the arrival of children, trade union organiser Jean Daley argued, served to 'complicate the situation'.[19] This dilemma could best be solved if the care of children was redefined as work, with all mothers rewarded accordingly.[20]

It was because mothers without reliable male breadwinners came to be valued for their whiteness that support could be garnered for policies which would support them to stay at home. Towards the end of the 19th century, state children's departments, influenced by the experience of women on boarding-out committees and state children's councils, began to grant some mothers boarding-out allowances for their own children. The payments were conditional—intended to 'assist' but not 'maintain', a recognition of 'merit' rather than an entitlement—but they quickly became the primary means by which the states assisted poor children.[21] It was the conditionality of such payments that effectively racialised access. If the employment of married women, as the overwhelmingly male 'experts' agreed, led to 'contraception, neglect of homes and husbands, abandonment of breastfeeding, farming out of babies and increased infant death', it followed that married women's employment threatened

---

[18] Factory inspectors in Victoria, for example, blamed mothers who needed to work for the prevalence of outwork arguing that they 'can afford to work at almost any rate of pay'. Report of the Chief Inspector of Factories on the 'Sweating System', 1235. For evidence as to the attitude of labour feminists to working mothers see Lake, *Getting Equal*, 74.

[19] Cited in Marilyn Lake, 'The independence of women and the brotherhood of man: debates in the Labour Movement over equal pay and motherhood endowment in the 1920s', *Labour History* 63 (1992): 12.

[20] Lake, *Getting equal*, 72.

[21] Item 3: Notes re work in the State Children's Relief Board, etc., c.1881–c.1920, Correspondence between Minister and Board on the subject of altering Monetary Regulations against the Recommendation of the Board, published in the forefront of the *Annual Report* 1913–14, 20 October 1914, President, State Children's Relief Board, to The Under Secretary, Department of Public Instruction, 9–10, Sir Charles Kinnaird Mackellar Papers, 1871–1922, ML MSS 2100.

the survival of white Australia.[22] Such concerns resonated with a sentimental idealisation of motherhood, which argued that motherhood and employment were incompatible because the mother was the best carer for her child, providing the grounds on which the old concerns about pauperisation and dependency could be overthrown, with women's maternal responsibilities increasingly seen as the essence of their claims to citizenship. The good mother was now defined as the mother who stayed at home. Infant welfare centres and kindergartens, which supported the stay-at-home mother in her mothering, replaced crèches as a focus of charitable effort, and pressure was exerted on government to transform the rudimentary payments for the support of children into pensions for widows and other unsupported mothers.

Working mothers of a different colour

In most such policy-making the imagined mother was implicitly white. The conditionality of the early state payments ensured that an applicant had to demonstrate her worth in order to gain access to the 'privilege'. The linking of maternalist arguments with wider concerns about white Australia ensured that part of that worth was the whiteness of her offspring. Outside the white community, older models of mothering continued to prevail. Amongst immigrant families of non-English-speaking background, a working mother was as often indicative of a sense of partnership as it was of male inadequacy. Mrs Chun See Tock migrated to Australia as a 20-year-old in 1890, settling in Melbourne's Chinatown where her husband was the manager of a cabinet-making factory. In addition to giving birth to four children over the period 1892 to 1909, she worked as a housekeeper and from 1915 served in the grocery store located on the ground floor of the family home in Lonsdale

---

[22] J. Kelly, 'Not merely minded: care and education for the young children of working women in Sydney: the Sydney Day Nursery and Nursery Schools Association, 1905–1945' (PhD thesis, University of Sydney, 1988), 43.

Street.[23] Amongst the first generation of Italian migrants a similar pattern prevailed, the women drawing on traditional skills and embracing new trades, eager to augment the family income in whatever way was available, with the children expected to help when they got in from school.[24] Giuseppina, for example, migrated alone in 1926, later sponsoring her fiancé to join her in Melbourne. They had three children together and ran a successful greengrocer's business which supported the family.[25]

Not surprisingly, working mothers struggled to keep state 'benevolence' at bay. Koori woman Olive Jackson recalled that her grandmother kept the family 'on the move, never staying anywhere long, always moving on before the welfare caught up with us ... It just wasn't safe for us to have a settled home'. She took work wherever she could get it, feeding the children from leftovers salvaged from the kitchens in which she was employed.[26]

Aboriginal families also often worked as a unit. In the more remote areas of the country, it was often women and children who came to perform hard physical work that would have been judged unsuitable for Europeans, digging post holes and foundations, carting materials and guarding stock, as well as undertaking domestic work in station homesteads.[27] In the more closely settled districts, Aboriginal families took work whenever it was available, relying on rations on the missions

---

[23] Sophie Couchman, '"Oh, I would like to see Maggie Moore again!"': Selected women of Melbourne's Chinatown', in *After the rush: regulation, participation, and Chinese communities in Australia 1860–1940*, eds. Sophie Couchman, John Fitzgerald and Paul Macgregor (Kingsbury: Otherland Literary Journal, 2004), 174–5.

[24] Julia Church, *Per l'Australia: the story of Italian migration* (Melbourne: The Miegunyah Press, 2005), 62.

[25] Ibid. 51.

[26] The Aboriginal Community Elders Service and Kate Harvey, *Aboriginal Elders' voices: stories of the 'tide of history'* (Melbourne: Aboriginal Community Elders Service, 2003), 18.

[27] Mary Anne Jebb, *Blood, sweat and welfare: a history of white bosses and Aboriginal pastoral workers* (Crawley: University of Western Australia Press, 2002), 93–4.

when it was not. Koori man Phillip Pepper remembered working alongside his parents from the age of six. 'Our family went hop-picking at Briagolong and I can remember Mum and Dad would be each side of the bin, and Dora and me were small and we'd be on the side plucking the hops off … We'd camp on the river or live in huts on the farms in picking times'.[28] Ellen Atkinson, whose four children were born between 1919 and 1927, supported her family in a similar way. 'Eddy used to do a lot of carpentering and fishing. We used to camp and fish along the Murray and sell fish in the towns'. In the harvesting season the family would 'go up for the good pea and bean picking in New South Wales', then move to the Victorian fruit-growing towns, camping for a few weeks wherever work offered but always going 'home to Cummera', where they could subsist on savings.[29]

Many Aboriginal mothers were compelled to support their children without the assistance of a male breadwinner. Pepper's mother-in-law taught her daughters to make the grass dilly-bags which she sold to support the family between bean-picking seasons.[30] At Coonabarabran Janet Robinson's mother and grandmother walked from the mission into the town to do laundry. As her mother also did domestic work it was the grandmother who took responsibility for the children:

> She used to do washin' at a boardin' place, Harper's, and that's where we used to come and learn how to hang the sheets out and the shirts, properly, they were all white things, and then Mum used to come and iron.[31]

The new ideal did not acknowledge such racial difference. As the good mother now stayed at home to care for her children, non-white mothers

---

[28] Phillip Pepper and Tess De Araugo, *You are what you make yourself to be: the story of a Victorian Aboriginal family 1842–1980* (Melbourne: Hyland House, 1989), 53–4.

[29] Diane Barwick, 'Aunty Ellen: The pastor's wife', in *Fighters and singers: the lives of some Aboriginal women*, eds. Isobel White, Diane Barwick and Betty Meehan (Sydney: George Allen and Unwin, 1985), 185.

[30] Pepper and De Araugo, 76.

[31] Margaret Somerville et al., *The sun dancin': people and place in Coonabarabran* (Canberra: Aboriginal Studies Press, 1994), 112.

were vulnerable to criticism for neglecting their children by continuing to work. Aboriginal women, uniformly excluded from all government benefits, were left even more firmly constrained within the older construction, all too often losing their children because it was assumed that they would be unable to support them.[32] Other women whose whiteness was open to dispute could faced a similar struggle if they came to the attention of child welfare officials to whom the absence of a mother at work was evidence of neglect.

Not quite the 50s' ideal families

In the immediate postwar era, the idealisation of the stay-at-home mother remained unchallenged, but access to the ideal continued to be racialised. While the postwar migration program allowed married women to be supported by their husbands, mothers who came alone had no such protection. Employment was important 'from an assimilation aspect', an official noted, lest the women's 'continued idleness ruin what slight incentive may remain to accept some responsibility for their own and their children's welfare'.[33] Coming from countries with very different constructions of motherhood, and quarantined by their lack of English from the dominance of domesticity as portrayed in the Australian media, many of the married women assumed that they would work in order to build the family's future in the new country as well. The willingness of the Australian government to advertise their availability to potential employers and provide child care centres in migrant holding centres would suggest that such women were seen as provisional or probationary

---

[32] *Royal Commission on National Insurance, third progress report: destitution allowances* (Melbourne: Government Printer, 1927), 9; Anna Haebich, *Broken circles: fragmenting Indigenous families, 1800–2000* (Fremantle: Fremantle Arts Centre Press, 2000).

[33] G. A. M. Edson to Secretary Department of Immigration, 1 November 1950, Widows with Dependent Children at Immigration Centres —Employment and Accommodation, Department of Immigration File, A434 (A434/1), 1950/3/27104, National Archives of Australia, Canberra.

whites, more valued for their productive than for their reproductive potential.[34]

Women of Greek, Italian and Yugoslavian origin constituted the first large cohort of married women with pre-school children to enter the Australian industrial workforce. By the 1960s they constituted 30 per cent of the married female workforce, clustered in the factory and service sectors.[35] Commentators struggled to explain this over-representation. 'I only work because of the money—we need it', was a common response, but why did migrant women see their families as more needy than their non-immigrant neighbours?[36] They had few other thoughts than finding ways to increase the household budget, in order to establish the family, buy a home and provide opportunities for their children. As one woman wrote bluntly on her survey form, she worked to ensure that her children wouldn't need to work in these 'shit' factories. Yet there was little recognition in the Australian community of the difficulties these women faced in a new country. Excluded, as provisional whites, from the ideals of domesticity embraced by the non-immigrant community, they were nevertheless criticised for 'choosing' to work and neglecting their families. When sub-standard child care arrangements were exposed, the media coverage that followed condemned the migrant mothers irresponsible enough to entrust their children to such inferior care, rather than highlighting the problem which the absence of reliable child care posed to mothers who wanted or needed to work.

---

[34] Debates about the use of such facilities placed additional strains on women who had only recently arrived in Australia. See: Letter from N.N. Drummond to Olga Leschen, 30 July 1952, A445 220/52/13, National Archives of Australia, Canberra; Letter to Mr Robson from N.N. Drummond, 19 May 1953, A445 220/52/13, National Archives of Australia, Canberra; and Analysis of Creche Services over the period 1 February–3 July 1953, A445 220/52/13, National Archives of Australia, Canberra.

[35] Katie Richmond, 'The workforce participation of married women in Australia', in *Social change in Australia: readings in sociology*, ed. Donald E. Edgar (Melbourne: Cheshire, 1974), 301–2.

[36] Ibid. 302.

Migrant women understood their work as struggle rather than selfishness. The 'struggle of having little kids, with latch keys, basically who let themselves in after school and working long, long hours … was what they did to get ahead'.[37] It was a struggle which they undertook on their own. Government services designed to assist mothers and babies assumed the presence of the mother at home. Australian kindergartens that emphasised child education and development, and opened only for brief morning or afternoon sessions, were part of another world. Most migrant women were not used to factory work and few enjoyed their jobs. Children were matter of fact about the experience of being latch-key children, recognising that their mothers 'were trying to supplement the family income as best they could'.[38] Unions were slow to recognise migrant women workers as part of their constituency rather than threats to white labour. The overwhelmingly male Anglo-Celtic leadership often did not see the women's concerns as legitimate industrial issues.

Aboriginal mothers were even more firmly excluded from the suburban maternal dream. In Brisbane, Aboriginal poet Kath Walker (Oodgeroo Noonuccal), left her children unattended while she did domestic work for Lady Phyllis Cilento. Freed from her domestic responsibilities, Cilento became the leading campaigner for maternal and infant welfare in Queensland, yet did not consider assisting her maid to test her eligibility for the government assistance which would have enabled her to care for her children at home.[39] Walker was one of the many Aboriginal women who, during and after the Second World War, had come to the cities in search of work. Young women educated on the missions might gain access to white-collar work, but most found

---

[37] Anne Sgro, interview with authors, 29 February 2003.

[38] Joy Damousi, 'Growing up in a Greek family', in *Fitzroy: Melbourne's first suburb* ed. Cutten History Committee of the Fitzroy History Society (Melbourne: Melbourne University Press, 1991), 253.

[39] Susan Mitchell, *The matriarchs: twelve Australian women talk about their lives to Susan Mitchell* (Melbourne: Penguin, 1987) 212.

themselves confined to laundry work and cleaning on temporary and sporadic contracts. They might take a young child with them or leave them with a relation or neighbour, and worked if possible while their older children were in school. In rural areas, Indigenous mothers worked alongside their male partners, looking to wider family and community networks for child care. Alongside the men, Aboriginal women undertook fruit picking and canning, vegetable harvesting (potatoes, tomatoes, asparagus, millet), rabbiting, and also heavier tasks such as fencing, burning off, droving and shepherding. These Aboriginal working mothers sought to enhance the family income, but a meagre subsistence was their usual achievement. They wanted to see their children get ahead and have better opportunities than they had had, but seldom enjoyed this satisfaction. The nearer such families moved to non-Aboriginal communities, the more closely their mothering was monitored by Aboriginal welfare officers who had the power to remove children they believed to be subject to neglect.[40] Mainstream services designed to support the mother at home condemned the Aboriginal mother for falling short of community standards, perpetuating a cycle in which Indigenous women, working to support the white economy, lost custody of their children who were in turn trained to perform similar marginal but supportive labour.

Ruby Langford, who was born in rural New South Wales in 1934, began to work as a casual cleaner at 15. At the age of 17, she had her first child. Subsequently she travelled with her partner through outback New South Wales, where the couple took what work they could find, returning briefly to relatives' communities for the births of her children, eventually eight in all. She described with graphic detail the trials of undertaking the hard work they were given, with young children around them and often pregnant into the bargain. On one occasion her partner heard there was a job on a property burning off. His mother lent them some pots and pans

---

[40] Haebich, *Broken circles*.

and a billycan, and they had an advance from the job to buy some food. All they had was the car, which broke down, and the clothes they wore. They lived in the car with four children under four, the youngest a small baby. 'We slept in the car. There was Gordon and me and the four children, and when it rained we locked ourselves in the car till it stopped'. The kids played around the camp all day. When she was pregnant again they built a lean-to out of hessian bags. It was, she said, hard, physical gut-busting work. She assisted with fencing, sawing wood and digging holes for the posts. When they had a job looking after a property, she fed the chickens and milked the cows while he ploughed and broke horses. But often she assisted in his tasks. Even when pregnant or newly delivered of a child the work had to be done. There was never enough money; they killed rabbits or stole a sheep when they were desperate for food. Despite their hard work they lived worse than the poorest whites, she thought. And they never seemed to get ahead: always, when they had a nest egg, some family crisis would absorb it and they would be again living day by day, virtually penniless.[41]

In the postwar era, the wages of both migrant and Indigenous mothers, while low, were essential to sustain household economies. The women seldom had much choice about whether to work, or what kind of occupation to take, and had no time to gain training or education. Most of these mothers considered themselves to be the primary carers of children, and the provider of family services. The aspirations they held related to their children, not to themselves. Their coping mechanisms for hard, alienating, low-paid work lay in their identification as 'mothers', but their understanding of good mothering was often in conflict with the dominant discourse within the Anglo-Celtic community.

---

[41] Ruby Langford, *Don't take your love to town* (Melbourne: Penguin, 1988).

Conclusion

The women's movement in the first half of the 20th century, whether liberal women working within female-only organisations or labour women aligned with the unionists, struggled to carve a place of dignity and just reward for their sex in their capacity as mothers. With limited fertility control, with restricted waged work for women, with little or no support for working mothers, their efforts made some sense. Worldwide in the West, only Marxists offered alternative models of married women's labour, and few in Australia listened to them. But their blindness had sad costs for many other women. The activists, immersed in discourses of whiteness, had little empathy with the numbers of Indigenous and migrant women, poor and marginalised, who escaped their sympathetic consideration.

When a new wave of feminism emerged in the 1960s, some sections of the women's movement, those who situated the right of women to work as central to their new campaign, would proceed initially in ignorance of such differences. Their claims would be marked by an assumed whiteness, recasting stay-at-home mothering as evidence of female oppression and arguing that women's liberation could only be achieved if barriers to their active participation in the workforce were removed, but paying little heed to the struggles of women who had always had to work. The response of such women would threaten to fracture the movement along ethnic and racial lines. Arguments that positioned children as an impediment to women's equality held little appeal to immigrant women who had constructed and justified their working lives around their desire to secure their children's futures, and campaigns for abortion rights and 24-hour child care were rejected by Indigenous women for whom the greater struggle was to have their rights to bear and nurture their children recognised. At the root of this conflict would lie the failure to recognise that the restrictive maternal role against which the new feminists protested had been but one manifestation of the privileges of whiteness from which they needed to step aside if their movement was not to similarly compromised.